AN INTRODUCTION TO INFORMATION ENGINEERING

AN INTRODUCTION TO INFORMATION ENGINEERING

From Strategic Planning to Information Systems

Clive Finkelstein
Information Engineering Services Pty Ltd

Addison-Wesley Publishing Company

Sydney · Wokingham, England · Reading, Massachusetts
Menlo Park, California · New York · Don Mills, Ontario
Amsterdam · Bonn · Singapore
Tokyo · Madrid · San Juan

The programs in this book have been included for their instructional value. They have been tested with care but are not guaranteed for any particular purpose. The publisher does not offer any warranties or representations, nor does it accept any liabilities with respect to the programs.

Many of the designations used by manufacturers and sellers to distinguish their products are claimed as trademarks. Addision-Wesley has made every attempt to supply trademark information about manufacturers and their products mentioned in this book. A list of the trademark designations and their owners appears on page xvi.

Cover designed by Hybert Design & Type, Maidenhead.
Typeset by Times Graphics, Singapore.
Text designed by Debra Myson-Etherington.
Printed in Singapore.

First printed 1989. Reprinted with corrections 1990. Reprinted 1993.

British Library Cataloguing in Publication Data
Finkelstein, Clive
  An introduction to information engineering: from strategic planning to information systems.
  1. Computer systems. Development
  I. Title
  004

  ISBN 0–201–41654–9

Library of Congress Cataloging in Publication Data
Finkelstein, Clive.
  An introduction to information engineering: from strategic planning to information systems/Clive Finkelstein.
      p. cm.
  Includes bibliographical references.
  ISBN 0–201–41654–9
  1. System design. 2. Data base management. I. Title.
QA76.9.S88F54 1989
004.2′1––dc20

                                                            89–37370
                                                            CIP

I dedicate this book to my wife Jill and our daughter Kristi.

PREFACE

The development of computer application systems using traditional data processing methods has been labor intensive, error prone, slow and extremely costly. Much skill is needed to marry the business knowledge of users with the computer experience of analysts and programmers. The developed systems have suffered from a lack of business understanding by data processing staff: they have not fully satisfied the information needs of managers and users. But a revolution is underway in the analysis, design and development of computer application systems. This addresses the entire systems development cycle. It also encompasses strategic planning. It fully automates the analysis and design process, and has the potential to generate required application systems automatically.

This automation of systems development is based not on technical computer experience but on the users' expert business knowledge. Programming, testing and maintenance, as we have known them, will eventually disappear. Instead, business changes will be made at the analysis level. *The changed systems will then be automatically regenerated.*

The revolution is based on a new discipline, called **information engineering**. This addresses strategic planning as well as analysis and design. It is mainly data driven, not procedure driven. Together with appropriate software, it provides expert support to users for development of application systems which support the strategic plan exactly.

Computer-aided software engineering (CASE) has emerged in the last few years as an important development in the software industry. The term CASE relates generally to the automation of software development. Many CASE products are now available. These automate systems development and improve the productivity of analysts and programmers, sometimes by as much as two or three times. However, they do not yet approach the productivity gains achieved by using information engineering and the software described in this book. Projects that have typically taken analysts 2–3 years using software engineering are now being analyzed and designed by managers and users in 2–3 months: with automatic generation of data bases designed also by these same managers and users. Effective productivity gains 10–20 times greater than software engineering are today being regularly achieved.

Information engineering is automated by software that provides expert computer knowledge. Managers and their staff provide expert business knowledge. The result is the automated analysis, design and generation of data bases today. This will lead to the automatic generation of information systems, as well as the development of a new class of intelligent systems: **expert business systems**.

A new approach is introduced: not only to systems development, but also to strategic planning – **computer-aided strategic planning (CASP)**. This automates systems development from the strategic plans and business plans set by management. It is used to develop application systems, information systems, decision-support systems and expert business systems which support these plans exactly. These systems can be developed for use on mainframes, minicomputers and microcomputers. Hundreds of organizations have designed and implemented these systems over the last few years. They represent every industry, including: manufacturing, distribution, law enforcement, banking, insurance, securities, health care, airlines, process, defense, telecommunications and Government. These systems were designed and developed by managers and users with no data processing knowledge, and with significantly less analyst assistance than with traditional systems development methods.

The productivity gains have indeed been impressive. But the upper limit of productivity gain has not yet been reached: the potential exists for development productivity *many times* greater than software engineering. This is now seen as an achievable target in the immediate future. The day when all analysis and design will be carried out by managers and users at the business level, with automatic generation of the supporting systems in hours, is on the horizon. This will change forever the data processing industry as we know it today.

Outline

This book provides an introduction to information engineering. It is organized in four parts:

Part One – Introduction: This introduces information engineering and its historical evolution. It is required reading.

- **Chapter 1** reviews the problems of growth in organizations, and discusses both traditional and new approaches to addressing those problems.

- **Chapter 2** outlines the evolution of information engineering – from its beginnings in data base design to its application by managers and staff, based on strategic planning.

Part Two – Basic Principles: This describes the basic concepts of information engineering. It establishes definitions and data modeling conventions. It provides an introduction to normalization and shows how normalization can be used as a business technique to define the future. It is also required reading.

- **Chapter 3** introduces data modeling.
- **Chapters 4 and 5** discuss the documentation conventions and concepts used in data modeling to establish business meaning and standard terminology.
- **Chapter 6** describes the basic dictionary documentation needed for an information engineering project.
- **Chapter 7** is an introduction to normalization.
- **Chapters 8 and 9** next use normalization as a business technique to define the future; to identify and structure data so that organizational change can be accommodated with minimum disruption.

Part Three – Information Engineering Projects: This discusses the conduct of an information engineering project. It first presents a treatment of strategic planning. Two methods are introduced to set strategic directions: one formal, the other informal. These provide the catalyst for a project. The planning, management and conduct of a project are then discussed in terms of a typical organizational example.

- **Chapter 10** introduces the concepts of strategic planning and strategic management. It discusses the separate roles of formal strategic planning and informal strategic planning, and the feedback provided by strategic management. It describes the formal strategic planning steps.
- **Chapters 11 and 12** discuss the strategic and tactical stages of informal strategic planning respectively. They describe the role of the strategic statements and the tactical statements in setting strategic directions.
- **Chapter 13** describes the use of the strategic statements for strategic modeling. It introduces goal analysis for refinement of those statements.
- **Chapter 14** provides an overview of the phases of information engineering.
- **Chapter 15** introduces the tasks which are carried out in the project scope stage. These are critical to eventual project success.
- **Chapter 16** describes preparation and project planning steps that must be performed before commencing the strategic modeling stage of a project.
- **Chapter 17** discusses the conduct of strategic modeling sessions. Using an example, it details the steps involved in identifying broad data subjects and then strategic data entities and attributes. It describes the development of a strategic data map.

Part Four – Automated Systems Development: This part introduces the basic principles of computer-aided software engineering (CASE) for automated analysis, design and development. A number of CASE products are covered which offer differing levels of automated support to information engineering. One of these products is used to illustrate processing of the organizational example discussed in Part Three.

- **Chapter 18** describes the characteristics of software for automated analysis, design and development. It introduces the basic principles of computer-aided software engineering (CASE).

- **Chapter 19** next introduces several CASE products which illustrate these principles.

- **Chapter 20** discusses one of these products in detail: a product that automates information engineering as described in this book – supporting the analysis, design and generation phases of the systems development life cycle.

- **Chapter 21** uses the software from Chapter 20 to process the example developed in Chapter 17. This covers automation of the analysis phase of the systems development life cycle.

- **Chapter 22** concludes the book by describing the productivity gains achieved using information engineering. It discusses future directions which will allow the automatic generation of menus, screens, reports and program code – in a variety of languages. These will be automatically generated directly from a data model developed by users and managers with no computer expertise.

The techniques discussed in this book can be learned in five days, and mastered in a few weeks. With that training, users can design and implement their own systems. It is far easier to train users in these techniques than train analysts in the business. But analysts also learn the same approach. The user knows the business, the analyst knows computers. Both draw on their respective expertise. With these techniques they work together in a design partnership. And if changes are needed, the users can modify the resulting systems immediately. And again, and again, until they are satisfied. The problems of communication disappear.

Acknowledgements

The methods described in this book represent the work of 17 years. They started with initial ideas I developed evenings and weekends from 1972 while I was employed by IBM in the USA and Australia. After this gestation period, information engineering had its birth when I left IBM in 1976 to set up my first company. The methodology evolved over the period 1976–1981 through use by many Australian, New Zealand and South East Asian organizations. 1981 saw its introduction first to the USA and Canada, and then elsewhere throughout the world. Today, many thousands of enterprises, government and commercial, use information engineering for strategic planning and systems development. Other organizations have also emerged to provide software, consulting and education services in information engineering.

Information engineering is not the work of one person, but of many. Their names are too numerous for special mention, except for one. Those who participated with me from 1976–1982 made their individual contributions at that point of evolution of the methodology. But then they moved on. Some today provide information engineering consulting services based on the methodology as it was then. But the greatest advances were made from 1983–1988. They are described in this book.

The most important acknowledgement I have left till last: my wife, Jill. She supported me from the first days with IBM. From formation of our first company, and for each subsidiary and related company, she has provided not only her organizational skills but also her encouragement, support and advice. The path has not been easy. Changing people's ways and thinking never is. But with her help and love she has smoothed the way. Jill, these thanks are but a small return: but they are given with all of my heart.

Clive Finkelstein
June 1989

CONTENTS

PART ONE

Introduction

CHAPTER 1

The Dawn of a New Era

Management is on the threshold of an explosive boom in the use of computers. A boom initiated by simplicity and ease of use. Managers and staff at all levels of an organization will be able to design and implement their own systems, thereby dramatically reducing their dependence on the data processing (DP) department, while still ensuring that DP maintains central control, so that application systems and their data can be used by others in the business.

The revolution removes the technical complexity of computer analysis and design by using, instead, *existing management experience* to develop application systems and generate data bases. The revolution, based on information engineering, starts with strategic planning, used not just at the highest management levels, but at all management levels. It bridges from strategic plans directly to computer systems which support achievement of those plans. This dramatically reduces the backlog of applications waiting for scarce analyst and programmer resources. The revolution supports the business needs of both managers and their staff, as well as the technical DP needs of data administrators, analysts and programmers. Using information engineering software, they can evaluate the impact of a strategic alternative in their orizanization and, if not suitable, change that strategic approach.

1.1 | TRADITIONAL APPLICATION DEVELOPMENT

Computer programming is labour intensive and prone to many errors. Each program is individually designed and hand-coded, tested and

3

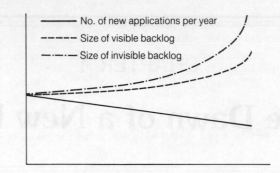

Figure 1.1 Application backlog with traditional development methods. Most DP departments find that current application development methods help the application backlog grow larger, rather than reduce it.

documented, with the result that programs can only be maintained – debugged or updated – if their design and construction has been adequately documented by the original designer. The intricate tapestry of logic that is woven into many programs has made them fragile construction indeed. Their logic is so interwoven that it is impossible to unravel. In fact, it may be faster to throw a program away and start again, than to try and change it.

Current application development methods are largely procedure driven (see Section 1.7). Such methods include systems analysis, structured analysis, structured design and business systems planning. We will refer to these as **traditional development methods**. The low productivity of traditional application development is illustrated in Figure 1.1. This examines the application backlog: the elapsed time from a user request for a new application system to when that application has been developed and is ready for use.

In many organizations, the application backlog may be two, three or more years. A new application project may have to wait many months, or years, for analysts and programmers to be allocated before the project can start. The application development cycle (requirements specification, analysis, design, coding, testing and system testing) may then take many more years. This is the **visible** application backlog, as shown in Figure 1.1. Once in production, these applications must be maintained, which requires programming resources. As fewer resources are available for subsequent applications, the backlog increases.

Figure 1.1 also illustrates the **invisible** application backlog. This represents other possible application requests that are not made by users, because of the time they must wait. Instead, the users acquire their own computing facilities, whether microcomputers, minicomputers, or outside service bureaux, and develop the applications themselves, if they are simple. If the application is complex, it is often abandoned.

As can be seen from Figure 1.1, the visible and invisible application backlogs increase as more applications are developed. Consequently, the rate of development of new applications progressively decreases. This is due to the problems of maintenance.

1.2 | PROBLEMS OF MAINTENANCE

A simple change required in a program may lead to other changes. Furthermore, these changes may introduce errors which require further change, so leading to yet more change and errors.

Maintenance modifications to production programs generally take precedence over new applications. In many organizations, some 70%–80% of programmer resources are engaged in program maintenance in its various forms (either systems maintenance, application maintenance or conversion), leaving only 20%–30% of programmers available for new application development. These statistics are the result of poor application development productivity, the true cause of which will be identified in the following pages.

The problems of maintenance have a cascading effect. Programmers are used to modify current applications, rather than to develop new applications, with the effect that the number of applications developed per year decreases, as shown in Figure 1.1. What is the cause of this maintenance workload? How can it be avoided, or at least minimized? The answer lies in an analysis of the errors that lead to change.

1.3 | SOME REASONS FOR MAINTENANCE

An analysis of the causes of many errors is shown diagrammatically in Figure 1.2(a). (This is based on surveys reported by De Marco [1].) As can be seen, maintenance due to program *coding* errors represents only 7% of errors. In contrast, errors in *design* represent 27%, while errors in *incomplete requirements* specification total 56%. Hence, contrary to what might be expected, errors are introduced long before coding even starts.

Figure 1.2(b) illustrates the effort required to correct these errors: the 7% coding errors require only 1% of the effort to correct; the 27% design errors require 13% of the effort; while the 56% requirements errors require 82% of the effort to fix!

It is clear, therefore, that most errors are introduced in the initial requirements specification and design stages, before any detailed program coding commences. But what is the cause?

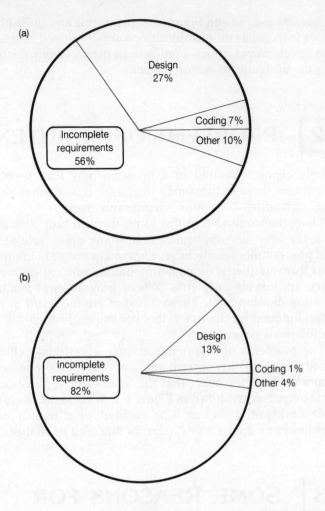

Figure 1.2 (a) The source of errors. More errors occur in requirements specification. Coding errors represent only a very small proportion. (b) The distribution of effort to correct errors. Errors due to incomplete requirements specification are far more difficult to fix than are coding errors.

1.4 PROBLEM OF COMMUNICATION

The problem is, largely, due to a lack of effective communication. DP analysts, data base administrators and programmers use a computer jargon that is foreign to most users and management. Similarly, the day-to-day terminology of business matters may be unintelligible to many analysts and DP staff. This communication problem is compounded by the long lead time before the developed systems are delivered to the users.

To overcome this problem, the DP industry has trained users and managers in computer fundamentals, while the organization has trained analysts in the details of the business. Such cross-training has certainly helped communication but has not solved the problem, since neither became sufficiently expert in the other's discipline. Subsequently, the software engineering technique of structured analysis was introduced. This provided some communication benefit, although it was still not sufficient. Fourth-generation languages (4GLs) reduced the lead time for the development of systems, but, more often than not, resulted in the *wrong* system being delivered sooner.

The real problem lay in determining the true information needs of users. Users were not aware of the potential of computers, and their initial definition of the information they needed was often incomplete. '*The users need more training in computer analysis!*' said DP. Most users rebelled at this suggestion. Managers and their staff did not want to be computer experts. They wanted techniques to express their business knowledge, *without* having to be experts in computer technology, so that other managers and users could review and understand their specification of information needs, regardless of whether they had computer experience or not. And DP staff wanted the users' documented needs, so they could be translated into detailed specifications for computer programs, application systems and data bases. This documentation, each said, must provide a common communication medium: one that enabled business and DP staff to draw on their respective expertise. The users know the business; DP staff know computing.

1.5 COMMON COMMUNICATION MEDIUM

The information engineering methodology evolved to provide this definition and documentation discipline. The techniques of strategic modeling and tactical modeling (see Part Three) allowed a clear expression by users of the data required by them to run the business. These techniques defined the data that *was* the organization. And the policies, objectives and strategies of the business were clarified and further refined, as a by-product.

In contrast to traditional application development, information engineering represents an integrated set of **strategic development methods.** It produces documentation that allows users to review the correctness of data definition. Then this documentation can be automatically translated into detailed data base designs, computer systems specifications and accurate program code.

But this is only part of the problem. The other problem is the enormous time and effort required to develop and modify these computer systems. Our techniques for computer system development must improve:

> *'We must automate the tasks of the analyst and the programmer. Not to eliminate their jobs, but to enable them and the users to work together more productively: to reduce the application backlog; to improve the effectiveness of the systems that are developed.'*

Software is now available to help solve these problems, in the form of 4GLs and expert systems software. We will discuss 4GLs now, but will leave the subject of expert systems software until Part Four.

1.5.1 Fourth-generation languages

The late 70s and early 80s saw the emergence of high-level, end-user languages suitable for use by DP staff, or by managers and users with no computer experience. These languages evolved to become closer to English than either the second-generation languages (assembly language) or the third-generation languages (COBOL, PL/I or Pascal). Examples of such 4GLs are FOCUS, MANTIS, UFO, LINC, MAPPER, ORACLE, and other implementations of SQL.

A benefit of 4GLs is their ability to dramatically improve application development productivity. These languages enable computer programs, even entire systems, to be implemented in days – and sometimes even hours. The same programs or systems may have taken months or years using 3GLs. Many of the consequent problems of maintenance tend to disappear in this new environment. Because of the productivity gains achieved, the development time is significantly reduced. The intricate logic patterns weaved by programmers using 3GLs become broad logic sweeps with 4GLs. Or merely statements of the results to be produced, with no specification of how to achieve those results. These latter languages are termed non-procedural. They are not concerned with specifying the detail of logic. They define *what* is to be produced, rather than *how*. These non-procedural 4GLs then generate the necessary computer instructions to achieve the result. An example of a simple specification based on structured query language (SQL), developed by IBM and now accepted as a standard, is as follows:

```
select    employee_number, employee_name,
          employee_address, employee_sex
from      employee;
```

This details what is needed, not how the computer is to do the required processing. With 4GLs a new support capability also began to emerge. This was promoted primarily by IBM. It is referred to as the information center.

1.5.2 Information center

This acknowledges the need for managers and users to specify their own information requirements. 4GLs have enabled non-DP personnel themselves to specify reports, or extract information from computer data bases. This helps to reduce the application backlog. With the information center, users can access their data. If needed, DP staff experienced in 4GLs can assist them in areas of technical difficulty, as internal consultants.

The results were spectacular! The users were at last freed from long application development times. They could satisfy critical information needs themselves. The application backlog dropped: simple applications were developed by users; complex applications by DP staff. And the invisible application backlog was also reduced.

However, the information center placed huge demands on computer resources. 4GLs were used to extract needed information from vast masses of data used for day-to-day production processing. But they did not exhibit the same performance efficiency of 3GLs. And the data were not structured for efficient processing. Such 4GL workloads wreaked havoc on the concurrent processing of high-volume production computer systems. This workload problem was often resolved by installing computers dedicated solely to the information center function.

With 4GLs and information centers, users resolved their own information needs. Urgent needs could be satisfied quickly, and if the resulting reports were not what was wanted, they could be discarded and respecified, again and again until a satisfactory result was obtained.

1.6 | ANOTHER PROBLEM

However, another problem began to emerge. Increasingly, data required for a particular information need was found not to be available in the computer data base, because it was not required for day-to-day processing. The data was not needed before, yet it was required *now*. How could these data needs be identified? How should they be satisfied? Where should the data reside? How could the data be captured? These questions had never arisen before. The data had not been needed previously and had never been specified. Missing data was painfully apparent. The wrong data was available. Management were frustrated again.

This frustration led to recognition. The use of 4GLs moved managers, users and DP staff to a different plane of understanding. With 4GLs, managers and users gained their computer 'driver's licence'. They learned a 4GL and used their new capability for tasks that had not been anticipated before.

But one more step lay ahead before an understanding of the *real* problem could be appreciated, by the late 70s: the decision-support systems era had begun to dawn.

1.6.1   Decision-support systems

The term **decision-support system (DSS)** has been applied to systems that provide information for management decision making. They are often specified, in many cases implemented, and most certainly operated, by the same people who use them: managers with no knowledge of computing.

The early DSSs were painfully developed by DP staff using 3GLs to satisfy a perceived information requirement [2]. They were designed so users could manipulate data; so they could extract information based upon their changing needs. Flexibility was provided, but within well-defined boundaries. The management information system of the early 70s with its promise of all the information the manager ever needed, had finally arrived. *Or so it was thought . . . .*

DSS developers found that satisfying one need led to other needs for different information. If anticipated and designed for, that new information could be extracted. But often the need had never been anticipated. 3GL-based DSSs were not productive enough, requiring too much time for coding and testing, and the manager could not wait.

With the advent of 4GLs, a more responsive decision-support environment evolved. Managers could address their own decision-support needs directly, and could utilize a 4GL to satisfy their changing needs. Some 4GLs used relational data base systems. They enabled new data structures to be readily introduced and the required information extracted. Other 4GLs, however, could not respond so quickly. Their ability to introduce new data structures was limited. The discovery mode encouraged by a truly responsive DSS was thus constrained. Where the data for operational processing was not adequate for the needs of management, additional data structures had to be defined. And only the managers could identify the data they needed. Hence, techniques were needed that would enable managers to specify their own data resource. Once defined, the data could then be loaded into the information center data bases by DP staff.

The *true* problem had begun to emerge. With horror, managers recognized that corporate policy was no longer set or controlled by senior management; they had abdicated that responsibility by default to the analysts, since where policies, goals and strategies were not clearly detailed, analysts and programmers had no direction. They had no alternative but to interpret those policies themselves; to become the final arbiters of corporate policy! They discussed possible interpretations with operational managers. However, these managers were also unaware of senior management's thinking. As a consequence, the decisions made were rarely the best for the future. They reflected only the environment of today. But such decisions were set in code, in concrete, which was difficult and costly to change if wrong.

1.7 | THE REAL PROBLEM

Much of the data needed was based on the strategic plans set by management. Only they could decide relevant data and associated goals, policies and strategies. They realized that there was no substitute for their active involvement; only they were sufficiently aware of alternative strategic directions; only they could determine the data needed; only they could specify their information needs. They needed techniques and business understanding to identify the data, to consolidate it and to document it so that it could be implemented by DP staff, and made accessible to all. Data base is a management concern. Management decisions depend on ready access to accurate, up-to-date data in a single repository.

Like operational users, senior managers found information engineering indispensable to identify data and policies to support their information requirements. Managers, users and DP staff recognized that they needed to work together in a design partnership to identify, implement and process the data that supported the business. This was based not on traditional application development, but on the strategic development methods of information engineering. With improved communication, with users and managers actively defining the data and information they needed, much of the design task was also accomplished by them. The dawn of a new era had arrived: an era of communication and mutual cooperation. No longer did management turn away from the computer. They would have been horrified with any suggestion that a new building project be constructed without their close review of its progress, to ensure that organizational needs were satisfied. Yet this same close-detailed review had been missing in the management of computer projects. Managers did not understand the computer jargon of DP staff,

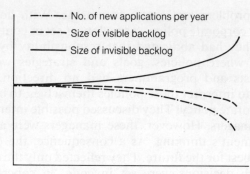

Figure 1.3 Strategic development methods of information engineering lead to increases in application development productivity and a decrease in the application backlog.

and they no longer abdicated their responsibility to DP staff who had no knowledge of the business.

The result was a dramatic improvement not just in implementation, but also in requirements specification and design. The problems of incomplete requirements specification disappeared, and the application backlog shrunk rapidly, as illustrated in Figure 1.3. The maintenance chaos of the traditional development methods dropped away and was replaced by the application development productivity gains of the data-driven strategic development methods, with decreasing maintenance, as illustrated in Figure 1.4(a). This should be compared with Figure 1.4(b) which shows the effect of the traditional procedure-driven methods at the six stages of computerization or automation (DP growth). These six data processing growth stages, on the introduction of computers to an organization, have been identified by Nolan [3]. They are as follows:

- **Stage 1 – Initiation**: The initial introduction of computers sees their use in functional cost-reduction applications such as accounting, inventory control and invoicing.

- **Stage 2 – Contagion**: As these applications succeed, there is a proliferation of user requests for new computer applications, and applications are combined to support operational systems. The organization moves from the first stage to the second stage.

- **Stage 3 – Control**: As new requests for applications grow, the DP department starts to lose control and the application backlog builds up. Consequently, DP management turn to formalized planning and control techniques, upgrading existing documentation and restructuring applications. At this stage, the need to consolidate data is recognized.

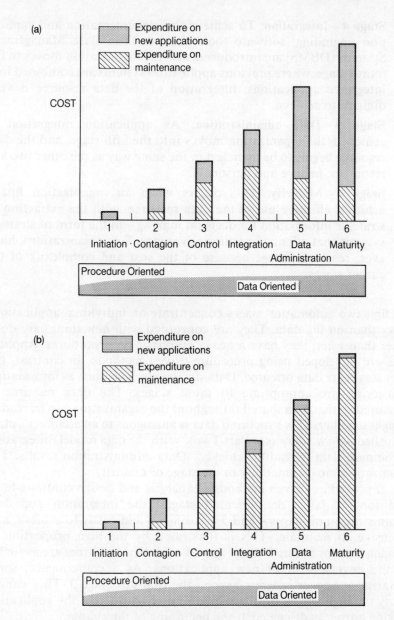

Figure 1.4   (a) Strategic development methods lead to increasing productivity of new application development and decreasing maintenance cost, as an organization moves to the later stages of DP growth. (b) The impact of using procedure-driven methods of analysis and design in the data-oriented stages of DP growth. Few resources are available for new application development, as most are committed to maintenance.

- **Stage 4 – Integration**: To achieve this documentation and application upgrading, software tools such as Data Base Management Systems (DBMS) are introduced, and the organization moves to the fourth stage, where previous application systems are combined into integrated applications. Integration of the data resource is very difficult to achieve.

- **Stage 5 – Data administration**: As application integration is achieved, the organization moves into the fifth stage, and the data resource begins to be managed in the same way as the other two key resources: finance and personnel.

- **Stage 6 – Maturity**: This occurs when an organization finally achieves effective use of the data resource, with the extraction of strategic information for decision making – in the form of strategic systems that offer competitive advantage. Few organizations, however, reach this stage because of the cost and complexity of the earlier stages.

The first two automation stages concentrate on individual applications rather than on the data. They are concerned with *how* things are done rather than *what*; they have a heavy emphasis on procedures. Applications are developed using procedure-driven methods. In contrast, the latter stages are data oriented. Data-driven methods such as information engineering are appropriate to these stages. The data resource is structured so that data shared throughout the organization can be readily brought together. This structured data is analogous to an architect's plan: it is called a *data model* (see Part Two). With the data model, integration of common data is readily achieved. Data administration results. The organization moves smoothly to the stage of maturity.

If procedure-driven methods of analysis and design continue to be used for the latter data-oriented stages, the integration and data administration of Stages 4 and 5 are difficult and costly to achieve, and expensive to maintain. This is illustrated by the high proportion of maintenance for Stages 4–6 in Figure 1.4(b). Few resources are available for the development of new applications. As a consequence, some organizations never progress beyond the chaos of Stage 3. They cannot justify the high expenditure needed to move ahead, and the application backlog grows, as discussed at the beginning of the chapter.

In contrast, Figure 1.4(a) illustrates the effect of data-driven methods used in the data-oriented stages. The data model provides the control needed in Stage 3. Integration occurs naturally, administration follows, and areas of high priority for management are identified clearly, so that they can be implemented early. Fewer resources are needed for maintenance and more resources are applied to new application development.

References

[1] De Marco, T. (1982). *Software Systems Development*. Yourdon Press: New York.

[2] Keen, P. and Scott-Morton, M. (1978) *Decision Support Systems*. Addison-Wesley: Reading, MA.

[3] Nolan, R. (1979). Managing the crises in data processing. *Harvard Business Review* (March–April).

CHAPTER 2

Evolution of Information Engineering

This chapter introduces the various component techniques within information engineering – not in detail, but chronologically. This highlights the way in which they evolved, to provide an integrated set of methods, which extend from strategic planning, at the highest levels of management, directly to generation of the information systems and expert business systems required to support those strategic plans.

Many people have contributed to the evolution of information engineering, both as users of the techniques, and as consultants and instructors. Some made major contributions, while others made refinements and improvements. Still others contributed quite independently to an evolving understanding of data modeling. The result is not the work of one person, but of many, as this chapter illustrates.

This chapter covers the first two five-year stages of the strategic plan for development of the information engineering methodology: 1976–1986.

2.1 STAGE 1 EVOLUTION (1976–1981)

Information engineering had its early roots in data base technology and relational theory. The pioneering work of Edgar (Ted) Codd, while a Research Fellow at IBM San Jose, then IBM Santa Teresa in California, formed much of its early base.

2.1.1   Data base management systems

The first data base management systems (DBMS) were introduced in the 1960s. Software products of the mid-60s, such as BOMP (by IBM: Bill of Material Processor), saw some of the early data base applications applied to manufacturing. This gave rise to a number of DBMS products, including Cincom's TOTAL.

During this period, early work carried out by North American Rockwell on an information management system (IMS) was continued by IBM, and introduced as a DBMS product. This used Data Language/1 (DL/1) to define the physical structure of the data to be stored in an IMS data base. In 1971, IBM issued a statement of direction which announced that IMS and DL/1 were to be its strategic data base products. They reconfirmed that direction in 1976.

During this same period, attempts were made by many organizations to establish a data base standard. A result of this was the emergence of the CODASYL (COnference on DAta SYstems Languages) data base specifications, which gave rise to a number of data base products in the early 1970s. Some of the more widely used CODASYL products included IDMS (as used by ICL and by Cullinane – now Cullinet), DMS 1100 (Univac, now part of Unisys), DMS 170 (CDC), DBMS 11 and DBMS 32 (DEC).

In the mid-70s, several DBMS products emerged based on an 'inverted list' architecture. This included ADABAS (Software AG), SYSTEM 2000 (MRI, taken over by Intel) and DATACOM (taken over by ADR).

The DBMSs of the 70s were characterized by great technical complexity, and required substantial training and experience for their effective use. Hence, the role of a data base administer (DBA) emerged, as a technical DBMS specialist.

During the 1970s, DBMS products were used to bring together redundant versions of data (when so identified) for high-volume operational computer processing. But the promise that data bases had offered – to provide a management information system (MIS) capability to senior management – was not yet realized. Its achievement depended on extensive knowledge of the organization and its business, as well as experience in data base design. Some DBAs had these skills, but they could not easily pass them on to others, as they were based on experience and intuition.

2.1.2   Relational theory

During this period of evolution of data base technology, highly innovative research was underway in the USA based on mathematical set theory. This was applied by Ted Codd and his colleagues at IBM to the problems of representation of data. He found it was possible to represent data in a data base more simply than had previously been achieved – as a two-dimensional table, rather than as a convoluted collection of data items, gathered together in computer files and records, as used by the DBMS products and data base designs of that time. This work led to the development of relational theory and normalization (see Part Two), first published in Codd's landmark paper [1]. However, the early application of these disciplines was heavily steeped in mathematical jargon, and they were of more interest to academics than to the real world of commercial data processing.

It was not until the mid-70s that efforts were made to bridge relational theory to practical reality. To the author's knowledge, by 1978, there were concurrent and independent efforts by at least three companies to make this bridge: one in Europe (CACI); one in UK (BIS); one in Australia (Information Engineering Services Pty Ltd – IES). The first two of these organizations applied relational theory, as a DP technique, to the problems of commercial data base design rather than strategic planning. They applied relational theory and normalization to the development of DP driven data analysis methods. But it was the Australian effort that gave birth to information engineering – bridging from strategic planning through to implementation, as described in the following chapters.

2.1.3   Data base design

Relational theory and normalization techniques were first used to develop logical data base designs, which could then be translated into physical data base designs by DBAs. These designs were implemented for different DBMS products by a formal data base design methodology. This used logical data models produced by data analysis, a formal technique developed by IES and based on normalization. Data base design and data analysis were the first of the information engineering techniques.

2.1.4   Data analysis

Data analysis (as used in information engineering) was based on a detailed examination of the existing documents used in an organization. These comprised source documents, reports, enquiries, manual ledgers, computer file formats, and other documentation designed to capture, record and report operational data in the organization. Such data were used for day-to-day operation, based on the experience of the past and the objectives set by management to operate and control the business.

Data analysis today exists as current systems modeling, part of operations modeling.

The early results of data analysis demonstrated that analysts, without a knowledge of data base design, could design data bases that were comparable to those defined by experienced DBAs, but with one difference: while the DBA 'knew' the design was 'right' (through intuition and experience), the analyst could explain *why* the design had to be represented in such a way. He or she used the formal rules of normalization to develop that data base design. The intuition of the DBA was in fact the unconscious application of normalization principles to the definition and structuring of data.

As data analysis began to be applied by more and more organizations, a curious situation emerged. Analysts used data analysis to develop logical data base designs, but it was found that *users* without a knowledge of computers were also able to apply this technique. In fact, in some cases, they developed logical data base designs that were more correct than those of either the analyst or the DBA. Using the technique of data analysis, users could identify the data they needed. Furthermore, they could establish relationships, which existed in their organization, between the data, and could represent those relationships in their logical data base design.

A significant breakthrough was emerging: users did not need to understand computers. Instead, they could draw on their detailed knowledge of the business and express that knowledge so it could be exactly interpreted and implemented by DBA staff. The search for user-driven methods was beginning to bear fruit.

However, the data that existed and was used at operational levels of an organization was not the only data needed to support an organization's future processing needs. Different data was also often needed to plan for the future. The problem was the inability of both the operational departments of an organization and the DP department to respond quickly and easily to changes in business directions, and to new management requests for information. The application development techniques used by DP prevented a timely response to these information requests.

The solution to these problems was found by merging data analysis with formal management theory. This evolved into the technique of information analysis, which started to point the way to involvement of senior management.

2.1.5   Information analysis

Data analysis was based on operational data, but such data was not always needed for the future, and future needs were not clearly identified.

So, data from the past was incorporated in computer systems and data bases for no reason other than 'the data has always been there'. From a study of management theory and strategic planning methods, it can be realized that these future information needs are capable of much earlier identification. The future is *not* unknown; in fact, it is based on the decisions taken today. Although all future requirements cannot be established with full certainty, many possible future alternatives can be identified. The source of this future was found in the strategic planning directions established by management.

Management theory has evolved since the Second World War, in parallel with, but independently of, the development of computer technology. Strategic planning and management objectives enabled managers to evaluate alternative directions for the future and select those that appeared to have the greatest chance of success. Management could at last gain some control over their destiny. They could identify and select from a number of options, and make appropriate adjustments as the organization moved into the future.

One of the most widely respected of the management theorists is Peter Drucker. Information analysis was based strongly on Drucker's work [2]. With the strategic planning guidance of Drucker, combined with the normalization and documentation conventions of data analysis, a highly productive definition environment was born: **information analysis**. Previously, with strategic planning, there had been much preoccupation with *how* the various functions and processes were carried out in an organization. However, it was found that managers could apply Drucker's guidance to identify, not *how* things were to be done in the future, but rather *what* was to be achieved, and from this they could determine the data needed by the organization. The data resource needed by management, and the information extracted from that data resource, was the main emphasis of information analysis.

Focusing on the what, rather than the how, was the reverse of previous analysis approaches such as software engineering and business systems planning (BSP). Information analysis used strategic plans as a catalyst to identify fundamental data needed for management decision making. With the experience of data analysis, and then information analysis, *it was now clear that this data-driven emphasis was the key to the development of user-driven techniques.*

2.1.6   Early feedback to strategic planning

As information analysis evolved and was applied in organizations, a by-product emerged. By concentrating on the data needed to support the organization, management could focus on fundamental issues independently of how those issues might be resolved later. The documentation conventions of information engineering (see Part Two) enabled them to see clearly the implications of different representations and relationships in the organization. It provided early feedback to management, which assisted in the establishment of strategic directions. This was not intended, but it is one of the greatest benefits of information engineering.

In the past, the only way to evaluate the effectiveness of a strategic plan was to introduce a 'pilot' version of the plan, using part of the organization as a guinea pig. Based on the experience gained after one, two or more years, the plans could then be refined and introduced across the rest of the organization. Information analysis showed that this feedback process could start much sooner. It enabled management to move through several evolutions of strategic planning thought and evaluate the implications of alternative directions based on feedback provided by information analysis. They could then select the most appropriate approach for implementation, in months rather than years.

Used in this way, information analysis was perceived as a management technique, rather than a *data processing* technique. Managers recognized that the people who should use information analysis were not the DP staff, but the managers themselves and their own staff (the users). They saw that it also provided an exact specification of the data resource needs to the DP department, to implement the data bases and computer systems needed to support management decision making.

In those organizations where strategic planning had not previously been used, information analysis was also seen as an alternative strategic planning approach. With its firm foundation in management theory, it introduced a formal management technique. Managers could identify alternatives for the future and select the most appropriate. Information analysis introduced strategic planning by default into those organizations. With the experience of information analysis, it was found that the strategic planning process itself could be significantly improved through the early feedback gained.

Information analysis, as just described, was in fact only tactical. With its focus on markets, products, services and channels, it today exists as part of tactical modeling.

2.1.7   Procedure formation

The evolution of information engineering during the Stage 1 period concentrated first on the definition of the data resource; that is, it was data driven. Only after the data had been defined (using information analysis or data analysis) was its processing considered. This gave rise to the information engineering technique of procedure formation.

It was found that the clear expression of management strategy and controls in a logical data model could be used formally by managers and users to derive procedures for their implementation. These procedures could be manual, or could be automated. As automated procedures, they were able to be translated into computer programs and computer support systems using 3GLs, or 4GLs. These procedures were designed by users, who had an expert knowledge of the business. The analysts, on the other hand, did not have this knowledge. Another user-driven technique had emerged.

It was also found that this formal derivation of strategies and procedures provided an essential cross-check of the data model. It clarified the effectiveness of policies, objectives and strategies as initially set by management. By concentrating on the data needed to support decision making and the policies by which the data was managed, it was found that alternative strategies could be identified for evaluation. This also aided the strategic feedback provided to management. Furthermore, computer-support systems could then be designed which precisely implemented management's strategies and controls, and the users themselves could check the correctness of the designed procedures. Where certain strategies were not precise enough, they could be clarified or changed, before they were implemented in computer systems.

Another significant advantage emerged from procedure formation in that a further step along the strategic path to the development of user-driven techniques had been taken: as much as 80% of the analysis and design previously carried out wholly by analysts could now be completed by the managers and users themselves. Users could evaluate the business implications of derived procedures and identify their processing needs more exactly. This was based on feedback gained from information analysis and procedure formation. The systems specified by the users, and implemented by DP staff, were able to satisfy the information requirements of managers and users more exactly. Procedure formation later evolved into procedure modeling, which is used today as part of the design phase of information engineering.

However, techniques were also needed by DP staff to select and configure the most appropriate hardware and software to implement these designed systems. This saw the development of data use analysis.

2.1.8 Data use analysis

This technique first evolved as part of data analysis, but was later moved outside this discipline. Data use analysis provided analysts and DBAs with a technique for early sizing and performance analysis of transactions and data base designs. Response-critical transactions were identified, and data base designs and procedures were optimized to improve performance of those transactions, perhaps at the expense of less critical transactions. Where data and processing were distributed geographically, communication loads were calculated. It allowed detailed and precise capacity planning and tuning to be carried out early in the design stage, based on data models developed by information analysis and data analysis, and procedure models developed by procedure formation. Required hardware and software facilities were defined, based on a detailed understanding of the work to be done.

The evolution of information engineering techniques to this point is documented in [3] and [4].

2.2 STAGE 2 EVOLUTION (1981–1986)

From 1981–82, information engineering saw little change. However, in the period 1983–85, several new breakthroughs occurred: firstly the senior management techniques of feasibility analysis and practical strategic planning appeared, to be followed by the development of information systems design and information systems implementation. These techniques were the early forerunners of strategic modeling and tactical modeling. This period also saw the evolution of procedure formation to procedure modeling.

2.2.1 Feasibility analysis

Feasibility analysis first emerged in late 1982, to satisfy a problem unique to large organizations; that is the size and complexity of such enterprises made it difficult to identify the most appropriate starting point. Feasibility analysis, on the other hand, enabled information engineering to be applied broadly, but quickly, to a large area of an organization [5]. It resulted in a critical information model which identified potential areas of technical and economic opportunity, and, based on early perceived benefits suggested by these opportunities, management priorities could be established for subsequent detailed information engineering projects. Feasibility analysis was the first step in the evolution of strategic modeling, as discussed in Part Three.

2.2.2 Practical strategic planning

The use of strategic plans as catalysts to information analysis led to the development, in 1983, of the practical strategic planning methodology of information engineering. An overview of this technique is presented in

Chapter 10. Part of its output, in terms of strategic statements, is used both as input and a catalyst for strategic and for tactical modeling.

2.2.3 Procedure modeling

Procedure formation underwent further evolution in 1983 with the discovery of generic procedures. This enabled standard common procedures to be defined and implemented, and used as a basis for processing any data model. It reduced the design and implementation of new computer systems from years to weeks, and in some cases to days. It resulted in the procedure modeling approach used today in the design phase of information engineering.

Much research effort had been invested in the 70s and 80s by universities and organizations in the development of the 'programmers work bench' – a set of logic building blocks that could be used to construct programs. The answer lay not in the analysis of programs, but in the analysis of data. The generic procedures of procedure formation were these logic building blocks. With them, common, reusable procedures and code could be automatically generated from a data model. Today, this reusable code is implemented using 3GLs or 4GLs, or by using object-oriented programming systems (OOPS) techniques and languages.

Still further improvements were made as information engineering continued to evolve through application by hundreds of companies. This led to the development of implementation strategies, information systems design and information systems implementation (1983–85), and their subsequent evolution to strategic and tactical modeling (1986–87).

2.2.4 Implementation strategies

As found earlier (with data use analysis), data models and procedure models could be used for selection of the most appropriate information systems architecture for implementation. This led to the technique of implementation strategies. The most appropriate physical implementation of data and procedures, whether through manual systems or automated computer systems, could be defined.

With the clearer specification of requirements, as indicated by the data model, more exact evalution could be made of the effectiveness of various software packages. Where a package could not satisfy specified requirements exactly, changes to that package could be identified. Not only could software packages be selected more effectively, but the most appropriate DBMSs could also be determined. Where an organization identified a requirement for high-volume processing, relevant DBMS software could be selected to support this processing. Where the environment was one of unpredictable change, DBMS software that could readily accommodate change was more appropriate.

But the most significant development came when it was found that the data model could be used as the basis for formal derivation of an **implementation project plan**. This derivation was extremely rigorous and led to the progressive implementation and delivery of prioritized subsets of the data model as completed systems to the user. This is discussed further in relation to software support for information engineering in Part Four.

In 1984, information systems design evolved. This was a highly productive combination of the previously separate information analysis and data analysis techniques developed in Stage 1. This was an intermediate step along the evolutionary path to tactical modeling.

2.2.5   Information systems design

As discussed earlier, information analysis enabled users to define the data needed for the future, based on the strategic directions set by management. Data analysis, on the other hand, enabled DP analysts to define the data needed at the operational level, based on the current systems used in an organization. These two techniques were used independently in the past, depending on the environment of each organization, either for the development of new systems or for the conversion of current systems. Information systems design evolved from an amalgamation of these two techniques. The combination resulted in data models of higher quality, defined some two times faster than had previously been achieved using either of the techniques individually.

2.2.6   Information systems implementation

As with information systems design, information systems implementation evolved from an amalgamation and modification of earlier techniques. It focused on improved productivity of design and implementation. It led to a high degree of automation and permitted the rapid implementation of data models using either 3GLs or 4GLs and DBMS products. This was an intermediate step in the evolution of the design and generation phases used today, as discussed in Part Four.

2.2.7   Strategic modeling and tactical modeling

During Stages 1 and 2 of the evolution of information engineering a consistency of organization terminology emerged. Organizational policies, goals, objectives and strategies were defined, which led to information systems that satisfied management's information needs exactly.

Table 2.1 Evolution of information engineering.

Plan	Period	Technique	Advantages	Disadvantages
1	1976–78	Data base design	• Formal data base design technique • DBMS independent • Develops flexible design	• Knowledge of DBMS architecture • High manual content • Extensive optimization needed
	1977–78	Data analysis	• Develops logical data model • Easily translated to data base design • Operational information • Reflects current environment • Data-driven approach • Applies to Stages 1 and 2 of DP growth	• Predominantly DP driven • Focuses on current business • Management information missing • Strategic directions not considered • High manual content • Time consuming
	1978–79	Information analysis	• Develops logical data model • Easily translated to data base design • Middle management information • Middle management environment • Data-driven approach • Applies to Stage 3 of DP growth only	• Operational, user driven • Focuses on middle management • Strategic information missing • Strategic directions not considered • Time consuming, manual effort • Manual integration of data difficult
	1978–79	Procedure formation	• Develops logical procedure model • Easily translated to program code • Operational procedures • Reflects current environment • Data-driven processing • Applies to Stage 3 of DP growth only	• Operational, user driven • Focuses on operational users • Strategic processing missing • Strategic procedures not included • Time consuming, manual effort • No integrated procedures
	1979–80	Data use analysis	• Transaction response time calcs. • Response-critical transactions • Optimized data base designs	• High manual content • Time consuming • Recalculate for business changes

Table 2.1 Evolution of information engineering.

Plan	Period	Technique	Advantages	Disadvantages
2	1983–85	Information systems design	• Develops logical data model • Easily translated to data base design • Middle management information • Middle management environment • Faster data-driven approach • Applies to Stage 3 of DP growth only	• Operational, user driven • Focuses on middle management • Strategic information missing • Strategic directions not considered • Still time consuming, manual effort • Manual integration of data difficult
	1983–85	Information systems implementation	• Develops logical procedure model • Easily translated to program code • Data-driven, generic procedures • Both management and operational user-driven • Operational and strategic procedures • Both strategic and current environment • Integrated, shared procedures • Applies to Stage 3 of DP growth only	• Needs DP acceptance of approach • Needs management commitment • Needs management direction • Needs management review
	1986 to present	Strategic modeling	• Users design data model and systems • Automated generation of systems • Expert systems support for design • Senior management information • Computer-aided strategic planning • Rapid strategic planning feedback • Applies to all DP growth stages	• Needs DP acceptance of approach • Needs management commitment • Needs management involvement • Needs management review
	1986 to present	Tactical modeling	• Users design data model and systems • Automated generation of systems • Expert systems support for design • Middle management information • Applies to all DP growth stages	• Needs DP acceptance of approach • Needs management commitment • Needs management involvement • Needs management review

They provided the essential foundation for eventual migration to expert business systems, and established the basis for Stage 3 of the strategic information engineering plan. By the beginning of 1986, information engineering had evolved to strategic modeling and tactical modeling. Then the most dramatic breakthrough of all occurred! User-driven expert systems were developed to automate information engineering, resulting in an immediate leap in productivity. Project durations dropped from 2–3 years to 6–12 months and then to 2–3 months. Senior management became actively involved in strategic modeling, providing direction for detailed tactical modeling. Implementation plans were automatically derived from data models, enabling senior management to rapidly identify priority areas, and resources were allocated for early implementation and delivery.

The systems developed to this point of the evolution of information engineering far surpassed the capability of software engineering, CASE and BSP. These latter procedure-oriented methods took an application-focus. In contrast, information engineering took a corporate-wide emphasis. Systems that were being delivered in 2–3 months by information engineering were too complex to have even been attempted with any confidence by the procedure-driven methods for delivery in any time less than 3 years.

2.3 | SUMMARY OF EVOLUTION

Table 2.1 puts the evolution of information engineering in context, indicating the advantages and disadvantages of each evolutionary step. It illustrates the progressive refinement of these methods to their present, automated, user-driven form. It relates each technique to the six stages of DP growth, as discussed in Chapter 1.

For example, data analysis, data use analysis and data base design were found to apply only to those organizations in either Stage 1 or Stage 2 of DP growth – because of the DP-driven nature of these techniques. This emphasis was quite appropriate during the period 1976–80, but was increasingly less effective in the 1980s because of their strong DP focus: they addressed individual applications; their data models reflected current operational systems; management was not involved; and there was no opportunity to design for the future. But when changes did occur, they were accommodated with less disruption than for systems developed using the procedure-oriented methods of software engineering or BSP.

With the evolution to information analysis and procedure formation (1978–79), user involvement increased. Strategic directions set by management provided input, which resulted in data models and systems that focused more on the future. These techniques applied well for organizations at Stage 3 of DP growth, as they provided the control needed at this stage. They identified information for both middle and operational management, but senior management was not involved. There were benefits for those managers who participated; there was little or no benefit for senior management. The data models and systems were tactical, not strategic, and were still strongly DP driven.

References

[1] Codd, E. (1970). A relational model for large shared data banks. *CACM*, **13** (6), 377–87.

[2] Drucker, P. (1974). *Management: Tasks, Responsibilities, Practices*. Harper & Row: New York, NY.

[3] Finkelstein, C. (1981). Information engineering. Published as six InDepth articles. *Computerworld* (May–June).

[4] Martin, J. and Finkelstein, C. (1981). *Information Engineering*. Savant Institute: UK.

[5] Finkelstein, C. (1983). *Information Engineering in Manufacturing*. Future Directions in Manufacturing Technology Symposium, Unilever Research Laboratories: Port Sunshine, UK.

PART TWO
Basic Principles

CHAPTER 3

Data Modeling: Introduction

This chapter introduces and defines the terminology, and some of the documentation conventions, used in data modeling. These conventions are used for strategic modeling, tactical modeling and operations modeling. They are also used to design information systems and expert business systems.

Expert systems take an application-specific focus, while expert business systems may address an entire organization. This wide divergence is due to the different approaches used to define expert rules. The development of expert systems, to date, has reflected a *DP-driven* emphasis. In contrast expert business systems are *user-driven*. The users are the experts. They use the techniques of information engineering to express this knowledge.

3.1 DATA FOUNDATION OF ORGANIZATIONS

Information engineering identifies data fundamental to an organization. For example, if we are interested in orders received from customers, there are certain data that we must know about customers and about the orders they place, such as the customer's name and address, a customer number to identify each individual or company customer, or the customer's account balance. *Customer number, customer name, customer address* and *customer account balance* are (data) attributes that identify the customer (*customer number*) and tell us certain things about that

33

customer (his name, where he is located and how much he owes); that is, they describe the customer (see Section 3.1.2). Such attributes are grouped together in data entities and stored for later reference.

3.1.1 Data entities

When grouped together, the foregoing attributes represent the CUSTOMER data entity. Similarly, the ORDER data entity may be comprised of data attributes such as *order number*, *order date* and *delivery address*, and attributes that identify *quantity ordered* and *product number* of each of the products making up the order. Each reference to CUSTOMER or to ORDER implies a reference to a single occurrence of a customer and an order. There may be many occurrences of customers or orders in total (perhaps millions), but we are concerned with each occurrence. Hence, we always use the singular (CUSTOMER) in naming an entity, rather than the plural (CUSTOMERS).

We will define a data entity as follows:

> A **data entity** represents some 'thing' that is to be stored for later reference. (The storage medium may be either a disk or tape, or it may be on paper for manual systems.) It may be referred to as an entity or a record. It is always uniquely named in the singular and is written in capitals. For example, each of CUSTOMER, ORDER, SUPPLIER and PRODUCT are data entities.
>
> The term **entity** refers to the *logical* representation of data, while the term **record** refers to the *physical* representation (on disk, tape or on paper). We will use entity, as we are concerned with logical design.

When each entity is defined, as well as a unique name, it is also given a **purpose description**. This is a narrative statement that indicates the business reason for the data represented by the entity. That is, the narrative is data oriented: it indicates *what* the entity represents (its purpose in each part of the organization), rather than how it is used.

The purpose description may be a brief statement of one line, in which case it is called a **basic** purpose description, or it may require several lines, or pages, in which case it is called an **extended** purpose description. An agreed purpose description for each entity is essential for later strategic, tactical and operations modeling: it ensures that all interested personnel are referring to the same data. It leads to definition of policies for management and control of those parts of the business represented by each entity. It may, however, be refined during normalization (see Chapters 7–9).

3.1.2   Data attributes

As we saw earlier, an entity comprises a number of data attributes. We will define a data attribute as follows:

> A **data attribute** is a 'piece' of information that describes a data entity. It may be referred to as an attribute or a data item. It is always uniquely named in the singular and is written in lower case italics. For example, the data attributes *customer number* and *customer address*, provide details about a CUSTOMER entity, while *product description* and *order date* provide details about PRODUCT and ORDER entities respectively.
>
> The term **attribute** refers to the *logical* representation of data. The terms **data field**, **data item** or **data element** are used to refer to its *physical* representation. Attributes are grouped together in entities, while data items are grouped together in records. We will use the logical term attribute.

To distinguish between similar attributes, they are often qualified. Thus, we refer to *customer address* and *supplier address*, rather than the unqualified, ambiguous attribute name *address*. In many cases, the attribute name can be qualified by prefixing it with the name of the entity in which it resides, as for the two address attributes above which reside in the CUSTOMER and SUPPLIER entities respectively.

As for entities, each attribute is given both a unique name and a purpose description (either basic or extended) which indicates the agreed meaning. As for entities, the purpose description is data oriented and may be further refined during normalization. As will be seen later, an attribute purpose description leads to the definition of objectives.

3.1.3   Data associations

Extending our example, it is obvious that we are not only interested in customers and orders; we need, for example, to identify each order placed by a customer and, for a given order, the customer to whom we should send an invoice. We see that there is a relationship or data association between a customer and an order. Given the customer number, we are able to determine, through the association between CUSTOMER and ORDER, all of the customer's orders. Conversely, given the order number for a specific order, we can, through the association, determine the customer who placed that order.

We will define a data association as follows:

A **data association** indicates that a relationship exists between two entities. It may be called an association or a relationship. For example, a CUSTOMER–ORDER association may exist between a CUSTOMER entity occurrence and a specific ORDER entity occurrence. This indicates that a particular order belongs to that customer. Similarly, a PRODUCT–SUPPLIER association may exist between a PRODUCT entity occurrence and a SUPPLIER entity occurrence. As with entities and attributes, an association may also be named. However, while entities and attributes are named with a singular noun (such as CUSTOMER) or a qualified noun (such as *customer address*), associations may be named by a verb (such as 'places') or a phrase (such as 'customer places orders').

The term **association** refers to the *logical* connection between two entities, while the term **relationship** refers to the *physical* connection between two records. We will use the logical term association.

As for entities and attributes, each association is also given a unique name and a purpose description (basic or extended). As discussed earlier, entity and attribute purpose descriptions are data oriented; that is, they indicate *what* data is represented. By contrast, the association purpose description is procedure oriented: it describes *how* the association is used. It is a representation of business strategy. It allows us to define *how* we want to manage two related entities, by providing a detailed definition of controls (business conditions) to be satisfied and the procedures to be implemented (or automated) to carry out the defined strategy within the established controls. As will be seen later, an association purpose description leads to a discussion and evaluation of alternative strategies. As before, the association purpose description may be further refined during normalization.

3.1.4   Common communication medium

Using these building blocks (data entities, data attributes and data associations), we can represent the fundamental data needed in an organization and show strategies established to manage that organization. They provide the data plan: the data model. The data model provides a common communication medium, viewed from different perspectives throughout the organization. It provides management with an organization blueprint for immediate strategic planning feedback. It also provides the conceptual schema, the logical data base design essential to DBAs for the development of data bases and information systems. It provides a definition of knowledge bases and expert rules for subsequent generation of expert business systems. We will now examine the data model in more detail.

3.2 THE DATA MODEL

Two pieces of documentation are produced by strategic, tactical and operations modeling which represent the data used by an organization. These are the entity list and the data map, which are collectively referred to as the **data model.**

3.2.1 The entity list

An **entity list** documents data entities and their attributes using a free-form representation (see Section 3.5). It helps managers, users and DP staff to identify the separate data attributes in a data entity. For example, an entity list may document a CUSTOMER entity and indicate that it is comprised of the following data attributes: *customer number, customer name, customer address, customer account balance, customer credit limit.*

The entity list establishes an agreed, standard terminology to be used by the organization. Together with the purpose description (basic and extended) of each entity and attribute, this terminology becomes the basis for a clear, unambiguous representation of data, which is essential for the design of information systems and expert business systems.

3.2.2 The data map

A **data map** schematically documents data entities and associations. It graphically illustrates the business strategy established to manage those associations and entities. A simple data map is illustrated in Figure 3.1 for the example introduced earlier.

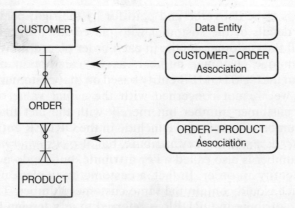

Figure 3.1 Example of a data map. This shows data entities and the associations between entities. (The symbols on the association lines are discussed later.)

3.3 | KEY ATTRIBUTES

In defining the attributes of a data entity, we need to know a number of things. Firstly, what distinguishes one occurrence of an entity from other entity occurrences? To answer this we will introduce the concept of keys, which are data attributes used to identify entities.

3.3.1 Primary keys

We usually identify different customers by allocating each a unique customer number. The *customer number* attribute is called a **key attribute**. In particular, as it is the unique identifier of a customer, it is referred to as the **primary** key attribute of the CUSTOMER entity. Similarly, we can distinguish between different orders by allocating each order a unique order number. Thus, *order number* is the primary key attribute of the ORDER entity.

3.3.2 Candidate keys

Several attributes may identify an entity. For example, if each customer name was unique, it would also be a candidate (with customer number) for selection as a primary key. Both *customer name* and *customer number* attributes, in this example, are called **candidate keys**. The candidate key selected becomes the primary key attribute (for example, *customer number*).

3.3.3 Foreign keys

If an order is to be delivered and paid for by the right person, we may need some details of the customer who placed the order. Rather than repeating all the customer details in each order placed, we only need to know the unique customer number, as we can obtain other details directly from the CUSTOMER entity based on that customer number. At this point, we are not concerned with the actual value of the order number or customer number but merely with the fact that there is a customer number. Therefore, we include in the ORDER entity, not only *order number* as a primary key attribute, but also *customer number*. This customer number is also called a key attribute, but we do not need it to uniquely identify an order. In fact, a customer may place many orders, each of which would contain the same customer number. The *customer number* key attribute in ORDER is referred to as a **foreign key**. We can use that foreign key to obtain details from the entity that has the same key attribute as its primary key – in this case the CUSTOMER entity.

Table 3.1   Quantity ordered depends on order number and product number.

Order Number	Product Number	Quantity Ordered
10	15	12
	16	20
75	15	1000
	16	2500

3.3.4   Compound keys

As we have seen, a primary key must uniquely identify each entity occurrence. However, in some cases, we may not be able to establish a unique primary key very readily. For example, consider the following problem: An order (order number 10) is placed for two products. It requires 12 items of product number 15 and 20 items of product number 16. Another order is received (order number 75) which also requires product numbers 15 and 16. This requires 1000 items of product 15 and 2500 items of product 16. Table 3.1 illustrates this example. What can we use to allocate the correct quantities of each product? If we use *product number* as the identifier, who receives 12 items of product 15 and who receives the 1000 items? If instead we use *order number* as the identifier, we cannot tell which product request is for 12 items and which is for 20.

It is obvious from Table 3.1 that we need to know *both* the order number and the product number to determine the correct quantity ordered. We say that the quantity ordered is dependent on both the *order number* and *product number*. Uniqueness is only established by using both key attributes as the primary key. We call this a **compound primary key**, referred to generally as a compound key. Alternatively, we could define another key attribute, *order line number*, to uniquely identify each line in the order. In this case, the compound key would be *order number* and *order line number*, with *product number* as a foreign key.

3.4 | NON-KEY ATTRIBUTES

Non-key attributes do not uniquely identify an entity; rather, they tell us something about that entity. For example, quantity ordered in Table 3.1 is a non-key attribute.

3.4.1   Selection attributes (secondary keys)

Some non-key attributes may be used to select certain entity occurrences. For example, we may wish to select all customers who live in a certain postal area, as indicated by the attribute *postcode* (or *zipcode*). However, as many customers may live in the same area, *postcode* is not unique and so cannot be defined as a primary key. We call it a **selection attribute**. It may also be called a **secondary key**; this term originated as a technical data base design term.

3.4.2　Group attributes

Sometimes we may wish to group a number of attributes under a single name, such as *customer address*; for example, there may be additional details relating to customer addresses, such as the street number, street name, suburb, city, state, postcode (zipcode) and perhaps country. We call the general term, *customer address*, a **group attribute**. This group attribute is made up of a number of detailed attributes. The group attribute name *customer address* can be used as a shorthand reference to the detailed attributes. We may initially identify *customer address* as a group attribute, but not concern ourselves with defining the underlying detailed attributes until some later time.

3.4.3　Repeating groups

There is one final term we must cover. When we discussed orders in Section 3.3.4, we referred to the number of products making up the order and the quantity ordered of each individual product. An order may comprise a request for a certain quantity of only one product, or it may include a number of requests for different products – with different quantities ordered of each of those products. For each product ordered, therefore, we may need *product number*, *product name* and *quantity ordered*. Although this also represents a group of attributes, it is different from the group attribute just introduced. Because there may be one or many occurrences of this group of attributes, we call it a **repeating group**. Each occurrence of the repeating group in our example records each separate product number, product name and quantity ordered of that product.

3.5　ENTITY LIST DOCUMENTATION

Strategic, tactical and operations modeling all concentrate on identifying entities and the attributes that comprise those entities. Business normalization is used for progressive attribute identification (see Chapters 7–9). As initial attributes are identified, new attributes may be discovered and noted in an entity list. The entity list documents, for each entity, the primary key or compound key attributes, non-key (data) attributes, secondary keys (selection attributes), group attributes, repeating groups and foreign keys.

Information engineering uses a specific entity list documentation convention to represent the various components comprising an entity. This allows convenient differentiation of attribute types when manually documenting entities (such as on a white board or on paper). These conventions can also be used by software to capture entity and attribute definitions.

Key attributes (whether primary key, compound key or foreign key) are identified as such by a '#' following the key attribute name. For example, customer number is shown as a key attribute by *customer number#*, where the '#' is spoken as 'key', as in 'customer number key'. Similarly, order number would be shown as *order number#* and spoken as 'order number key'.

Primary keys are differentiated from foreign keys by underlining them. Any key attribute (with a # at the end) that is not underlined is therefore a foreign key. A compound key brings together each of the separate primary key attributes needed to establish uniqueness. Each of those compound key attributes is underlined if it is a compound primary key; it is not underlined if it is a compound foreign key.

A selection attribute (secondary key) is identified by surrounding the selection attribute name by single left and right square brackets. For example, the selection attribute *postcode* is represented as *[postcode]*.

A derived attribute is identified by surrounding the attribute name with single left and right curly braces. For example, the derived attribute *customer account balance* is represented by *{customer account balance}*. This indicates that it is calculated from other attributes.

A group attribute (which may represent many detailed underlying data attributes) is indicated by surrounding the group attribute name with single left and right parentheses. For example, the group attribute *customer address* is represented as *(customer address)*.

A repeating group is shown by grouping each of the repeating data attributes together with the key attribute of that repeating group. In our example of *product number, product name* and *quantity ordered, product number#* is the repeating group key. A repeating group is identified by surrounding the entire group of repeating attributes with double left and right parentheses. Thus, the repeating group would be represented as *((product number#, product name, quantity ordered))*.

In documenting the entity, the entity name is written in capitals. This is followed by an initial left parenthesis and the primary key (or compound key attributes), which is underlined. The primary key is followed by any selection (secondary key) attributes, group attributes, derived attributes, repeating groups or non-key data attributes – so indicated by square brackets, single parentheses, curly braces, double parentheses or no brackets/parentheses respectively. Finally, any foreign key attributes are documented. This convention is illustrated in the following example:

ENTITY   (primary key-1#, primary key-2#, ...
        [selection attribute-1], [selection attribute-2], ...
        (group attribute-1), (group attribute-2), ...
        {derived attribute-1}, {derived attribute-2}, ...
        ((repeating attribute-1)), ((repeating attribute-2)), ...
        non key attribute-1, non key attribute-2, ...
        foreign key-1#, foreign key-2#, ...

The exact sequence of selection attributes, non-key attributes, group attributes, repeating group attributes and foreign keys as illustrated here need not be followed rigorously. They may be scattered throughout the entity list notation for a specific entity. The only real requirement is that the primary key attributes be underlined and precede all other attributes. The following examples illustrate this convention:

ORDER   (order number#, [order date], date required, customer number#, ((product number#,
        product name, quantity ordered)), {sale price} delivery address)

EMPLOYEE (employee number#, [employee name], employee title, ((course number#, course name,
        course start date, exam result)), manager number#, manager name)

This notation is a free-form representation of the attributes in each entity. This representation is useful during initial discovery of entities and attributes in strategic, tactical and operations modeling. More formal documentation is produced using an expert design dictionary (see Part Four).

There is no restriction on the way in which each attribute or entity is named, apart from the need for each name to be unique. However, the name should not be abbreviated, but written out in full to avoid misunderstanding. Furthermore, the use of mnemonic names or acronyms (such as CUSTNO) is discouraged, as what may be an obvious abbreviation to one person may be totally unintelligible to another. The need to abbreviate data names because of the limitations of computer languages does not exist here.

The entity list enables us to record the detailed attributes making up each entity. The other documentation conventions used relate to the data map. This illustrates the associations that exist between different entities in the organization, and the management strategy used to manage those entities.

CHAPTER 4

Data Modeling:
Conventions

This chapter builds on the terminology introduced in Chapter 3. It focuses first on conventions used for data modeling. Once we have covered these conventions, we will be equipped to examine the different data modeling approaches that have emerged since the introduction of Codd's relational model. Several approaches are discussed at the end of the chapter: entity–relationship modeling, extended entity–relationship modeling, semantic modeling and binary modeling.

4.1 INTRODUCTION

Initially, data modeling focused on data used for operational systems. Such data existed in the form of source documents, reports, enquiries, file formats and manual ledgers used for existing manual and automated systems. These were used to identify entities, attributes and associations. Entities and attributes are documented in an entity list format, as shown in Figures 3.2 and 3.3, while entities and associations are illustrated in data map format, as shown in Figure 3.1. We will now look at the conventions for drawing data maps.

Entities are represented in a data map as rectangular boxes, with the name of each entity in capitals inside the box. Associations between two or more entities are indicated by lines joining those entities. A simple data map representing customers and orders, and the association between each customer and each order, is represented in Figure 4.1.

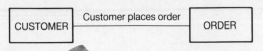

Figure 4.1 A simple data map. This represents a CUSTOMER entity and an ORDER entity, and shows that an association exists between them, named 'Customer places order'.

As a typical organization may have hundreds of entities in its data map, for graphical clarity, an association name is not written on large data maps. Instead, it is separately documented in an association dictionary in conjunction with the entities that are interrelated and the description of the strategy represented by the association. A manual association dictionary is discussed in Chapter 6.

The simple data map in Figure 4.1 can be used to represent many entities and the associations between them. In most organizations, the association lines represent formal strategies established by management to ensure related entities are properly managed. We can graphically represent strategies by including symbolic notations on the association lines. This notation schematically documents often quite complex strategies and management controls. It is introduced in the following section.

4.2 BASIC ASSOCIATIONS

Basic associations are classified into three categories, referred to as the degree or cardinality of an association. We will use the term *degree* in this book.

- One-to-one associations.
- One-to-many associations.
- Many-to-many associations.

4.2.1 One-to-one associations

A one-to-one association between two entities is represented by a single straight line. It indicates that an occurrence of one entity is related to only one occurrence of another entity. Figure 4.2 illustrates this convention.

As discussed in Chapter 3, an association purpose description is a procedure-oriented statement; that is, it indicates *how* the association is used. Consequently, there may be several extended purpose descriptions

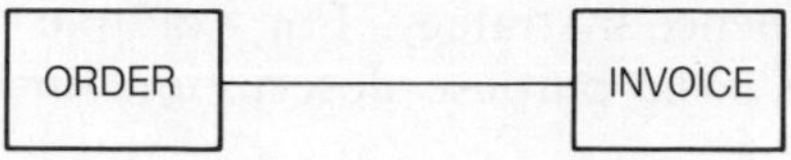

BASIC PURPOSE DESCRIPTION

Every order has one invoice and
every invoice applies to one order.

STRATEGY

*An order is not invoiced until it can be fully satis-
fied, and then only one invoice is prepared for
that order.*

Figure 4.2 A one-to-one association, with a basic purpose description and a possible strategy used by an organization for that association.

for the same association. For example, the following purpose description indicates the use of this association by the warehouse department:

> *'When all products have been selected and the order has been packed for shipment, a copy of that order is sent to the accounts department who prepare a single invoice for payment of the order. If any products cannot be supplied to complete the order, it is not shipped, and the accounts department is notified that the order is incomplete.'*

An association extended purpose description provides a more detailed definition of the business rules expressed by the association. In this form, it can be used for preliminary specifications of the logic to be carried out by programs that use the association. It also provides a preliminary definition of expert rules to be attached to the association.

The exact interpretation of this association, and the definition of its purpose, depends on the organization, its business rules or expert rules, and the logic to be attached to those rules. Different parts of the business may use the association in different ways. For example, the accounts department may define an extended purpose description for this same association as:

> *'All orders are invoiced at the end of the month. One invoice is prepared for each, but only if all products requested in that order have been shipped. If any products cannot be supplied, the order is incomplete and no invoice is prepared.'*

Thus, the data map initiates discussion; it is a catalyst for uncovering and evaluating alternative strategies. Managers and users discuss different interpretations of the association and eventually agree on a particular interpretation, and hence a strategy. For example, an overall strategy developed from the basic purpose description for all departments of Figure 4.2 is:

> *'An order is not invoiced until it can be fully satisfied, and then only one invoice is prepared for that order.'*

Each association is named and its purpose description is documented in an association dictionary. Similarly, each strategy is documented in a strategic planning dictionary. Both of these dictionaries are discussed in Chapter 6. Each strategy is related (linked) back to its relevant association. When referencing that association, the agreed interpretation of the strategy is therefore available, and vice versa.

ORDER and INVOICE are tactical entities that are used for day-to-day operations. Senior management, however, is not interested in this level of detail; they are more interested in aggregated data such as SALES REVENUE and ACCOUNTS RECEIVABLE, which are strategic entities. Tactical entities lead to tactical associations and to the definition of relevant operational tactics, just as strategic entities lead to strategic associations and to the definition of senior management strategies. (These concepts are discussed further in Part Three.) To avoid confusion, we will use the generic term 'strategy' to refer to either strategy or tactic statements derived from the association purpose description, as illustrated in Figure 4.2. In addition, we will only use the *basic* purpose description when defining a strategy from an association. The different extended purpose descriptions that may apply to an association from various parts of an organization will not be considered.

4.2.2   One-to-many associations

Figure 4.3 illustrates a one-to-many association between ORDER and INVOICE. The many end of the association line is represented by a 'crowsfoot' at the end of the line touching the entity that has many occurrences (INVOICE). The other end of the line touches the entity with only one occurrence (ORDER); it has no crowsfoot, so representing **one.**

The part of the association that represents *one*, or *many* occurrences of the related entity, is called the **degree** of the association. This is one characteristic of an association. We can see that, by changing the association degree from one in Figure 4.2 to many in Figure 4.3, we can represent quite a different business strategy.

4.2.3   Many-to-many associations

Figure 4.4 represents a rather complex association between orders and products. We discussed previously that an order may be made up of one

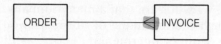

PURPOSE DESCRIPTION

An order may have many invoices,
but each invoice applies to only one order.

STRATEGY

*An order will be progressively invoiced, as back-
ordered products are delivered to the customer
in fulfilling that order.*

Figure 4.3 A one-to-many association. The many invoices belonging to an order are represented by the crowsfoot on the association line at the INVOICE end. The single order that each invoice applies to is represented by no crowsfoot at the ORDER end of the line.

or many products. We may have represented this in the entity list as a repeating group of *product number, product name* and *quantity ordered* within the ORDER entity. Similarly, the product might be requested in many orders. The PRODUCT entity would therefore have a repeating group of *order number*. This is certainly a real-life situation: one where we hope that a specific product will be requested in many orders, where each order may also request many other products. These reciprocal repeating groups result in the **many-to-many association**, with crowsfeet at each end indicating this association.

PURPOSE DESCRIPTION

An order is for many products, but a
product may be ordered in many orders.

ISSUE

*We cannot determine which products are to be
supplied for each order. We cannot determine
which products are in demand, and which are
slow movers.*

Figure 4.4 A many-to-many association. This represents a poorly defined business strategy: it is not clear which products belong to each order, and vice versa. In its present form, it is not a clear strategy. It indicates potential problems if used this way. It is expressed as an issue.

In Chapter 7, we will learn that a many-to-many association can be decomposed through the technique of normalization into two, one-to-many associations with an intermediate entity, as illustrated in Figure 4.5. The intermediate entity in this figure, between the ORDER and the PRODUCT entities, may be named by its associated entities, such as ORDER–PRODUCT. An intermediate entity is also called an **intersecting entity**. We may need to think of a more appropriate name for this intermediate entity: one that is more descriptive of the data it contains. The entity in fact comprises the repeating groups ((product number, product name, quantity ordered)) and ((order number)) which we discussed earlier. These were the ORDER entity repeating group ((*product number*, *product name*, *quantity ordered*)) and the PRODUCT entity repeating group ((*order number*)). The content of the ORDER–PRODUCT entity is the combination of these two repeating groups, namely:

ORDER–PRODUCT   (order number#, product number#, product name, quantity ordered)

This representation of attributes in an intersecting entity will be discussed in more detail in Chapter 7, in relation to first normal form.

Examining the attributes in ORDER–PRODUCT, we may decide that a more appropriate name would be ORDER LINE ITEM. It represents, for example, each line on an order form detailing for that order: the product number, the product name and the quantity ordered of that product. In this case, we may choose to use as part of the compound primary key *order line number* with *product number* now defined as a foreign key, and change the name of the entity more appropriately to ORDER LINE ITEM:

ORDER LINE ITEM   (order number#, order line number#, product name, quantity ordered, product number#)

The decision whether to use *product number* or *order line number* as the second part of the compound primary key depends on the business requirements. For example, use of order forms with preprinted line numbers may suggest that *order line number* is an appropriate key. The product is then identified by the foreign key *product number*.

Figure 4.5 illustrates the decomposition of the many-to-many association in Figure 4.4 to two, one-to-many associations with the intermediate ORDER LINE ITEM entity. This is a graphical representation of one of the normalization rules; it represents application of the first normal form rule.

An intersecting entity is used to determine which
products relate to which orders.

ORDER LINE ITEM (order number#, order line number#,
product name, quantity ordered,
product number#)

So data map is . . .

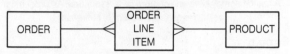

PURPOSE DESCRIPTION

An order is made up of one or many order line
items, and a product may be requested in one or
many order items.

Figure 4.5 Decomposition of a many-to-many association into two, one-to-many
associations with an intersecting entity.

4.2.4   Management controls

We are now able to represent some of the intrinsic associations and
strategies that exist between various data entities in an organization.
However, one of the key ingredients is missing: **management controls**.

For example, we may wish to represent the fact that related entities
must be present; that is, they are **mandatory**. In other circumstances,
related entities may be absent; in other words, they may be **optional**. For
example, an order must be associated with one, and only one, customer.
This is mandatory. The order can then be delivered to the correct
customer and subsequently paid by that customer. On the other hand, a
customer who is presently inactive may currently have no orders to be
filled. In this case, the association of the customer with the order is
optional. These clarify the **nature** of the association (that is, whether it is
mandatory or optional). Hence, an association is described by its degree
(or cardinality, as discussed earlier) and its nature. These represent
additional controls that apply to the association.

Management controls are represented by additional notations on
the association lines between entities. We show the mandatory nature of
an association by drawing a short line, at right angles, across the end of
the association line close to the entity that must be present. We indicate
an optional nature by drawing a small circle across the end of the
association line close to the entity that need not be present. Figure 4.6

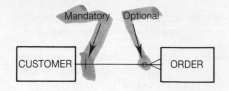

PURPOSE DESCRIPTION

A customer may have one or more orders, or none. An order must belong to one, and only one, customer

STRATEGY

Our customers are considered customers regardless of the number of orders they currently have on the books – even if they are presently inactive. An order can only be accepted if it is placed by a customer who is on our books, and who has sufficient credit available such that the total cost of this order will not cause the customer's account balance to exceed the credit limit.

Figure 4.6   A mandatory one-to-optional many association between CUSTOMER and ORDER.

illustrates the conventions for representing an association nature. Note that the mandatory association of ORDER with CUSTOMER is expressed in the strategy statement to ensure that certain checking of the customer is carried out before the order is accepted. The specific interpretation of this mandatory association may differ from organizaiton to organizaiton. For a company that makes tailor-made clothes, it may be interpreted instead by the strategy:

> *'We must measure the customer before we will accept and make the order: therefore the customer must visit the tailor.'*

Another interpretation is illustrated in Figure 4.6. Because the organization is not a 'cash' business (such as the retail store earlier), an invoice is prepared, to be subsequently paid by the customer. The organization establishes a credit control strategy to ensure the customer can subsequently pay the invoice before it will accept the order.

Figure 4.7 illustrates an appropriate strategy for a cash business, using an optional one-to-optional many association. Note the interpretation of the optional indicator close to the CUSTOMER entity in the strategy statement documented below the data map. This indicates that customer details are not required if the customer has already selected and paid for the goods. (We will see, in Chapter 9, that the optional one association in this example indicates incomplete normalization.)

Let us now consider more strict control: a mandatory one-to-

PURPOSE DESCRIPTION

A customer may have one or many orders, or none.
An order may belong to one customer, or none.

STRATEGY

We will accept an order from a customer once the customer has
selected the goods and paid for them. We do not need to know
anything else about the customer.

Figure 4.7   An optional one-to-optional many association between CUSTOMER
and ORDER.

mandatory many association. Figure 4.8 represents a strategy in which no
order is allowed to leave the organization unless it is accompanied by an
invoice. Because there may be many invoices for an order, it further
indicates that an order is to be progressively invoiced as back-ordered
items are received from suppliers to satisfy the original order. Each of
these invoices must be produced at the time the order (or back-order) is
shipped and must accompany that order (or back-order), as indicated by
the mandatory nature at INVOICE. Figure 4.8 therefore represents the

PURPOSE DESCRIPTION

An order must have one or many invoices, but at least
one. An invoice must belong to one, and only one, order.

STRATEGY

If any products in an order cannot be supplied, those products
will be back-ordered and sent later. An order must have at least
one invoice but there may be many invoices, one for each
back-order. On the other hand, each invoice applies to one and
only one order and is shipped with the relevant order or a sub-
sequent back-order.

Figure 4.8   A mandatory one-to-mandatory many association between ORDER and
INVOICE. The invoice must be prepared and sent when an order or back-order is
shipped. This applies to a pre-billing (pre-invoicing) organization.

PURPOSE DESCRIPTION

An order may have one or many invoices, or none.
An invoice belongs to one, and only one, order.

STRATEGY

An order may have one or many invoices, but those invoices need not be prepared until a later time. An invoice relates to one, and only one, order and must be prepared and sent after the order is shipped.

Figure 4.9 A data map with a post-billing association between ORDER and INVOICE. Invoices may be sent after the order has been shipped.

strategy of a 'pre-billing' ('pre-invoicing') organization – a company that sends the invoice included with the products requested in the order.

A post-invoicing organization, on the other hand, which sends the invoice at a later time, separate from the shipped order, might be represented by Figure 4.9. Because of the optional association of the order to the invoice, an invoice need not exist when the order is first placed. The invoice may be prepared at a later time and mailed to the customer some time after the order is shipped – perhaps at the end of the month.

However, while correctly representing post-invoicing, Figure 4.9 does leave the organization open to a potential problem. For example, it implies an order may be processed and no invoice need ever be prepared and sent for that order. This might be the case for orders that are to be donated to charitable institutions, but for most customers management will require at least one invoice to be prepared for each order, even if it is at a later time. This extra control can be represented by a further notation: an optional circle and a mandatory line on the association, both close to the entity to which this additional control relates. This situation is called '**optional tending to mandatory**' or '**transitional**' **association** nature. Figure 4.10 illustrates the additional control that this places on the example used in Figure 4.9.

In the foregoing examples, we documented the basic purpose description of each association as a narrative statement, including its degree and nature. Additional details of how the association is used and how the controls are applied are expressed in the extended purpose description for the association, which offers further perspective. As we

PURPOSE DESCRIPTION

An order may initially have no invoices, but must at
some time have at least one, or many invoices.
Each invoice belongs to one, and only one, order.

STRATEGY

*An order will have one or many invoices. Initially an invoice
need not exist, but at least one invoice must be prepared at a
later time. Each invoice relates to one, and only one, order.*

Figure 4.10 A data map representing post-billing, with control to ensure that at least one invoice is produced for each order.

saw earlier, it is useful in establishing an agreed strategy. Each strategy indicates how the association is used by different interested parts of the organization. The exact interpretation of an association and the strategies it supports will usually differ from organization to organization, due to the differences that exist between enterprises in the way they conduct their business.

Each association and its controls are used subsequently by management as input to define business conditions, or controls. In modeling terminology, these are called **constraints**. Conditions must be satisfied, as they ensure that the strategy is carried out and the controls are enforced. For manual systems, strategies are followed by staff who manually check that each defined condition is observed. For automated systems, conditions are translated into conditional logic tests. These tests are carried out by programs that implement the specified strategy and ensure the controls are enforced.

Business conditions are defined during the analysis phase, as we have seen with the purpose descriptions and strategy statements. They are derived from the data map, association purpose descriptions and strategy statements in the relevant dictionaries. If the business conditions (rules) change at a later time, managers and users may make these changes in the data map: the affected programs are then changed.

We can now use these basic association conventions to represent rather detailed strategies and controls. This will help us to identify possible alternative strategies: whether they indicate new business opportunities or permit greater (or less) control to be exercised. As indicated earlier, associations require interpretation. They provide a catalyst for discussion of business alternatives from which comes agreed meaning and use. In their expanded form, as extended purpose descriptions and strategies, they become the input for expression and implementation of the expert rules of the business, for development of expert business systems.

4.3 IDENTIFICATION OF ALTERNATIVE STRATEGIES

The data map conventions we have covered so far allow us to represent the associations that exist between entities. The *one* or *many* degree and *mandatory* or *optional* nature at each end of an association line is used as a catalyst to express the purpose of that association. Different areas of the business may interpret an association differently: how they manage the data represented by the related entities; how they use the data; how they refer to the data or process the data. These interpretations indicate how the data is related and how the association is used by them. This can suggest alternative strategies as described in the following.

We will change the degree, and then the nature, at each end of an association. For example, if the degree of one end is many, we will change it to one; if it is one, we will change it to many. Similarly, if the nature is mandatory, we will change it to optional, and vice versa. By changing the one or many and mandatory or optional representations of an association, some interesting strategies can emerge for consideration. Some changes may not have much meaning to the business, but other changes may suggest situations that should not occur, but which could arise; hence, additional controls may need to be defined to prevent them. Still others may suggest possible future business changes, thereby giving management the opportunity to discuss these and agree on appropriate strategies. Some changes may even suggest completely new business opportunities.

The basic association conventions already discussed represent the strategy for management of parts of the organization. The management strategy reflects the way the data is interrelated, since the data represents the organization. Using the data map and association conventions, we can identify alternative strategies. The data map illustrates alternative strategic planning directions relating to the data – and hence the part of the business that manages that data. Let us investigate how this might work.

As an example, we will use part of a data map from a manufacturing organization showing one association between two entities: PRODUCT and PART. This represents parts that are used to manufacture a particular product. We will observe a modeling session conducted by the

STRATEGY

Each of our products consists of one or many parts. However each part is made for only one product, and is not used in any other products in our range.

Figure 4.11   A strategy relating to products and parts used in their manufacture.

General Manager, the Manufacturing Manager, and the Warehousing and Marketing Managers of the organization. We will listen as they change the association to identify alternative strategies. In this and the following examples, we will only document the statement of strategy as interpreted by management. We will not also show its purpose description.

The association between PRODUCT and PART is illustrated in the data map in Figure 4.11. This data map represents the business as it is today: a manufacturing organization with a limited number of products. Each product has been designed to be manufactured by assembling unique parts, specially designed for that product. The organization is growing and will shortly introduce additional products, at which time other strategies may be appropriate. The data map provides a useful aid to consider some of these alternatives.

The managers first change the PRODUCT end of the association from one (in Figure 4.11) to many (in Figure 4.12). Figure 4.12 shows that this represents an important change in strategy; an interesting variation has been introduced. What does this suggest to management? The Manufacturing Manager immediately sees an opportunity from this:

'This is interesting, and something I have been thinking about for some time. An interpretation is the use of interchangeable parts that can be used for the

STRATEGY

Each of our products is manufactured from one or many parts. Furthermore, each part stocked must be used in at least one of the products we manufacture, but may be used in more than one product.

Figure 4.12   A different manufacturing strategy from that of Figure 4.11.

Each of our products is manufactured from one or many parts. Furthermore, parts that we stock may be used in one or more products, but we will also stock parts that are not used in the manufacture of any of our products.

Figure 4.13   Another manufacturing strategy.

manufacture of more than one product. This way we can standardize on a small number of parts. Some products may need some redesign and retooling, but not a great deal. This reworking cost can be recovered from the substantial savings in lower inventory carrying costs and more efficient manufacturing which will result from this alternative manufacturing strategy. I believe we should investigate this opportunity further.'

Together they make another change. The mandatory nature at the PRODUCT end of the association is next changed to optional, as shown in Figure 4.13. But this change seems to be suggesting something rather strange: that they will stock parts for products they do not manufacture! Why would they want to do that? It seems quite inappropriate. This is an alternative that management had not considered before, so they discuss it further. It seems unnecessary to the Manufacturing Manager; it takes up valuable warehouse space for the Warehousing Manager; but it suggests an intriguing marketing strategy to the Marketing Manager. He reminds the other managers of certain facts: they all know that the products they manufacture are of exceptionally high quality and that those of their competitiors are of poor quality. He goes on to say:

'If we stock not only parts used in the manufacture of our own products, but also high-quality spare parts that can be used to repair our competitors' products, we can then offer those spare parts for sale. Our competitors' customers can purchase the spare parts from us, to repair their defective products. They will gain first-hand experience in the quality of our spare parts. They may then choose to purchase future replacement parts and products not from the competitors but from us.'

This has identified a market opportunity: do-it-yourself kits for repairing their competitors' products! The Manufacturing Manager then adds:

'It also suggests that we might want to contract for other organizations to manufacture low-volume products which represent high cost and low margins to us. It would be cheaper to buy them in, than make them ourselves.'

Similarly, we can discuss the interpretation of changes made to the PART end of the association. Instead of a product manufactured from many parts, what would it mean if it was manufactured from only one part, or even no parts – that is, the nature is optional? The Warehousing Manager joins in:

'We have problems with consistent quality and prompt delivery from several of our parts' suppliers. If we contracted for manufacture of those relevant products outside, we could concentrate on the remaining products where we can be confident of reliable supply and quality. And of course we would be saving a lot on inventory carrying costs for the parts we no longer have to stock.'

The General Manager then takes up the discussion:

'This is all suggesting that not only should we have some products manufactured outside, but perhaps even overseas. Material and labour costs are lower. Some countries can manufacture complete products for less than we can buy the parts from our suppliers. And the quality of other products in our industry manufactured in those countries is high. In fact, why not license some of our products for manufacture and sale in countries that we never intend to expand into? This all bears further investigation. It's an exciting thought!'

We will see in Parts Three and Four that the data and strategies used to manage an organization, as represented in the data map, offer a very useful tool for identification and feedback to management of strategic alternatives. Such interactive strategic planning allows management to undertake a 'what if' investigative approach to strategic planning. They can analyze the data map representation of the organization and identify new business opportunities.

When we cover the steps of strategic modeling and tactical modeling in Part Three, we will see how varying associations in this way can be used as an extremely effective strategic planning tool. Often, quite complex variations are found to exist in real life in most organizations. The data map allows management to see clearly the implications of these strategic variations.

The complexity of these associations sometimes extends beyond the capability of the basic associations we have discussed. For example, we may find not only associations between entities, but also associations betweens associations. These are documented using extended associations and are addressed in Chapter 5.

4.4 | EVOLUTION OF THE RELATIONAL MODEL

Codd's relational model provided a new way for representing data through the use of tables [1]. Both DP professionals and users alike found his method easier to understand than the previous methods of data representation. By the early 70s, a number of methods had emerged to represent data, all of which were based on the structure of the data. Four main approaches were in common use: hierarchical (for example, IBM's IMS); network (for example, IBM's BOMP, Cincom's TOTAL); CODA-SYL (IDMS from ICL and Cullinet); or inverted list (Software AG's ADABAS). Each of these depended on embedded pointers in computer files to relate data in other files. These pointers physically implemented associations (relationships) between files. In contrast, in the relational model, data was interrelated based on the existence of common data columns, such as keys. (We will discuss this further in Chapters 7–9.)

Codd's work spawned considerable research in the 70s into data modeling techniques and also into the development of relational data base management systems (RDBMSs). Both of these research efforts are discussed here.

4.4.1 Relational data base

In parallel with research into data modeling techniques, activity was also focused on the physical implementation of the relational model on computers. IBM initiated its System R project for the development of a prototype RDBMS product. This also led to the development of a 4GL designed to be used for processing against an RDBMS – structured query language (SQL).

Oracle Corporation was the first company to release a commercial RDBMS product, in 1979, which was called ORACLE. IBM followed in 1981 with the release of SQL/DS, and then DB2 in 1983. SQL was integral to each of these products, so with this endorsement by IBM, SQL was adopted as a standard 4GL by the American National Standards Institute (ANSI) in October 1986. Consequently, almost every DBMS vendor today supports the relational model through SQL. We will leave any further discussion of relational data base management systems until Part Four.

4.4.2 Extensions to the relational model

In the late 70s, Codd developed several extensions to the relational model to capture more data meaning [2]. These were published a few months after he had traveled to Tasmania, possibly explaining for this version of the relational model – the RM/T model: relational model/ Tasmania. The extensions (together with their parallels in information engineering) were as follows:

- The need for mandatory and optional nature at each end of an association, and the development of extended associations (which signify incomplete business normalization – see Chapters 5 and 8). The integrity rules defined in RM/T reflected these needs.

- Definition of the kernel entity, characteristic entity and associative entity, which had some parallel in the information engineering principal, secondary and intersecting entity types respectively (see Chapters 7–9).

- The need to normalize to the level of fourth normal form, to model the existence of subtypes (see Chapter 8) and supertypes.

- The need to establish a single internal (unchangeable) primary key in place of compound keys for physical data base design and automatic data base generation (see Chapter 9). RM/T addresses this with surrogate keys.

4.5 | DATA MODELING APPROACHES

Data modeling offers an analysis and design method. It helps to define the requirements of users, and then to design systems that satisfy those needs. Data modeling leads to development of logical data base designs based on users' needs. These logical designs can be converted to physical data base designs using many available hierarchical, network, CODA-SYL, inverted list or relational DBMS products in the market place.

As we have seen, data modeling focuses on the logical representation of data. To assist this, Codd introduced the formal process of normalization. We will address both formal normalization and business normalization in detail in Chapters 7–9.

From the early 70s, research was undertaken both in academia and in commercial organizations to apply Codd's work to the development of data models that could then be used for data base design. As discussed in Chapter 2, by the mid-70s at least three organizations had made the bridge from normalization to data base design: CACI in Europe, BIS in UK and Information Engineering Services Pty Ltd in Australia. This bridge was initially based on the Bachman notation to represent data.

4.5.1   Bachman notation

The Bachman notation was named after Charles Bachman, an early pioneer of the CODASYL data base specification (see Chapter 2). This notation was used for the schematic representation of a physical CODASYL data base design. A Bachman diagram is illustrated in Figure 4.14.

The Bachman notation, while useful for illustrating entities (as record types) and associations (as set relationships), was not adequate to represent the considerable business meaning generally applied to each association. There was no concept of association nature: mandatory, optional or optional becoming mandatory.

Data modeling has evolved dramatically since these early years, with more meaning having been incorporated into the data model.

4.5.2   Entity–relationship modeling

In 1976, Peter Chen introduced the entity–relationship model, called the E–R model [3]. This extended the Bachman notation to show explicitly the data meaning of relationships. Relationships are modeled as diamonds; and entities as boxes. This model can also illustrate identifying attributes (primary keys) and descriptive attributes (non-key attributes), if desired. Figure 4.15 provides one example of the E–R notation, based on evolution since Chen's initial paper [4].

Figure 4.15 shows that a CUSTOMER places one or many ORDERS made up of one or many ORDER LINEs, each for a PRODUCT. This notation uses a crowsfoot for *many* and no crowsfoot for *one*. Additionally, a solid circle represents *mandatory*, while an open

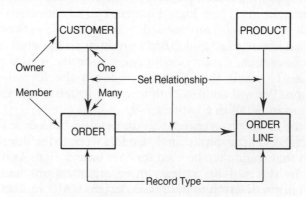

Figure 4.14   A simple example of Bachman notation. This was used to represent schematically a CODASYL data base design.

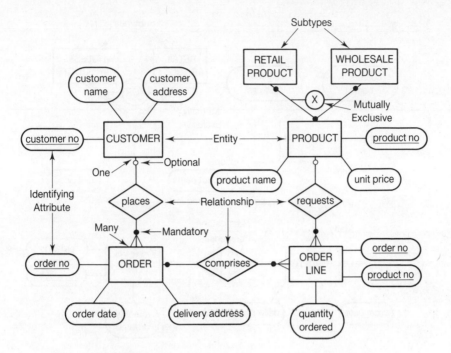

Figure 4.15 An entity–relationship diagram.

circle represents *optional*. This representation of mandatory and optional is used at the end of the line close to the referring entity, rather than at the referenced entity end as is described in this book. A different notation is sometimes also used, as illustrated in Figure 4.16 for extended E–R modeling.

Figure 4.15 further shows that there are subtypes of PRODUCT: RETAIL PRODUCT and WHOLESALE PRODUCT. Lines join PRODUCT to its subtypes, each with a mandatory solid circle. These lines are then joined by another line, with a circled X to represent *mutually exclusive*. This is referred to as a constraint and represents the business rule 'a product is either retail or wholesale, but cannot be both'. We will see another way of indicating subtypes and constraints, when we cover extended associations in Chapter 5.

4.5.3 Extended entity–relationship model

The E–R model has since been further extended to capture still more meaning. This is referred to as the extended E–R model, sometimes called the EER model [5, 6]. Figure 4.16 illustrates one EER representation of Figure 4.15.

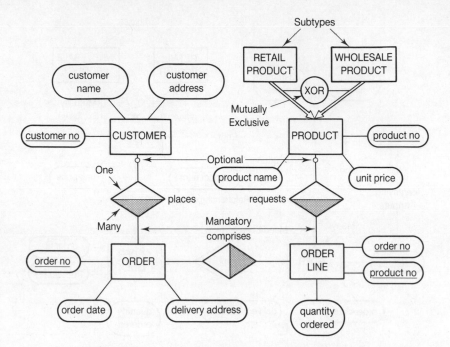

Figure 4.16 An extended entity–relationship model.

The notation for the EER model leaves the relationship diamond 'open' closest to an entity that is *one*, and 'solid' (shaded) closest to an entity that is *many*. An *optional* association is shown with an open circle on the line, while a *mandatory* association has no circle on the line – but is close to the referring entity rather than the referenced entity as described in this book. A subset (subtype) association is shown as an open arrow (see PRODUCT, with the subtypes RETAIL PRODUCT and WHOLE-SALE PRODUCT). These are mutually exclusive which is represented by XOR on the line joining the subtype open arrows. It shows the business rule discussed in conjunction with Figure 4.15.

Note that, in these examples of E–R and EER notation, mandatory and optional nature apply to the whole line; there is no opportunity to represent mandatory or optional at each end of the line to identify alternative strategies, as we saw earlier in the chapter.

The E–R and the EER model can represent binary relationships (between two entities), as shown in Figures 4.15 and 4.16, ternary relationships (between three entities), quaternary relationships (four entities), and so on. These are referred to as *n*-ary relationships (between *n* entities). Figure 4.17 illustrates a ternary relationship between PERSON, SKILL and PROJECT. It shows that: a project *must* (mandatory)

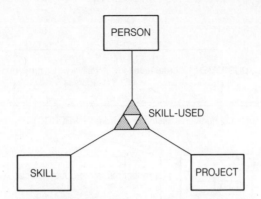

Figure 4.17   A ternary relationship.

use many skills and many persons; a person *must* work on many projects (over time) and have many skills; and a skill *must* be used on many projects and be held by many persons. The ternary relationship is called SKILL–USED. This is represented in entity list notation as follows:

SKILL–USED   (person number#, skill number#, project number#, project skill allowance)

This indicates that a skill held by a person in relation to a specific project may result in a special *project skill allowance* to be paid to the person.

Represented in this way, we can see that *n*-ary relationships in E–R or EER notation are analogous to intersecting entities, as illustrated in Figure 4.5 for ORDER LINE ITEM. We will further see, in later chapters, that an intersecting entity can have any number of other entities related to it. Each of these entities is related to the intersecting entity by an association, and that association can represent many different business strategies, through varying the degree and nature at each end of the association line, as we have seen in this chapter.

4.5.4   Semantic modeling

This chapter, and each data modeling extension just described, has focused on providing more data meaning; that is, to capture greater semantic information relating to business. As this has been achieved, the term *data modeling* has evolved to *information modeling*. At the same time, the process of *data analysis* (used to develop data models) has also evolved to *information analysis* (used to develop information models). Chapter 2 discussed these evolutionary stages of information engineering.

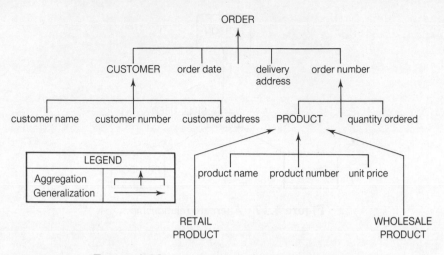

Figure 4.18   An example of semantic modeling.

In recent years, a further modeling approach, called **semantic modeling**, has emerged. This uses entities and relationships, both of which are characterized by **properties** (that is, attributes). Entities, relationships and properties are further classified into **types**: the entity–type CUSTOMER; the relationship–type REQUESTED–ORDER; the property–type CUSTOMER NAME [7].

In modeling, it is sometimes difficult, initially, to distinguish between an entity and an attribute. The same data may be an attribute in one part of an organization, while it is an entity in another part of the same organization. For example, when an order is first placed, the order department needs to know the *customer number* for that order. The accounts department is also interested in the *customer number*, but is much more concerned with the *customer account balance, customer credit limit* and *customer address*. To the order department, *customer* is only an attribute of the order, needed to determine ownership of the order. For the accounts department, however, CUSTOMER is an entity: they require more detail so they can decide whether, first the order, can be accepted based on the customer's account balance in relationship to his credit limit, and, later, so they can send an invoice to the customer.

To overcome this initial difficulty in data definition, semantic modeling avoids the distinction between entity–type and property–type. Instead, it uses two abstraction forms: **aggregation** and **generalization**. This approach allows easy representation of entities, subtypes and relationships, as illustrated in Figure 4.18. This clearly shows all related information, and is particularly useful at the application level. Different variants of semantic modeling use a single-headed arrow to represent *one* and a double-headed arrow to represent *many*. Not all variants have implemented the concept of *mandatory* or *optional* nature on the aggregation or generalization links to represent business meaning, as we have discussed in this chapter. However, this will only be a matter of time.

Normalization (see Chapters 7–9) is an integral step in Codd's RM/T model, in E–R and EER modeling, and also in semantic modeling. It is used to decompose data into a stable representation. However, in the late 70s, another data modeling technique emerged: binary modeling.

4.5.5   Binary modeling

Binary modeling does not depend on initial normalization; rather, it decomposes the natural language sentences that describe the business meaning into a diagram. This diagram is then converted to a data base design. While E–R and EER modeling allow two or more entities to participate in *n*-ary relationships, binary modeling always uses two entities and binary relationships, hence the name.

Binary modeling [8] uses **object types** and **fact types**. An example of an object type is CUSTOMER. This is called a **non-lexical object type** and corresponds generally to an entity. A non-lexical object type may have a number of **lexical object types**, such as CUSTOMER NUMBER, CUS-TOMER NAME, CUSTOMER ADDRESS, which generally correspond to attributes.

There may be two kinds of fact types: an **idea type** and a **bridge type**. An idea type connects two non-lexical object types and carries informa-tion. 'A CUSTOMER places an ORDER' is one example; thus, it corresponds generally to an association. On the other hand, a bridge type does not carry information; it merely names the association. Each fact type has two roles, one for each object type in the relationship; for example 'a CUSTOMER places an ORDER' and 'an ORDER is placed by a CUSTOMER'.

The binary model uses **generalization hierarchies**, which correspond to subtypes in the E–R and EER models. Constraints are used to represent business meaning. Figure 4.19 illustrates Figure 4.15, now using binary modeling.

The focus of binary modeling is to decompose natural language statements into a schematic representation, as shown in Figure 7.19. It does not rely on normalization, but is totally dependent on the accuracy of the original statement that is decomposed. We will see (in Part Three) that such statements need considerable refinement before all interested areas of an organization agree on its meaning. Only then is it appropriate to decompose it through binary modeling. We will see in Chapters 7–9

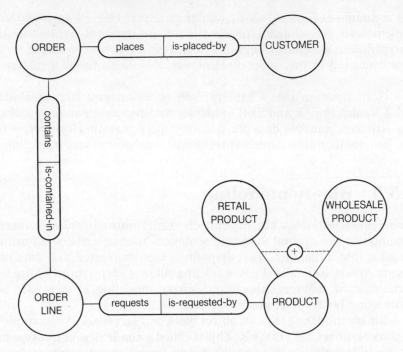

Figure 4.19 A binary model of the example in Figure 4.15.

that normalization is a powerful tool, when used by business experts to identify alternative representations of data. It allows them to evaluate different data interpretations and agree on the data and their meaning. Used in this way, it helps define the future.

4.5.6 Summary of data modeling approaches

Data modeling, and later information modeling, has evolved along a consistent path, at all times moving to capture more business meaning – that is, greater information semantics. The extension of the relational model to RM/T used normalization to achieve this objective. E–R and EER modeling use a rich variety of schematics, including entities, attributes and relationships on the data map together with subtypes and business constraints. Similarly, semantic modeling uses generalization and aggregation to show relationships, business constraints and subtypes.

The schematic inclusion of attributes in a data model is extremely beneficial, as it allows users to see at a glance the available data. This is particularly effective for the design of individual applications. However, the clarity that this offers at the application level represents a confusing mass of detail at the corporate level. To overcome this problem, most of the approaches discussed here eliminate attributes from large schematic data models. They rely on principles of abstraction. Entities that are shown as a box at one level of a data model can be expanded into the component attributes at a more detailed level of the model.

Information engineering has also evolved along a similar path since its beginnings in 1972. By 1978 it had reached the point where it could represent substantial business meaning in a data model, first through data analysis, then through information analysis (see Chapter 2). Apart from the influence of Codd, its evolution was independent of the approaches discussed here. But following the publication of *Information Engineering* in 1981 [9, 10] it may have influenced some of the later evolution that we have discussed.

Each of these modeling approaches is converging towards a more precise representation of business rules and constraints. Using the nature at each end of an association line of *mandatory* and *optional*, or (the often time-dependent) *optional becoming mandatory* as described in this chapter, offers one method of precisely capturing these rules. Further constraints are represented through extended associations as described in Chapter 5.

Any schematic representation of rules requires precise business interpretation. As seen in this chapter, many alternative strategies can be uncovered using data modeling as a catalyst. The agreed strategy is attached to the relevant associations. Similarly, entities are documented with relevant attribute detail using the entity list notation introduced in Chapter 3. These are further defined through basic and extended purpose descriptions.

References

[1] Codd, E. F. (1970), A relational model for large shared data banks. *CACM,* **13** (6), 377–87.

[2] Codd, E. F. (1979). Extending the database relational model to capture more meaning. *ACM Trans. on Database Systems*, **4** (4), 397–434.

[3] Chen, P. (1976). The entity relationship model: Toward a unified view of data. *ACM Trans. on Database Systems,* 9–36.

[4] Dampney, C.N.G. (1987). Specifying a semantically adequate structure for information systems and databases. In *Proc. of 6th Int. Conf. on E–R Approach*, New York, pp. 143–64.

[5] Kozaczynski, W. and Lillien, L. (1987). An extended entity–relationship (E^2R) database specification and transformation into the logical relational design. In *Proc. of 6th Int. Conf. on E–R Approach*, New York pp. 497–513.

[6] Teory, T. J., Yang, D. and Fry, J. P. (1986). A logical design methodology for relational data bases using the extended entity–relationship model. *Computing Surveys*, **18**(2), 197–222.

[7] Rolland, C. (1988). Recent techniques for information modeling. In *Proc. of Joint Int. Symp. on Information Systems*, Sydney, pp. 345–60.

[8] Thompson, P. S. (1987). The object and role of binary modeling. In *Proc. of 6th Int. Conf. on E–R Approach*, New York, pp. 55–64.

[9] Finkelstein, C. (1981). Information engineering. Published as six InDepth articles. *Computerworld* (May–June).

[10] Martin, J. and Finkelstein, C. (1981). *Information Engineering*. Savant Institute: UK.

CHAPTER 5
Extended Associations

So far, we have covered basic associations, which represent the strategy used for managing two data entities. In identifying strategies, we find that some associations must not exist together at the same time, whereas other associations may need to exist together, to correctly represent the full strategy. Extended associations have been used to represent these additional levels of control. They are used to represent more detailed business rules or constraints, as discussed in Chapter 4.

It is important to note that extended associations are important in the historical evolution of information engineering to its present form. However, as they are only transitional – they indicate incomplete business normalization as covered in Chapters 8 and 9 – they are now no longer used. They are discussed here only to illustrate their part in the historical evolution of business normalization.

5.1 | INTRODUCTION

There are three main classes of extended associations:

- Inclusive associations.
- Exclusive associations.
- Subset associations.

Each of these is concerned with associations that exist between two or more basic associations themselves, rather than between entities. While

69

basic associations involve only two entities, extended associations involve three or more entities, as will be described later.

Extended associations are useful for representing the more complex strategies and controls that exist in real life. However, they do not represent the final form of the data map; they are transitional; they act as a catalyst in uncovering additional business meaning. For example, extended associations indicate a need to further decompose the entities they interrelate by more extensive business normalization, as discussed in Chapters 7–9. By their presence, they suggest the existence of more detailed fourth business normal form and fifth business normal form entities. These disappear following detailed business normalization.

The discussion in the following pages introduces extended associations between three entities A, B and C. In each of these examples there may be a basic association between A and B, as well as a basic association between A and C. Extended associations indicate ways in which these three entities may, or may not, exist and how they are interrelated.

The principles discussed in this chapter may be equally applied to many entities, not just to three entities. Thus, there may be a basic association between A and B and another basic association between C and D. These two basic associations may be further interrelated through an extended association, so linking the four entities and their associations together in a complex representation of strategy and control.

5.2 INCLUSIVE ASSOCIATIONS

In the following discussion we will not be concerned with identifying whether any basic associations are one to one or one to many. We will only show the association line joining two entities. Furthermore, we will only include the nature of a basic association (mandatory or optional) when it is particularly relevant to the extended association we are discussing.

There are four types of inclusive associations:

- Optional inclusive OR.
- Mandatory inclusive OR.
- Optional inclusive AND.
- Mandatory inclusive AND.

5.2.1 Optional inclusive OR

Let us consider basic associations between three entities AIRCRAFT, CARGO and PASSENGER. Figure 5.1 is an example of an inclusive

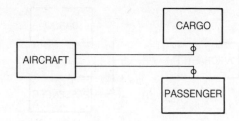

An aircraft may carry cargo or passengers, or both, or it may travel empty.

Note: Basic associations are not shown in full in this example.

Figure 5.1   An optional inclusive OR association.

extended association, as the two entities CARGO and PASSENGER are included in an association with AIRCRAFT. The optional nature indicates 'weak' control between the three entities; hence, the name **optional inclusive OR association**.

The association of AIRCRAFT with CARGO is optional, as is its association with PASSENGER. If there is neither cargo nor passengers, there is nothing to prevent the aircraft from taking off empty. Perhaps the aircraft may still need to make the flight, to be at its destination by a certain time to pick up passengers or cargo for ongoing flights. This points to more detailed entities relating to flight schedules.

5.2.2   Mandatory inclusive OR

On the other hand, the airline may wish to establish a stronger control if it has alternative aircraft available at the destination for the ongoing flights. This stronger control may prevent the aircraft from taking off if there is neither cargo nor passengers to carry. This can be represented through the **mandatory inclusive OR association**, as illustrated in Figure 5.2. As can be seen, the joining of the two associations is not at AIRCRAFT. Instead, they merge to establish a single association line with AIRCRAFT. This enables us to include a refinement at the merging fork, the mandatory indicator which imposes a control that one of the associations *must* exist. For example, an aircraft may normally carry either cargo or passengers, or both. But when there is neither passengers nor cargo, the mandatory indicator prevents the aircraft from taking off and flying empty. This mandatory indicator can also be used to merge three or more associations, not just two association lines as here.

The inclusive OR extended associations, both mandatory and optional, represent weak interdependencies between three or more

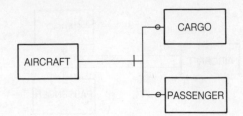

STRATEGY

*An aircraft may carry cargo or passengers, or both, but it must
not travel empty.*

Note: Basic associations are not shown in full in this example.

Figure 5.2 A mandatory inclusive OR association, which imposes additional control.

entities and their basic associations. In other cases, this interdependency may be very strong. In such cases, inclusive AND extended associations are used.

5.2.3 Optional inclusive AND

Certain entity occurrences may need to remain interrelated throughout their life because they are contingent upon each other. Such entity occurrences are said to be **mutually contingent**. These mutually contingent associations are called **inclusive AND associations**. They represent stronger control than with the earlier inclusive OR associations.

Figure 5.3 illustrates that an invoice can exist without a sales person. Furthermore, an invoice need not result in a commission being paid. The double line joining the associations between the entities INVOICE and SALES PERSON and between INVOICE and COMMISSION is interpreted to mean AND. It represents a strong control: if an invoice is produced by a sales person, then the commission (if it is to be paid) will be paid specifically to that sales person responsible for the invoice, and to none other. The extended association is 'contingent' on specific occurrences of the entities INVOICE, SALES PERSON and COMMISSION.

Without the extended association there is no control to prevent a commission being paid on an invoice even when there is no sales person to receive it. Furthermore, if a sales person is responsible for an invoice and a commission is paid, there would be nothing to prevent the commission being paid to a sales person not responsible for that

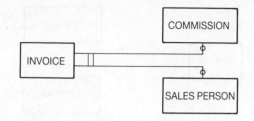

STRATEGY

If an invoice is allocated to a sales person, a commission must be paid for that invoice to the relevant sales person. Some invoices do not have a sales person associated with them.

Note: Basic associations are not shown in full in this example.

Figure 5.3 An optional inclusive AND association between INVOICE, SALES PERSON and COMMISSION.

particular invoice. Or, alternatively, the commission may be calculated on a different invoice for payment to the sales person, rather than on the specific invoice amount. The optional inclusive AND association enforces a strong commission strategy to prevent such situations from occurring.

We will later learn through business normalization that such a situation will subsequently result in two subtypes of SALES PERSON entity: a COMMISSION SALES PERSON and a NON-COMMISSION SALES PERSON. The association would thus be with COMMISSION and COMMISSION SALES PERSON. These two SALES PERSON entities are fourth business normal form entities.

5.2.4 Mandatory inclusive AND

Figure 5.3 enforces the control that a commission must be paid to the sales person responsible for the invoice. However, this example would enable some invoices to exist for which no sales person is responsible, and therefore for which no commission should be paid. This may be quite valid in many organizations, but in others it may represent lack of control. Management may tighten this control by means of the mandatory inclusive AND association.

The inclusive AND extended association has been strengthened in Figure 5.4 by the mandatory nature of the association between INVOICE and COMMISSION, and between INVOICE and SALES PERSON. It has been further reinforced by the mandatory line through the double

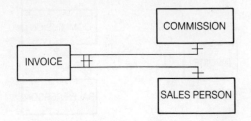

*All invoices must have a commission paid, and must have a
sales person responsible for each invoice. The commission is
paid on the specific value of the invoice.*

Note: Basic associations are not shown in full in this example.

Figure 5.4 A mandatory inclusive AND association represents strong mutual
contingency.

lines representing AND. This is interpreted to mean that the INVOICE:
COMMISSION and INVOICE:SALES PERSON associations both relate
to the same invoice. It is called a **mandatory inclusive AND association**
and represents strong control. Both a sales person and a commission
must exist for *every* invoice. After business normalization, mandatory
basic associations will exist between the COMMISSION and INVOICE
entities, and between COMMISSION and COMMISSION SALES PER-
SON. In such an organization it would not be acceptable for invoices to
be issued that do not have a commission paid and a sales person to receive that commission. This would apply to an organization that has
established a strong commission incentive for sales people, to increase
sales.

We have discussed inclusive associations, which interrelate several
entities. However, we may wish to impose controls that *prevent* certain
entities from being associated. This leads us to consider exclusive
associations.

5.3 EXCLUSIVE ASSOCIATIONS

Certain controls may need to be imposed in an organization to prevent
specific circumstances arising. These controls can be shown in a data
map by basic associations together with extended associations. Certain
entities and associations may be mutually exclusive. The exclusive OR,

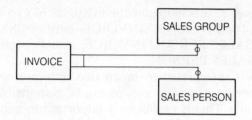

STRATEGY

*If an invoice is prepared, either a sales person or a sales group
is allocated responsibility, but not both. Some invoices are allocated to neither.*

Note: Basic associations are not shown in full in this example.

Figure 5.5 An optional exclusive XOR association between INVOICE and SALES
PERSON or SALES GROUP.

called the exclusive XOR, represents mutual exclusion. There are two
types of exclusive associations, optional exclusive XOR and mandatory
exclusive XOR, illustrated in Figures 5.5 and 5.6. They indicate a need
for extensive business normalization, as we have discussed for other
extended associations.

The single line joining both the INVOICE:SALES PERSON association and also the INVOICE:SALES GROUP association in Figures
5.5 and 5.6 is interpreted to mean 'either one, or the other, but not both'.
It is an exclusive association. Sales persons and sales groups cannot both
be associated with the same invoice: they are mutually exclusive. As we

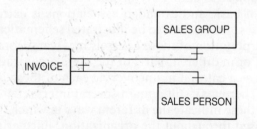

STRATEGY

*All invoices must be allocated to either a sales person or a
sales group, but not both.*

Note: Basic associations are not shown in full in this example.

Figure 5.6 A mandatory exclusive XOR association with strong control.

will see in Chapter 8, this indicates the existence of two fourth business normal form (4BNF) subtype INVOICE entities: SALES GROUP INVOICE and SALES PERSON INVOICE, with associations to SALES GROUP or to SALES PERSON.

Figure 5.5 is interpreted to mean that only one sales occurrence (either a sales person or a sales group) can be responsible for a specific invoice occurrence. This is particularly important to avoid commission disputes as only the individual or the sales group responsible for the invoice would receive that commission. This example, however, also shows it is possible for some invoices to exist that are allocated to neither a sales person nor a sales group. That is, there is a potential third 4BNF entity – UNSOLICITED INVOICE – with no association to any sales person. The optional nature of each basic association between INVOICE and SALES PERSON and between INVOICE and SALES GROUP indicates this. If every invoice is to be attributable to either a sales person or to a sales group, but not both, this can be represented by the mandatory exclusive XOR association as shown in Figure 5.6. In other words, the entity UNSOLICITED INVOICE *must not* exist. The basic associations (INVOICE:SALES PERSON and INVOICE: SALES GROUP) are now mandatory, and this is further reinforced by a mandatory line across the exclusive XOR line which enforces the control that there must be at least one sales person or sales group related to each invoice. No invoices can exist that are unassigned to sales representatives.

The exclusive associations enforce control to prevent possible circumstances from arising. The inclusive associations, on the other hand, ensure that certain circumstances occur together. Each of these situations may occur in real life and must be represented clearly. To describe strategy and controls in narrative form only can be quite complex, and subject to ambiguity or misinterpretation. The data map representation of basic and extended associations is extremely precise, enabling strategies and controls to be illustrated schematically. However, the specific interpretation of those controls may vary from organization to organization, or in different parts of the same organization. Extended associations act as a catalyst in uncovering each of these interpretations for discussion. There may still remain several interpretations even after discussion, and these indicate the different ways in which the relevant associations are used throughout the organization. Further normalization to fourth business normal form will clarify this (see Chapter 8).

The agreed interpretation is documented in narrative form as the extended purpose descriptions in the association dictionary for each of those associations. The strategies they represent are documented in the strategic planning dictionary. Both of these dictionaries are discussed in Chapter 6. From these associations and strategies, complex conditional logic can be automatically generated in computer programs. If extended associations are used as a catalyst for further business normalization,

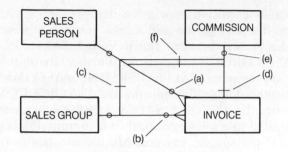

STRATEGY

A sales person may sell goods which bring about the production of one or more invoices (a). Some sales people may not be successful: they may have no invoices for which they are responsible.

Similarly, sales groups may sell one or many invoices (b), or none.

An invoice must be related to a sales person or a sales group, but cannot be related to both (c). Only one sales person or one sales group can claim responsibility for an invoice.

A commission amount is paid to a sales person for an invoice, when the invoice itself is paid (d). Commission payment relates to the specific invoice, but it is not paid if the invoice itself is never paid (e). Furthermore, commissions are paid only to sales people, and not to sales groups (f). Therefore, some invoices (due to sales groups), and other invoices which are not paid, will never give rise to a commission.

Figure 5.7 An example of several extended associations used to represent the strategy and controls for payment of sales commission.

much logic – which would otherwise be embedded in programs where it is difficult to change – is incorporated in the data model.

It will help at this point to illustrate a real-life example to bring together several of the extended associations examined so far. Figure 5.7 provides this example.

The extended associations in Figure 5.7 represent a 'design note' in graphical form to be resolved through later business normalization. They represent the strategy and controls for managing the allocation of invoices to sales people and sales groups, and for payment of commissions. All basic associations and extended associations are fully represented in the figure. As can be seen, the narrative description of the strategy and controls is lengthy and subject to misinterpretation. The data map, together with the narrative, illustrate the strategy and controls more clearly. This provides valuable design input for identification of a more detailed representation through business normalization, and leads to easy development of program logic.

The mutually exclusive association that prevents an invoice being allocated to both a sales person and a sales group is represented by the mutually exclusive line between the INVOICE:SALES PERSON and INVOICE:SALES GROUP associations. Further, the mutually contingent association between SALES PERSON and COMMISSION is represented by the double line joining the INVOICE:COMMISSION association with the INVOICE:SALES PERSON association. If an invoice is allocated to a sales person, then a commission is paid to that sales person for the specific invoice. Mutual exclusivity (and mutual contingency) was used by information engineering only up until 1983 [1,2]. Since that time, business normalization has resulted in more precise definition of data. These concepts are represented by the integrity rules of the RM/T model, the E–R model, the extended E–R model, binary modeling and semantic modeling (see Chapter 4) [3–7]. These other data modeling approaches can be expected to eventually evolve beyond these representations, also.

5.4 | SUBSET ASSOCIATIONS

So far, we have considered associations that apply to every entity occurrence nominated. However, there are instances where an extended association may apply to only specific instances (occurrences) of certain entities. To represent this situation, the subset association is used. Figure 5.8 illustrates an example. This indicates that of all the orders placed through the Sales Agreement association, not all of those orders may give

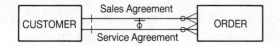

STRATEGY

A customer may have one or many orders (or none) which were purchased. Each order relates to only one customer. This is represented by a Sales Agreement.

Similarly, a customer may have one or many orders (or none) for which a Service Agreement is entered into. Each of these orders is related to only one customer.

Not all Sales Agreements give rise to Service Agreements. The Service Agreements are a subset of the Sales Agreements.

Figure 5.8 A subset association between customer sales orders and customer service orders.

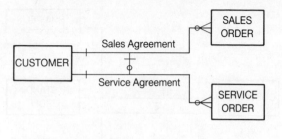

Note: The Sales Agreement and Service Agreement subset
associations indicate existence of more specific entities. These relate to two types of orders: sales orders
and service orders.

Figure 5.9 A subset association suggests more specific entities. (Compare with Figure 5.8.)

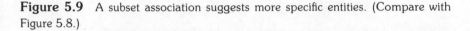

rise to a Service Agreement. The Service Agreement association is said to be a **subset** of the Sales Agreement association, while the Sales Agreement is a **superset** of the Service Agreement. The subset association is indicated by a single line joining the basic associations in Figure 5.8, but with an optional indicator on that line close to the basic association that is the subset (Service Agreement). The mandatory indicator on the subset line close to the superset (Sales Agreement) indicates that a sales agreement must exist before a service agreement can be issued. Such a subset association generally indicates specific differences in handling one, or both, of the related entities.

In Figure 5.8, it is essential in the organization concerned to ensure that a Service Agreement is not entered into for goods that were not purchased from the organization. This may be more readily represented by breaking the ORDER entity into two separate entities, a SALES ORDER entity and a SERVICE ORDER entity. Figure 5.9 illustrates this refinement, with further refinement in Figure 5.10. With the two entities SALES ORDER and SERVICE ORDER in Figure 5.9, together with the subset association, the true intent now becomes clearer. We can see that

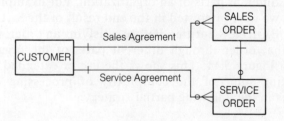

Figure 5.10 The subset association after further refinement (from Figure 5.9) is now seen clearly to be the basic association between the two entities SALES ORDER and SERVICE ORDER.

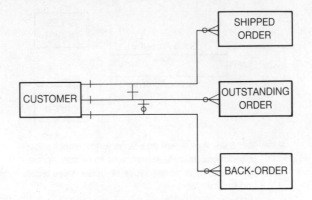

STRATEGY

An order when first placed is an outstanding order. As a result of processing this order, there may be insufficient stock on hand to satisfy the quantity ordered: it may therefore result in a back-order. Not all orders are back-ordered, however.

Once an order is fully processed, it is shipped and so becomes a shipped order. An order cannot be both outstanding and shipped, but can be both outstanding and back-ordered.

Figure 5.11   An example of extended associations. This illustrates the strategy in managing the progress of an order throughout an organization.

the subset association in Figure 5.9 is in fact a basic association between SALES ORDER and SERVICE ORDER, as shown in Figure 5.10.

The subset association was the catalyst in uncovering these two entities and the basic association between them. We will learn in Chapter 8 that they are fourth business normal form (4BNF) entities. They lead to the definition of a fifth business normal form (5BF) entity, called ORDER STRUCTURE. 5BNF is discussed in Chapter 9.

Extended associations are useful for representing specific strategies in managing different parts of an organization. For example, in Figures 5.9 and 5.10 we were interested in the end result of the SALES ORDER and SERVICE ORDER entities. Before satisfying an order, we may have to manage that order through different parts of the organization, as illustrated in Figure 5.11. This shows the use of extended associations in representing some of the complexity of processing orders from customers, as in the following partial strategy:

'An order when first placed is an OUTSTANDING ORDER. As a result of processing this order, there may be insufficient stock on hand to satisfy the quantity ordered: this may give rise to a BACK-ORDER.'

This is the reason for the subset association joining the CUSTOMER: OUTSTANDING ORDER association to the CUSTOMER:BACK-ORDER association. Next:

'Once an order is fully processed, it is shipped and so becomes a SHIPPED ORDER. An order cannot both be outstanding and shipped.'

This is the interpretation of the mutually exclusive association between CUSTOMER:OUTSTANDING ORDER and CUSTOMER:SHIPPED ORDER associations.

The use of extended associations in this context illustrates some of the management controls that must be implemented: all outstanding orders must be processed and shipped; any outstanding back-orders must be eventually satisfied and also subsequently shipped. In real life, these controls are generally implemented by appointing staff to manage the progress of orders through each of the order department, the back-order department and the shipping department. The extended associations in this example represent these job functions.

Instead of referring to the general entity ORDER, we found that it was more useful to separate an order into three component entities. It became clear where management had to place responsibility by appointing personnel to ensure that the defined strategy was applied correctly. This is yet another example of fourth business normal form, as discussed in Chapter 8.

References

[1] Finkelstein, C. (1981). Information engineering. Published as six InDepth articles. *Computerworld* (May–June).

[2] Martin, J. and Finkelstein, C. (1981). *Information Engineering*. Savant Institute: UK.

[3] Dampney, C. N. G. (1987). Specifying a semantically adequate structure for information systems and databases. In *Proc. of 6th Int. Conf. on E–R Approach*, New York, pp. 143–64.

[4] Kozaczynski, W. and Lillien, L. (1987). An extended entity–relationship (E^{2}R) database specification and transformation into the logical relational design. In *Proc. of 6th Int. Conf. on E–R Approach*, New York, pp. 497–513.

[5] Teory, T. J., Yang, D. and Fry, J. P. (1986). A logical design methodology for relational data bases using the extended entity–relationship model. *Computing Surveys*, **18**(2), 197–222.

[6] Rolland, C. (1988). Recent techniques for information modeling. In *Proc. of Joint int. Symp. on Information Systems*, Sydney, pp 345–60.

[7] Thompson, P. S. (1987). The object and role of binary modeling. In *Proc. of 6th Int. Conf. on E–R Approach*, New York, pp. 55–64.

CHAPTER 6

Dictionary Documentation

In the previous chapters, we have discussed the documentation of entities, attributes and associations. The schematic documentation of entities and associations is provided by the data map, while the detailed documentation of entities and attributes is provided through the entity list. The entity list indicates the existence of primary keys, foreign keys and data attributes in each entity. However, in practice, more detail must be provided in the form of a **design dictionary** for each entity, attribute and association.

We have also discussed, in the previous chapters, the different meaning given to entities, attributes and associations throughout an organization. These are documented as basic purpose descriptions and extended purpose descriptions in the design dictionary. Association purpose descriptions lead to further interpretations of strategy, as discussed in Chapters 4 and 5. We will see, in Part Three, that entity purpose descriptions provide a catalyst for the definition of policies; attribute purpose descriptions provide a catalyst for the definition of goals and objectives; association purpose descriptions provide a catalyst for the definition of strategies. These policy, goal, objective and strategy statements are documented in a **strategic planning dictionary**.

6.1. INTRODUCTION

The design dictionary and the strategic planning dictionary may be maintained on paper for small data models comprising less than 50 entities. Alternatively, use may be made of data dictionary or design dictionary software products, as discussed in more detail in Part Four. In our discussion here, we will concern ourselves with the description of a design dictionary and strategic planning dictionary which can be used for very small projects of less than 50 entities.

This chapter includes forms that can be used for a manual design dictionary and strategic planning dictionary. Sample entries are included in these forms to illustrate their use. These allow for the manual documentation of defined entities, attributes and associations. In addition, a form is included for a strategic planning dictionary that supports the documentation of text defining the extended purpose for entities, attributes and associations. It supports the documentation of policies, issues, goals, objectives, strategies and tactics, and relates these strategic statements to the data that supports their achievement.

Blank forms are also included at the end of the chapter. These can be used as a starting point for designing forms appropriate to your specific use, if you wish to document a small data model manually. Alternatively, Part Four describes software that can be used for this documentation.

6.2 MANUAL DESIGN DICTIONARY

6.2.1 Manual entity dictionary

Figure 6.1 illustrates a typical manual entity dictionary. This documents, for each entity, the entity name, its attribute content in entity list form and a purpose description of the entity. Using this simple format, each entity is uniquely named and documented, together with its purpose description. The purpose description may be an agreed basic purpose, or it may include one (or several) extended purpose descriptions.

The definition of an entity, together with its basic and extended purpose descriptions, may extend over as many pages as necessary. Each subsequent page is numbered, and the page number and total number of pages are written in the top right-hand corner of the form.

At the bottom of the form, the person who prepared it signs, together with the date of preparation. The first time the form is prepared the version number is 1. Whenever it is changed, the version number is updated.

The entity dictionary helps to identify entity synonyms and homonyms. These are defined as follows: two entities with different names, but with essentially the same attributes and purpose description, may be **synonyms** for the same data. One standard name is chosen to

	ENTITY DICTIONARY	Page ___ of ___
Entity Name	Entity Content	Entity Purpose
CUSTOMER	(customer no#, customer name, customer address, customer phone number, credit limit, salesperson#)	Records details about customers for credit control, invoicing and account management.
Prepared By:	Date Prepared:	Version No:

Figure 6.1 An example of a manual entity dictionary.

represent the separate synonym names. On the other hand, two or more entities may have the same name. If they are truly the same, they will have similar attribute content and a similar purpose description. However, if the attribute content is quite different, or the purpose description indicates the entity is used for another purpose, the existence of **homonyms** is indicated; that is, the same name is used for different data. Unique names are selected for each of the homonyms.

6.2.2 Manual attribute dictionary

Each attribute within an entity is further documented in an attribute dictionary. Each attribute is uniquely identified and its existence in various entities is indicated. We will see when we discuss business normalization in Chapters 7–9 that a non-key attribute can exist in only one entity. Otherwise, if it exists redundantly, whenever the value of that attribute changes, each redundant copy must be changed. On the other hand, key attributes (primary keys and foreign keys) may exist in many entities, indicating an association between those entities and the other entities in which the key attribute exists as a primary key or a foreign key. Such key attributes indicate the presence of an association and give rise to entries in the association dictionary (see Section 6.2.3).

ATTRIBUTE DICTIONARY			Page ___ of ___
Attribute Name	Used in Entity	Attribute Type	Attribute Purpose
Customer number#	CUSTOMER	Primary key	Identifies customer account for credit control and for invoicing and account management.
	ORDER	Foreign key	Identifies customer who placed the order, and the address to which the order and invoice are to be delivered.
Prepared By:		Date Prepared:	Version No:

Figure 6.2   An example of a manual attribute dictionary

Figure 6.2 illustrates a typical manual attribute dictionary. This shows the key attribute *customer number#*. It shows that this key attribute exists in the CUSTOMER entity as a primary key and in the ORDER entity as a foreign key. A purpose description indicates the purpose of the attribute. Although this is a basic purpose description, it may also include one (or several) extended purpose descriptions.

The *Attribute Type* column in Figure 6.2 can alternatively include a code which indicates whether an attribute is a primary key (P), a foreign key (F), a selection attribute or secondary key (S), a group attribute (G) or a repeating group (R). If this column is blank, it is a non-key attribute. Additional codes in this column indicate whether the attribute is mandatory (M) or optional (O). The mandatory or optional type indicates whether the attribute must be present in the entity (mandatory), or need not be present (optional). For example, a mandatory foreign key is represented by the code FM.

This indication of mandatory or optional attributes indicates the possible existence of more detailed fourth business normal form entities, which are uncovered by business normalization (see Chapter 8). This is also useful subsequently for derivation of procedures and program logic from the data model. It assists in the development of program code, input screens and output reports from the data model (see Part Four).

The definition of an attribute, together with its basic and extended purpose descriptions, may extend over as many pages as necessary.

The attribute dictionary also helps to identify attribute synonyms and homonyms. Two attributes with different names, but with essentially the same purpose description and residing in the same entity after completion of business normalization, are **synonyms** for the same data. One standard name is chosen. On the other hand, two or more attributes may have the same name. They may reside in the one entity or in several entities. If these are truly the same attribute, they will also have a similar purpose description. If the purpose descriptions are different, the attributes are **homonyms**; that is, the same name is used for different data. Different unique names are therefore selected.

6.2.3 Manual association dictionary

We have seen that associations are represented by primary key attributes and foreign key attributes. These are documented with other attributes in an attribute dictionary and also exist as part of the attribute content in the entity dictionary. However, neither of these dictionaries indicates the degree or nature of the associations concerned. This detail is documented in the association dictionary, as illustrated in Figure 6.3.

Associations may be identified by a short name or by the entities that are interrelated. Thus, an association between the CUSTOMER and

ASSOCIATION DICTIONARY				Page ___ of ___
		Association		
Related Entities	Association Name	Degree	Nature	Association Purpose
CUSTOMER:ORDER	Customer Places Order	Many	Optional	A customer may have many orders outstanding, but may presently have none and yet will still remain on the books
ORDER:CUSTOMER	Order Placed By Customer	One	Mandatory	An order is accepted for only one customer, who is on our books and whose credit limit is not exceeded by the amount of the order. The order will be delivered and invoiced to the customer's address.
Prepared By:		Date Prepared:		Version No:

Figure 6.3 An example of a manual association dictionary.

the ORDER entities may be referred to as the CUSTOMER:ORDER association or by a name as the 'places' association. The association name is sometimes useful as a description of how the association is used; for example, 'customer places order' and 'order placed by customer'.

The degree of an association is indicated in the *Degree* column of Figure 6.3 either by words or by codes such as one (1) or many (M). The *Nature* column indicates that the association is either mandatory (M) or optional (O). The degree and nature codes relate to the end of the association close to the entity which is right of the colon in the *Entities* column. The other end of the association is then documented in the next entry in Figure 6.3.

A basic purpose description for the association is documented to describe how it is used. This can be expanded in one (or several) extended purpose descriptions to provide more detail, as implied by the degree and nature of the association. Thus, Figure 6.3 shows that the CUSTOMER:ORDER association is a *mandatory one* (at CUSTOMER) to *optional many* (at ORDER) *association* which signifies the acceptance of an order. The purpose description in this example may be further extended as follows:

> *'A customer may have one or many orders outstanding, or none. An order, if it exists, is related to only one customer. Furthermore, that customer must be on our records and must have sufficient credit left to pay for the order based on its total value.'*

The definition of an association, together with its basic and extended purpose descriptions, may extend over as many pages as necessary.

6.3 MANUAL STRATEGIC PLANNING DICTIONARY

We have seen that associations lead to the definition of strategies. The basic purpose description of an association suggests an overall strategy across all areas of the organization. However, an association may have several extended purpose decriptions, which in turn will suggest specific strategies in different parts of the business. The basic and extended purpose descriptions are documented in the association dictionary just discussed, while the relevant strategy statements for an association are documented in a strategic planning dictionary.

The extended purpose descriptions and strategy statements are discussed by all relevant parties interested in the association. All become aware of their common interest, which leads to a greater business understanding among the managers, their staff and the DP staff who attend these review sessions. From this understanding, an agreed purpose description and an overall strategy statement is defined to reflect their common interest.

A strategy statement comprises narrative that details the strategy. It may describe how the association supports that strategy and how the association is used to implement it, and can contain text detailing the intent of the strategy. This statement of strategy will later provide input for the definition of conditions to be satisfied. These subsequently lead to conditional logic in application programs used in information systems, or to expert rules used in expert business systems. In conjunction with the associations, this leads to the development of program logic (see Part Four).

Figure 6.4 illustrates the strategic planning dictionary form. This may be used to document the text for several strategic plan items: policies, goals or objectives and strategies. We will discuss its use for documentation of strategies here.

The text in italics in Figure 6.4 illustrates a typical strategy statement. This is based on the strategy defined in Figure 4.6. As it documents a strategy, the relevant *Strategic Plan Item* is circled and a unique name is allocated – *Customer Credit Checking Strategy*.

The functional areas or *Area* interested in the strategy are listed: only *Accounts* is interested here. The entities involved are then listed in the *Entity* column: *CUSTOMER* and *ORDER*. These are the entities that establish the association. The association that implements the strategy is documented in the *Association* column: *Confirm customer credit status OK*. The association name may be a verb, a phrase or a statement, as appropriate.

If the statement to be documented is a policy, rather than a strategy as shown here, then the entities that implement it are listed. If it is a goal or objective, the attributes that measure achievement of the goal or objective, and the entities in which they reside, are listed. Finally, the agreed text of the strategy, or the text of a policy or of a goal or objective, is documented. This may extend over as many pages as necessary.

6.4 SAMPLE DICTIONARY FORMS

To assist you in small projects, the manual dictionary forms used in Figures 6.1–6.4 have been reproduced at the end of this chapter. These can be used as examples of forms you may wish to design for use in your own projects.

		Page ___ of ___
	STRATEGIC PLANNING DICTIONARY	

Strategic Plan Item: Policy   Objective   (Strategy)

Plan Item Name: *Customer Credit Checking Strategy*

AREA	ENTITY	ATTRIBUTE	ASSOCIATION
Accounts	*CUSTOMER*		*Confirm customer*
	ORDER		*credit status OK*

PLAN ITEM TEXT

Our customers are considered customers regardless of the number of orders
they currently have on the books – even if they are presently inactive. An order
can only be accepted if it is placed by a customer who is on our books, and
who has sufficient credit available such that the total cost of this order will not
cause the customer's account balance to exceed the credit limit.

Prepared By: [   ]   Date Prepared: [   ]   Version No: [   ]

Figure 6.4   A manual strategic planning dictionary.

This manual design dictionary and strategic planning dictionary is adequate for small projects with less than 50 entities. In a typical project which may involve perhaps 800–1000 entities, however, an automated design dictionary and strategic planning dictionary is essential to capture the evolving data design and check it for consistency. These dictionaries are described in Part Four, where they are used to document an example.

ENTITY DICTIONARY		Page ___ of ___
Entity Name	Entity Content	Entity Purpose
Prepared By:	Date Prepared:	Version No:

ATTRIBUTE DICTIONARY			Page ___ of ___
Attribute Name	Used in Entity	Attribute Type	Attribute Purpose
Prepared By:	Date Prepared:		Version No:

ASSOCIATION DICTIONARY				Page ___ of ___
Related Entities	Association Name	Association		Association Purpose
		Degree	Nature	
Prepared By:		Date Prepared:		Version No:

| | | | Page ____ of ____ |

STRATEGIC PLANNING DICTIONARY

Strategic Plan Item: Policy   Objective   Strategy

Plan Item Name: _____

AREA	ENTITY	ATTRIBUTE	ASSOCIATION

PLAN ITEM TEXT

Prepared By: [   ]   Date Prepared: [   ]   Version No: [   ]

CHAPTER 7

Introduction to Business Normalization

In Chapter 2, we discussed the evolution of information engineering. These techniques permit the identification and communication of information needs between management, users and DP personnel. In Chapters 3–5, we discussed the information engineering documentation conventions. These represent business strategies using data models (comprising entity lists and data maps), which provide the necessary data details that support those strategies. The data map and entity list introduced in these chapters are two of the tools of information engineering. A further tool is normalization: a technique used to identify data needed to support business needs. This chapter introduces the concepts of business normalization and shows how this technique can be used to establish the essential meaning of data throughout an organization, as well as identify possible future business alternatives.

Because of its emphasis on business and its application by users with no knowledge of computing, the business normalization rules used by information engineering differ from the precise definitions (and their extensions) used in formal normalization theory. The rules introduced in this chapter first are therefore from a business perspective. A definition of the rules of formal normalization is left until the end of the chapter.

7.1 | NORMALIZATION

Normalization had its origins in mathematical set theory. It was first used in the late 60s by Edgar Codd, who was with IBM in San Jose, California at that time, as a means of defining data. He proposed a relational theory, together with a relational algebra and a relational calculus [1]. This stirred considerable interest in academic circles in the early 70s as it provided a very clear way of defining and representing data used in computer application systems.

The formal discipline of normalization is well documented in technical articles and papers [2–5]. The purpose of this chapter is not to add to the excellent technical literature, but rather to show how normalization is used as a business technique to define data required by both government and commercial organizations. Because of this emphasis on business, rather than on theory, we will use the term *business normalization* to distinguish from *formal normalization*, as described at the end of this chapter. We will see how business normalization can be used to define future data and information needs [6].

7.1.1   The purpose of normalization

Normalization was cloaked in technical complexity throughout most of the 70s. It was applied by DP staff, but often with great difficulty as it depends upon a detailed understanding of the data used by an organization, and such an understanding is rarely held by DP staff. Rather, it is normally held by managers and users who work with the data on a day-to-day basis. To them, normalization represents 'common sense'.

The purpose of normalization can be stated in a non-technical way as:

> *The application of a formal set of rules which determine those key attributes which uniquely identify each data attribute, and which place each attribute in an entity where it is fully identified by the whole primary key of that entity.*

Expressed more simply, the purpose of normalization is to put each attribute into the entity in which it 'belongs'. Or, more memorably:

> *Each attribute is placed in an entity where it is dependent on the key, the whole key, and nothing but the key . . . so help me, Codd!*

Normalization leads to an exact definition of entities and data attributes, with a clear identification of homonyms (the same name used to represent different data) and synonyms (different names used to repre-

Product	Product	Supplier Details							
Number	Name	No	Name	Address	No	Name	Address	No	Na

Supplier Details (Cont'd)			Cost	Selling	Whse	Warehouse	Quantity
ss	No	Name	Address	Price	Price	Number	Address	On Hand

Figure 7.1   A product stock computer record.

sent the same data). It promotes a clearer understanding and knowledge of what each data entity and data attribute means.

7.1.2   An unnormalized entity

To illustrate the steps of business normalization, we will use a simple example based on a product inventory application:

> PRODUCT   (Product number#, product name, ((supplier number#, supplier name, supplier address)), cost price, selling price, warehouse number#, warehouse address, quantity on hand)

The data entity PRODUCT, expressed here in entity list format, is said to be '**unnormalized**'. It contains attributes relating to products, suppliers and warehouses, and a repeating group of supplier details.

A physical implementation of this entity as a computer disk or tape record is shown in Figure 7.1. It may be represented as a Product Stock Form in Figure 7.2. Both enable ready reference (on paper or in a computer) to relevant details relating to products and their suppliers.

7.1.3   Problems of changes

The *product number*# primary key identifies each unique product. Thus, a requirement to change the name of a product can be readily accommodated given the appropriate product number. For example, the specific Product Stock Form or relevant computer record can be directly located and the change in product name made immediately.

Consider, however, a need to change the address of a supplier of various products to the organization. If the products provided by the supplier are known, each product record can be referenced directly by the product number. The suppliers of that product (in the repeating group of supplier details) can then be used to identify the specific supplier whose address has changed. Figures 7.1 and 7.2 indicate that the address of each supplier of a product is stored with that product. If the products are unknown, it would be necessary to refer to *every* product record, whether

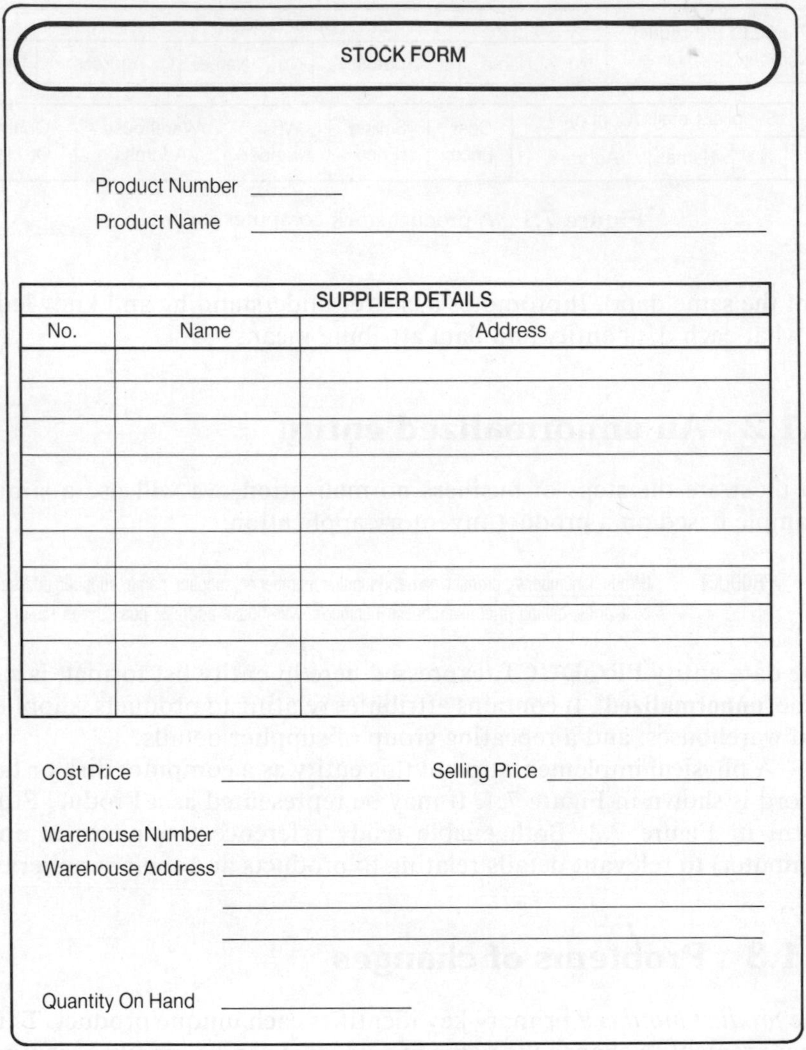

Figure 7.2 A product stock form.

on paper or in the computer. *Every* supplier of *every* product must be examined and the address changed as appropriate. Only when we have examined *every* product can we be sure that all instances of the supplier address have been changed. A similar problem arises in changing a warehouse address. Unless the specific products for that warehouse are known, every product record must be examined to change the warehouse address stored with each product.

As this situation often arises, it is beneficial to separate supplier details and warehouse details from product details. We can do this by allocating a supplier number, and a warehouse number, that can be

Table 7.1 Rules of normalization

Formal Normalization	Abbreviation	Business Normalization	Abbreviation
First Normal Form	(1NF)	First Business Normal Form	(1BNF)
Second Normal Form	(2NF)	Second Business Normal Form	(2BNF)
Third Normal Form	(3NF)	Third Business Normal Form	(3BNF)
Fourth Normal Form	(4NF)	Fourth Business Normal Form	(4BNF)
Fifth Normal Form	(5NF)	Fifth Business Normal Form	(5BNF)

stored in each product record as a key to identify the relevant supplier and warehouse. This supplier key or warehouse key is used to refer to separate supplier and warehouse records to obtain details of suppliers and warehouses.

In this example, the removal of supplier and warehouse details from the product record is an obvious thing to do. It is common sense. It is an example of intuitive normalization. But other similar examples may not be so simple. Hence, we need a set of steps to enable us to identify and move such data attributes into different entities. These are provided by the rules of business normalization.

7.2 | RULES OF BUSINESS NORMALIZATION

There are, in fact, six rules of normalization but we will confine ourselves, in this and following chapters, to the first five rules. These are called the **normal forms** and are numbered as shown in Table 7.1. We will distinguish between the rules of formal normalization and of business normalization by prefixing normal form with business and by prefixing the abbreviation *NF* with *B*. The non-prefixed name and abbreviation refers to formal normalization (see Table 7.1).

7.2.1 First business normal form

The first rule of business normalization is called **first business normal form** (abbreviated to **1BNF**). It is stated as follows:

*Identify and remove repeating group attributes to another entity. The
primary key of this other entity is made up of a compound key, comprising
the primary key of the entity in which the repeating group originally resided,
together with the repeating group key itself, or instead another unique key
based on the business needs. The name of the new entity may initially be
based on a combination of the name of the repeating group and the name of
the entity in which the repeating group originally resided. It may be later
renamed according to its final attribute content after business normalization
is completed.*

The repeating group in the PRODUCT entity given earlier is readily
identified, as it is surrounded by double left and right parentheses. It
contains supplier details: *supplier number#*, *supplier name* and *supplier
address*. The repeating group key is *supplier number#*. Using our first
rule, this is combined with the primary key of the entity in which the
repeating group resides – namely, *product number#*. The result is as
follows, where the new entity name is PRODUCT–SUPPLIER:

PRODUCT   (Product number#, product name, cost price, selling price, warehouse
                       number#, warehouse address, quantity on hand)

PRODUCT–SUPPLIER   (Product number#, supplier number#, supplier name, supplier address)

The two entities here are said to be in first business normal form; that is,
they represent two first business normal form entities following removal
of the repeating group of supplier details from the PRODUCT entity.
Note that the sequence of the PRODUCT–SUPPLIER keys is not
significant here. The alternative SUPPLIER–PRODUCT entity is identical, as in:

SUPPLIER–PRODUCT   (Supplier number#, product number#, supplier name, supplier address)

Our original PRODUCT entity has now been broken down into two
entities: PRODUCT and PRODUCT–SUPPLIER. We can illustrate this
schematically as shown in Figure 7.3. This is not a data map, but rather a
key map. A key map only shows the association lines joining related
entities, not their degree and nature. It later becomes a data map when
the degree and nature at each end of the association are defined. It
therefore represents a transitional stage in the development of a data map
from an entity list.

Figure 7.3 shows the two entities joined by a single line. They are
related by the common reference in each entity to *product number#*.
Product number# is the primary key of PRODUCT and is also part of the
compound primary key of PRODUCT–SUPPLIER.

Figure 7.3   First business normal form key map.

7.2.2   Second business normal form

We can apply the second rule of business normalization to clarify our two
first business normal form entities further. This rule (called **second**
business normal form, or **2BNF**) is stated as:

> *Identify and remove attributes into another entity which are only **partially***
> *dependent on the primary key and are also dependent on one or more other*
> *key attributes, or which are dependent on only **part** of the compound primary*
> *key and possibly one or more other key attributes.*

In applying this rule it is first easier to examine those entities with a compound primary key. PRODUCT–SUPPLIER is such an entity; its
compound key is made up of *product number#* and *supplier number#*. We
now determine whether each of the attributes of this entity is wholly (or
only partially) dependent upon the key attributes. What is the identifying
key for supplier name and supplier address? *supplier number#* immediately springs to mind! A product number is not needed to identify a
supplier, unless that supplier provides only that one specific product and
no other products to the organization! We only need *supplier number#*.

The second business normal form rule indicates that we must move
supplier name and supplier address into a new entity with *supplier*
number# as its key. We will name this entity SUPPLIER. The second
business normal form entity list at this stage is as follows, but note that it
is not yet complete:

PRODUCT   (Product number#, product name, cost price, selling price, warehouse
                   number#, warehouse address, quantity on hand)

PRODUCT–SUPPLIER   (Product number#, supplier number#)

SUPPLIER   (Supplier number#, supplier name, supplier address)

The representation of these three entities in a key map is shown in Figure
7.4. This illustrates the interrelationship between PRODUCT and
PRODUCT–SUPPLIER based on the key *product number#* and between
PRODUCT–SUPPLIER and SUPPLIER based on *supplier number#*.
We have not as yet been able to determine the degree and nature of the as-
sociations between these entities, merely the fact that they exist.

Figure 7.4   A second business normal form key map.

Looking at this entity list, it appears that we have a rather artificial situation, with PRODUCT–SUPPLIER comprised solely of a primary compound key. What about other attributes for this entity? Do they exist? Let us look at PRODUCT. Are we satisfied with the attributes left in this entity? Look at *cost price*. Our representation implies that each product has a single cost price, established for each product regardless of the suppliers of that product. This suggests a standard cost price, as well as a standard selling price. A standard selling price for a product is reasonable, and would certainly reside as an attribute in PRODUCT. But a standard cost price is most unusual! It may be valid for a giant corporation able to insist upon a standard cost price from each supplier of a product (which is illegal according to the anti-monopoly laws of many countries), but the more normal situation is a potentially different cost price for each separate supplier of a product. This suggests that *cost price* is dependent on both product number and supplier number. As PRODUCT–SUPPLIER has a compound key made up of *product number#*, and *supplier number#*, cost price should reside not in PRODUCT, but instead in PRODUCT–SUPPLIER. We should also give it a more meaningful name, such as *supplier product cost price* to clarify its real meaning. Does this mean that cost price is to be removed completely from the PRODUCT entity? Not necessarily. Its presence there might also be valid, but would represent a different attribute: perhaps renamed more specifically as *maximum supplier cost price*. The resolved second business normal form entities are now as follows:

PRODUCT   (Product number#, product name, selling price, warehouse number#, warehouse address, quantity on hand, maximum supplier cost price)

PRODUCT–SUPPLIER   (Product number#, supplier number#, supplier product cost price)

SUPPLIER   (Supplier number#, supplier name, supplier address)

In this example, we found that *cost price* had been used as a homonym (same name for different data) for both of these attributes. We identified two cost price attributes: *supplier product cost price* and *maximum supplier cost price*. This also represents a discussion opportunity. We can achieve greater control over profits! The next paragraph illustrates.

We can now satisfy a profit objective set by management. A minimum profit margin can be achieved for each separate product. We will establish a maximum supplier cost price for each product. The difference between this maximum cost price and the product's selling price is the minimum profit margin. Suppliers whose product cost price is less than the maximum cost price will result in a higher profit than the defined minimum. If the maximum supplier cost price is exceeded, the supplier is not acceptable. We can so exercise more control over the acceptance of new suppliers for specific products.

Second business normal form, therefore, is useful for identifying homonyms. It can also help to clarify business opportunities and set objectives, as was done in our example with the meaning for *cost price*.

During this discussion you may have been concerned that we overlooked *warehouse address*. Why did we not move this out into another entity? This leads us to consider the third rule of business normalization.

7.2.3   Third business normal form

The rule for **third business normal form (3BNF)** is more obvious than that for second business normal form. It is stated as follows:

> *Identify and remove into another entity those attributes which are dependent on a key other than the primary (or compound) key.*

The reason for leaving *warehouse address* in the PRODUCT entity during second business normal form now becomes apparent. *Warehouse address* is not partially dependent upon *product number#* (2BNF rule) or dependent at all on *product number#* (3BNF rule). Instead, it is wholly dependent on *warehouse number#*. It is therefore moved into another entity WAREHOUSE for third business normal form as illustrated in the following (partial) third business normal form entities:

PRODUCT	(Product number#, product name, selling price, maximum supplier cost price, warehouse number#, quantity on hand)
PRODUCT–SUPPLIER	(Product number#, supplier number#, supplier product cost price)
SUPPLIER	(Supplier number#, supplier name, supplier address)
WAREHOUSE	(Warehouse number#, warehouse address)

Note, however, that we have left *warehouse number#* as a foreign key in the PRODUCT entity, so we can determine the warehouse where each product is stored.

But what about *quantity on hand* in PRODUCT? Is this wholly dependent on *product number#*? If not, where does it belong? If we left *quantity on hand* in PRODUCT, it would imply a *total* quantity on hand for a product across all warehouses. Thus, it is now apparent that we may have one or more warehouses, since we have certainly found it necessary to number them! But are we more interested in the quantity on hand for a specific product in *each* warehouse that contains that product? Perhaps we should refer to it as *warehouse product quantity on hand*. But where does it belong? If we placed it in the WAREHOUSE entity, it would suggest a total quantity on hand of *all* products in a warehouse – not the quantity on hand of each separate product in that warehouse. From this discussion, quantity on hand seems dependent on both *product number#* and *warehouse number#*. But there is no entity with this compound key! Therefore, we must create such an entity, calling it PRODUCT–WAREHOUSE, and place *warehouse product quantity on hand* in that entity. The final third business normal form entity list is then as follows:

PRODUCT   (Product number#, product name, selling price, maximum supplier cost price)

PRODUCT–SUPPLIER   (Product number#, supplier number#, supplier product cost price)

SUPPLIER   (Supplier number#, supplier name, supplier address)

PRODUCT–WAREHOUSE   (Product number#, warehouse number#, warehouse product quantity on hand)

WAREHOUSE   (Warehouse number#, warehouse address)

Referring to our partial and final third business normal form entity lists, it can be seen that *warehouse number#* appears in the PRODUCT entity in the partial form, but it is not present in that entity in the final form. In the former, *warehouse number#* was needed to establish an association between the PRODUCT and WAREHOUSE entities. In the latter, however, it formed part of the compound primary key of PRODUCT–WAREHOUSE. The association between a product and the warehouse that stocks that product was thus explicitly defined. With this entity list representation we are now able to indicate the quantity on hand of a product in every warehouse that stocks that product. We could also keep total quantity on hand of a product across all warehouses, if required, by including the attribute *total warehouse quantity on hand* in WAREHOUSE.

Let us review again these three attributes: *warehouse number#*, *warehouse address* and *quantity on hand*. Only when we moved these warehouse attributes from PRODUCT, did we question leaving *quantity on hand* within PRODUCT. There, it implied a total quantity on hand across all warehouses for the product. It became apparent that these attributes were in fact repeating group attributes, as they applied to more than one warehouse, but this fact had not been identified in our entity list before we started normalizing the PRODUCT entity. If we had identified these as repeating group attributes, we would have moved them and formed a new entity called PRODUCT–WAREHOUSE during application of the first business normal form rule. Nevertheless, we eventually achieved the same result, when we applied the second and third business normal form rules. This illustrates an interesting quality of business normalization:

> *Business normalization cross-checks the accuracy of data interpretation.*

We found the need for additional entities during third business normal form, even though we had apparently missed them during first business normal form.

We now need to represent these entities schematically.

7.2.4 Deriving a key map from an entity list

We have seen how a key map can be derived from an entity list. A formal set of steps is used to achieve this derivation. In this section, we will apply these steps to our third business normal form entities to give the resulting key map of Figure 7.5, also in third business normal form.

The key map in Figure 7.5 establishes associations between suppliers, products and warehouses. It is formally derived from the third business normal form entity list as follows:

(1) Locate each entity in the entity list that has a compound primary key. Draw that entity as a box, with the name of the entity within it.

(2) Locate each entity in the entity list in which the component key attributes of the compound key entity are themselves *primary key* attributes of the other entity. Draw the entity boxes for those

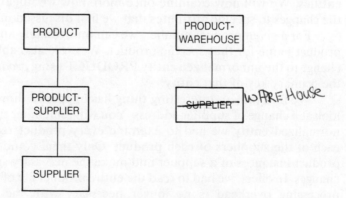

Figure 7.5 Third business normal form key map.

primary key entities adjacent to the compound key entity, and join
the compound key entity with each primary key entity.

(3)   Locate any entities in the entity list that have foreign keys, where the
foreign keys themselves are primary keys of other entities. Draw
those primary key entities close to the foreign key entities. Join each
foreign key entity with the entity where the foreign key exists either
as a primary key or a foreign key.

Following these rules, we first identify PRODUCT–SUPPLIER as a
compound key entity (step 1). The first component key attribute is
product number#, which is the primary key of the PRODUCT entity
(step 2). We draw the PRODUCT entity box close to the PRODUCT–
SUPPLIER box (see Figure 7.5). The second component key attribute of
PRODUCT–SUPPLIER is *supplier number#*, which is the primary key
of the SUPPLIER entity (also step 2). We draw the SUPPLIER entity box
adjacent to the PRODUCT–SUPPLIER entity (see Figure 7.5).

Similarly, we draw the PRODUCT–WAREHOUSE compound key
entity. We position it adjacent to the PRODUCT entity as the *product
number#* component key attribute of PRODUCT–WAREHOUSE is also
the primary key attribute of PRODUCT. Finally, the *warehouse
number#* attribute of PRODUCT–WAREHOUSE is the primary key of
the WAREHOUSE entity (again step 2). Thus, the WAREHOUSE entity
is also drawn adjacent to the PRODUCT–WAREHOUSE entity. There
are no foreign keys (step 3). Therefore, the final result is the key map in
Figure 7.5.

7.2.5   Changes are now easier

We have applied the business normalization rules to decompose the
unnormalized PRODUCT entity to five third business normal form
entities. We will now examine once more how we might accommodate
the changes to specific attributes that we first discussed in Section 7.1.3.

For a given product number, we can immediately apply a change of
product name for that specific product. We were also able to apply this
change to the unnormalized entity PRODUCT using *product number#* as
the primary key of that entity.

We find that an interesting thing has happened, however, when we
look at a change of supplier address. You will remember that with the unnormalized entity we had to examine every product record, and then
each of the suppliers of each product. Only then, could we identify all
product instances of a supplier and make the necessary supplier address
changes. In effect, we had to read the entire product file of records. Such a
processing overhead is no longer necessary with the third business
normal form entities as, given the supplier number, we can refer to the

specific supplier record and change the address directly. All products provided by that supplier (in PRODUCT–SUPPLIER) thus automatically refer to the new supplier address. Similarly, instead of examining the warehouse number for each product to make a warehouse address change, we can apply that address change directly to the specific warehouse record.

Not only can changes be applied more directly to the third business normal form entities, but the data have been structured so that we can now more readily answer the following questions. (You may wish to consider these questions first using the unnormalized entity, then apply the questions to the third business normal form entities.)

(1)   Are we tied to one supplier?

(2)   Can we negotiate cost price?

(3)   Do some or all products require special warehousing?

(4)   Do we intend to expand the number of warehouses?

Both the unnormalized entity and the third business normal form entities indicate that we can use more than one supplier for the product–represented by the repeating group in the unnormalized entity, and by PRODUCT–SUPPLIER in the third business form entities. This satisfies the first question.

On the other hand, we can now see that the unnormalized entity enabled us to keep only one cost price for each product. We could not record different cost prices from various suppliers and we could not use those cost prices to negotiate the most advantageous price from each supplier. Only with the third business normal form entities can we satisfy the second question.

The unnormalized entity further implied that all products were held in a single warehouse, as the warehouse attributes were not identified as repeating group attributes. The ability to store specific products in certain warehouses was not possible. This is not the case with the third business normal form entities. Furthermore, we are able to represent the specific quantity on hand of each product in each warehouse. Thus, the third question is satisfied only by the third business normal form entities.

This also answers the fourth question. There is no provision in the unnormalized entity to expand the number of warehouses. The third business normal form entities, however, do not suffer from this restriction. Hence, the fourth question is satisfied.

This simple PRODUCT example has introduced the rules of business normalization. It has given us some insight into the potential power of this technique when used to clarify the meaning of data. We have also seen how we may formally develop a schematic representation of a third business normal form entity list in the form of a key map. In the next chapter, we will use these business normalization rules to illustrate the identification of synonyms and homonyms.

. Business normalization rules do not provide answers; rather, they provoke questions. Business experts should be the only people who provide answers to those questions. Business normalization can certainly be used by analysts to assist in the interview process. However, in contrast, information engineering uses business normalization as a tool mainly for users, to define their needs for the future. It is an integral component of information engineering for the development of data models which capture business expertise. These rules are applied directly by the business experts, rather than indirectly by analysts through interview.

We need to understand the formal rules of normalization – called formal normalization – to appreciate the theoretical base on which this method rests. The remainder of this chapter addresses the formal definitions of first, second and third normal form. Formal definitions of fourth and fifth normal form are discussed in Chapters 8 and 9.

7.3 RULES OF FORMAL NORMALIZATION

A useful treatment of formal normalization, with references to more detailed papers, is provided by Date's *An Introduction to Database Systems – Volume 1* [7]. We will review the rules of formal normalization here, to distinguish them from the rules of business normalization.

7.3.1 Functional dependency

Formal normalization is based on functional dependency. Date defines this as:

> *Given a relation R, attribute Y of R is functionally dependent on attribute X of R. In symbols, this is written:*
>
> $R.X \rightarrow R.Y$

A **relation** in formal normalization is equivalent to an entity in business normalization. This definition indicates that $R.X$ functionally determines $R.Y$. That is, attribute X is the complete, unique primary key of attribute Y in relation R. Further, if X is a candidate key of relation R, and is in fact its primary key, all attributes Y of relation R must necessarily be dependent on attribute X. For example, consider the

Table 7.2   Relations used for formal normalization examples

Relation	Entity List Form	Functional Dependency Form	
SUPPLIER	(supplier#, sname, status, city)	supplier#	→ sname, status, city
SUPPLIER PART	(supplier#, part#, quantity)	supplier#, part#	→ quantity
PART	(part#, pname, color, weight, city)	part#	→ pname, color, weight, city

SUPPLIER relations (entities) in Table 7.2, expressed in entity list form and functional dependency form. An entity list is represented schematically in a data map, while functional dependency is illustrated in a functional dependency diagram, also called an FD diagram, as shown in Figure 7.6. In this figure, each attribute is represented in a box. An arrow extends from the primary key box to each functionally dependent attribute box. The compound primary key of SUPPLIER PART is shown at the far right of Figure 7.6. The larger box encloses each (compound) key attribute box. The functional dependency arrow extends from this larger box to attribute boxes that are functionally dependent on the compound primary key – in this case *quantity*.

We will now discuss the first three rules of formal normalization and relate them to the equivalent rules of business normalization. We will use as an example the unnormalized entity and FD diagram in Figure 7.7.

The arrow from *city* to *status* in Figure 7.7 indicates that *city* is a candidate key, with *status* functionally dependent on *city*. This presents a problem, as the status that applies to a city cannot be defined until there is at least one supplier in that city. This is referred to as an **insert anomaly**. Similarly, if a supplier provides only one part and that part is deleted, the fact that the supplier is located in that city is lost. This is called a **delete anomaly**. Problems associated with update are similar to the discussion at the beginning of this chapter with the PRODUCT entity. For example, if

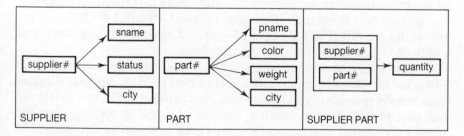

Figure 7.6   Functional dependency diagram for relations of Table 7.2.

PART SUPPLIER STATUS   (supplier#, status, city, part#, quantity)

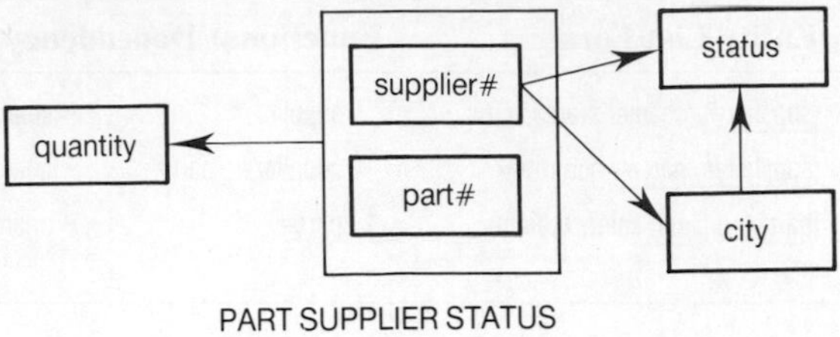

PART SUPPLIER STATUS

Figure 7.7 An unnormalized entity and FD diagram.

a supplier moves to a new city, every part provided by that supplier must be updated to refer to the new city. This is called an **update anomaly**. This latter term is also used as a collective term: insert, delete and update anomalies are all collectively referred to as update anomalies. Decomposing the entity to first, second and third normal form removes these anomalies.

7.3.2   First normal form

Date defines first normal form (1NF) as follows:

> *A relation R is in first normal form (1NF) if and only if all underlying domains contain atomic values only.*

The term **domains** (of a relation) in this definition is equivalent to attributes in an entity, while **atomic values** is equivalent to *remove repeating groups*. Both the formal and business normalization rules for first normal form are equivalent, but the business normalization rule (1BNF) is more explicit on the steps to take (see 1BNF rule as given in Section 7.2.1).

The FD diagram in Figure 7.7 shows that *status* and *city* are each functionally dependent on *supplier#*, which is part of the compound key of *quantity*. However, *quantity* is not atomic, as it is part of a repeating group, and so it is moved into a new entity SUPPLIER PART, leaving the entity SUPPLIER STATUS. Figure 7.8 shows the unnormalized entity of Figure 7.7 now in first normal form.

The update anomalies of Figure 7.7 have been removed. We can insert the fact that a supplier is located in a city, even though that supplier does not yet provide parts. There is no insert anomaly. We can delete the last part provided by a supplier without also losing the fact that the supplier is located in a particular city. There is no delete anomaly. The city for a supplier occurs only once (in SUPPLIER STATUS) and not many times redundantly, as in Figure 7.7. There is no update anomaly.

SUPPLIER STATUS   (supplier#, status, city)

SUPPLIER PART   (supplier#, part#, quantity)

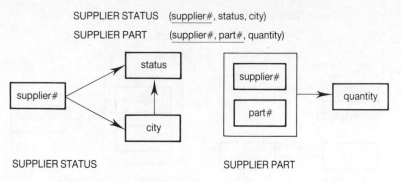

SUPPLIER STATUS   SUPPLIER PART

Figure 7.8   First normal form entities and FD diagram.

7.3.3   Second normal form

Date defines second normal form (2NF) as follows:

> *A relation R is in second normal form (2NF) if and only if it is in 1NF and*
> *every non-key attribute is fully dependent on the primary key.*

This is equivalent to the rule for business normalization, except that
2BNF defines the steps to be taken to establish that every non-key
attribute is fully dependent on the primary key (see 2BNF rule as given in
Section 7.2.2).

In the example of Figure 7.8, *quantity* is fully dependent on both
supplier# and *part#* (and no other key); that is, there are no partial
dependencies, only full, functional dependencies. SUPPLIER PART is
therefore in 2NF. Similarly, *city* is fully dependent on *supplier#*, which
means that, so far, some of SUPPLIER STATUS is also in 2NF.

Now, we will look at *status*, which (according to our example) is
fully dependent on *city*. Because *city* is dependent on *supplier#*, and
status is dependent on *city*, we say that *status* is transitively dependent on
supplier# (via the key *city*, which we should now show as *city#*). This
leads us to third normal form.

7.3.4   Third normal form

Date defines third normal form (3NF) as follows:

> *A relation R is in third normal form (3NF) if and only if it is in 2NF and every*
> *non-key attribute is non-transitively dependent on the primary key.*

This is also equivalent to the 3BNF rule for business normalization,

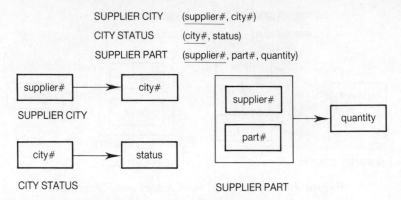

SUPPLIER CITY (supplier#, city#)

CITY STATUS (city#, status)

SUPPLIER PART (supplier#, part#, quantity)

Figure 7.9 Third normal form entities and FD diagram.

except that 3BNF defines the steps to be taken to establish non-transitive dependence on the primary key (see 3BNF rule as given in Section 7.2.3).

Figure 7.9 shows the 2NF entity and FD diagram of Figure 7.8 now decomposed to third normal form. In SUPPLIER STATUS of Figure 7.8, we cannot specify that a city has a status until there is a supplier located in that city. The transitive dependency of *status* on *supplier#* via *city#* is removed, according to the 3NF rule, by forming a new relation: CITY STATUS. This leaves *city#* fully dependent on *supplier#* in SUPPLIER CITY.

The rules of formal normalization were found to handle some situations inadequately; in particular, situations where a relation had multiple compound candidate keys, which overlapped. This led to the definition of Boyce/Codd normal form, which is a more precise definition of 3NF.

7.3.5 Boyce/Codd normal form

Boyce/Codd normal form is normally abbreviated to BCNF. It is stronger than third normal form [8]. In discussing this, we will define a new term: a functional **determinant** is any attribute on which another attribute is fully functionally dependent. BCNF is defined as follows:

> *A relation is in Boyce/Codd normal form (BCNF) if and only if every determinant is a candidate key.*

The main focus here is on candidate keys, not just on primary keys. It is potentially more powerful than 3NF because it forces the identification of candidate keys, and so helps uncover more business meaning.

Figure 7.10 uses an example where both *supplier#* and *sname#* (supplier name) are candidate keys, and where *status* is not dependent on

SUPPLIER   (supplier#, sname#, status, city)

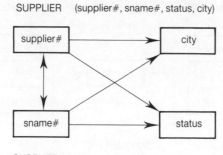

SUPPLIER

Figure 7.10   Example of Boyce/Codd normal form.

city (as in our previous example) but on either of the candidate keys. *City* is also dependent on the candidate keys. Note that the candidate keys are not underlined, as a primary key has not yet been determined.

In Figure 7.10, *supplier#* and *sname#* are candidate keys, indicated by the bidirectional arrow joining them, since each is a determinant of the other. The candidate keys also overlap, as they involve two or more attributes each, and have at least one attribute in common. However, they are not compound, as only one key is needed as a unique primary key. Thus, because the determinants *supplier#* and *sname#* are not compound candidate keys, SUPPLIER is in BCNF.

We will now look at an example of compound candidate keys (see Figure 7.11). *Part#* is a key. *Supplier#, part#* and *sname#, part#* are compound candidate keys (and so are not yet underlined) of *quantity*, which is dependent on either compound candidate key. This is resolved in BCNF by breaking the SUPPLIER PART relation into two alternative solutions, as follows:

SUPPLIER   (supplier#, sname)

SUPPLIER PART   (supplier#, part#, quantity)

or alternatively:

SUPPLIER   (supplier#, sname)

SUPPLIER PART   (sname, part#, quantity)

We can now see that BCNF helps to identify partial dependencies in the case of compound keys. This rule is applied in business normalization much earlier – in second business normal form. In fact, the second part of the 2BNF rule relates to BCNF. The focus here on only compound primary keys (rather than candidate keys) arises from the greater business knowledge applied to business normalization. There is usually no confusion over which candidate keys to make primary keys; they are

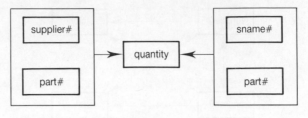

SUPPLIER PART

Figure 7.11 Example of compound candidate keys for BCNF.

generally identified long before the 2BNF rule is applied, based on the business environment.

Nevertheless, we can see that the same result is reached, whether formal normalization or business normalization is used. The only difference is in the extra guidance given by the business normalization rules. These rules define the steps to be taken in non-technical terms and so are understandable by managers, users and analysts, who become proficient, in less than a day, in the application of these rules to normalization of data in their business. This is generally not the case with the formal normalization rules. The formality of these definitions does not assist users, as they do not have the formal background of relational theory on which to base their understanding. Many users, even those who are already experienced at business normalization, never grasp the principles of formal normalization.

Because the business normalization rules are easy to apply, FD diagrams are not needed to determine full, non-transitive dependency. To use FD diagrams in a typical business data model comprising 800–1000 entities (relations) is overwhelming. Business normalization enables only data maps to be used.

This book therefore applies business normalization as a practical and powerful business technique, to be applied by managers, users and analysts, rather than aiming for the technical accuracy of definition used by formal normalization. The next chapter will demonstrate some of the power of normalization, when used as business normalization.

References

[1] Codd, E. F. (1970). A relational model for large shared data banks. *CACM*, **13**(6), 377–387.

[2] Codd, E. F. (1979). Extending the database relational model to capture more meaning. *ACM Trans. on Database Systems*, **4**(4), 397–434.

[3] Date, C. J. (1982). *Introduction to Data Base*, Volumes 1 and 2. Addison-Wesley: Reading, MA.

[4] Fagin, R. (1979). Normal forms and relational database operators. In *Proc. 1979 ACM SIGMOD International Conference on Management of Data.*

[5] Kent, W. (1983). A simple guide to five normal forms in relational database theory. *CACM*, **26** (2).

[6] Finkelstein, C. (1981). Information engineering. Published as six InDepth articles. *Computerworld* (May–June).

[7] Date, C. J. (1986). *An introduction to Database Systems – Volume 1.* 4th edn. Addison-Wesley, Reading; MA.

[8] Fagin, R. (1979). Normal forms and relational database operators. In *Proc. 1979 ACM SIGMOD International Conference on Management of Data.*

CHAPTER 8

Normalization as a Business Technique

Following the introduction to business normalization in Chapter 7, this chapter illustrates how business normalization can be used to help to define the future. Normalization used in this way is extremely powerful. Furthermore, it requires no computer experience; rather, it needs a detailed knowledge of the data, and this is held by the managers and staff in an organization – DP personnel rarely have this level of business experience.

This chapter also covers fourth business normal form. It introduces a business-oriented fourth normal form rule which has been found to be extremely effective with managers and users who have no knowledge of computing, or of the theoretical foundations of relational theory. This rule helps to identify subtype entities. Analysts and data administrators also find the business interpretation of 4BNF particularly productive. It allows business knowledge to be directly included in the resulting data models by the business experts, thereby avoiding problems of misinterpretation when the formal rules of normalization are applied without an expert knowledge of the business. The chapter ends with a formal definition of the fourth normal form rule of normalization.

8.1 BUSINESS NORMALIZATION EXAMPLE

We will now decompose another unnormalized entity EMPLOYEE into third business normal form. This entity is expressed in entity list format as follows:

EMPLOYEE	(employee number#, employee name, manager number#, manager name, start date, ((course number, course name, examination result))

First, we decompose this unnormalized entity to first business normal form by removing the repeating groups. The repeating group of *course number#*, *course name*, *examination result* is readily identified with the double left and right parentheses. We will move this repeating group to a new entity, with a compound key formed from the repeating group key ((*course number#*)), together with the key of the entity in which the repeating group resided (*employee number#*). This is formally called EMPLOYEE–COURSE. However, as it obviously deals with training of employees, we will call it TRAINING. The first business normal from entities are therefore:

EMPLOYEE	(employee number#, employee name, manager number#, manager name, start date)
TRAINING	(employee number#, course number#, course name, examination result)

Second business normal form requires those attributes that are only partially dependent on the primary key, or which are dependent on only part of a compound key, to be moved to another entity. The second business normal form EMPLOYEE entities are as follows:

EMPLOYEE	(employee number#, employee name, manager number#, manager name, start date)
TRAINING	(employee number#, course number#, examination result)
COURSE	(course number#, course name)

The course name is dependent on only part of the compound key of TRAINING – namely, *course number#*. However, the course name is not dependent on the employee unless it is a course that has been specifically developed for each separate employee. Course name is normally identified by course number; therefore, it is moved to the separate entity, COURSE.

We now examine the second business normal form entities using the rule for third business normal form. This identifies those attributes that are not at all dependent on the primary key of the entity in which they reside, but instead are dependent upon another key. In this example, *manager name* is dependent on *manager number#*, but not at all dependent on *employee number#*. *Manager name* is therefore moved to a new entity, MANAGER, leaving behind a foreign key of *manager number#* in the EMPLOYEE entity. The third business normal form entities are now:

EMPLOYEE	(employee number#, employee name, manager number#, start date)
MANAGER	(manager number#, manager name)

TRAINING   (<u>employee number#</u>, <u>course number#</u>, examination result)

COURSE   (<u>course number#</u>, course name)

Is this now a more complete representation of the data? How can we check? We will discuss the data with the Personnel Manager:

'*Yes, that seems reasonable*', he says. '*It enables me to determine the start date of an employee, and also identify the employee's manager*'.

However, discussing this with the Education Manager elicits a different reaction:

'*No, that does not meet my needs at all!*' says the Education Manager. '*How can I determine who is the manager responsible for a specific course? And how can I find who was the class manager responsible for a specific training class?*' *And while we are at it, you have only made allowance for one examination result per employee for a course! That implies, in the event of failing, that an employee cannot attend that course ever again! An employee may need to repeat a course several times until he gets a satisfactory examination result. How can you handle that situation?*

     Also another thing concerns me. I have no way of determining when a course was first introduced, or when a training class is scheduled. How would you handle that?'

These comments also cause the Personnel Manager to think further. He sees that there is no way of finding when a manager was appointed to his present (or any previous) position as the manager's start date in each management position does not exist.

     How did we miss so much data? Part of the reason for their concern lay in our original interpretation of the attribute *start date*. When *start date* was within the unnormalized EMPLOYEE entity, there was no concern as the Personnel Manager and the Education Manager could each apply his own unique interpretation to the attribute *start date*. It was only when the third business normal form entities emerged that we saw that *start date* was in fact *employee start date*. The original *start date* was in fact a homonym – that is, the same name being used to represent different data! We can now see that there are several start dates that are needed: *employee start date* (in the EMPLOYEE entity); *manager start date* (in MANAGER); *class start date* (in TRAINING); and *course start date* (in COURSE).

     Similarly, *manager number#* was a homonym. We need the following unique attribute names: *employee manager#* (in EMPLOYEE); *manager's manager#* (in MANAGER); *class manager#* (in TRAINING); and *course manager#* (in COURSE). The third business normal form entities, without homonyms, are now as follows:

EMPLOYEE   (<u>employee#</u>, employee name, employee manager#, employee start date)

MANAGER   (<u>manager number#</u>, manager name, manager start date, manager's manager#)

TRAINING   (<u>employee number#</u>, <u>course number#</u>, <u>class start date#</u>, examination result, class manager#)

COURSE   (<u>course number#</u>, course name, course start date, course manager#)

We have introduced specific start dates and manager keys in each relevant entity, using the name of that entity to establish a unique attribute name in each instance. Note in the case of the TRAINING entity that we have also established a further compound key attribute: *class start date#*. By making *class start date#* part of the compound key, we now have the ability to represent more than one examination result for an employee attending a course. So, an employee can attend a course several times on different dates, until eventually a satisfactory examination result is achieved.

It was not until the entity was in third business normal form that the true meaning of each data attribute became apparent. At that point, we gave homonym attributes unique names and placed them in entities where they belonged. A correct representation of the data meaning was the result.

Are we now satisfied that we have decomposed the original EMPLOYEE entity to a stable third business normal form? Not yet! We still have one more normalization cross-check to apply before we can be sure we have considered all likely data requirements.

8.1.1 Business normalization cross-check

We will cross-check the validity of these entities by applying the business normalization rules to each attribute in turn, instead of to each entity in turn as before. This is a useful check as it helps us to consider possible future changes that might occur in the data. Some examples will illustrate. We will apply the first business normal form rule to the *employee name* attribute in the EMPLOYEE entity. Is *employee name* a repeating group? Now that's interesting! Do we need to maintain the maiden name for each female employee, or previous married names? Do we need a record of an employee's previous name which was subsequently changed by deed poll? We would need clarification of these points from the Personnel Manager.

Let us follow this process further. Is *manager number#* a repeating group? This is also an interesting question! It forces us to consider the possibility of an employee having more than one manager. This might be the case in an organization that uses matrix management (where individual employees report to different managers for different functions involved in their job). Another example would be a need to maintain historical details of past managers for an employee. We may also want to keep other historical employee details for each past manager. For example, we may need the performance evaluation, the salary and the title the employee had when reporting to each past manager.

Employee history details

This suggests a need for another entity with a compound key of *employee number#* and *manager number#*, which we will call EMPLOYEE MANAGER HISTORY. It may also need to include additional attributes such as the date the employee first reported to the manager and the period of time he reported to that manager. It may also include further attributes such as *performance evaluation* and *salary* (if the salary changes when an employee first reports to a new manager).

Let us next cross-check the attribute *employee start date*. Is *employee start date* a repeating group? An example immediately comes to mind: an employee who previously worked for the organization is subsequently rehired. (This is increasingly encountered today.) Furthermore, some organizations may reinstate past employees with benefits accruing based upon the total period of employment with the organization; that is, as if that employment was a contiguous period. We find that a repeating group of *employee start date* is in fact quite feasible. But how would we represent such an attribute? It suggests a further entity, perhaps called EMPLOYMENT HISTORY (different from EMPLOYEE MANAGER HISTORY). This would have as its compound key *employee number#* and *employee start date#*. Likely attributes would include *termination date, salary at termination, benefit at termination*, and so on.

We have only applied the first business normal form rule so far in this cross-checking stage. We might equally apply the second business normal form rule to determine whether some attributes are more completely identified not only by the primary keys of the entity where they presently reside, but may require additional compound key attributes. Such partial dependency would suggest that these attributes should be moved into another entity where they are wholly dependent on the entire compound key of that entity. For example, is the *employee number#* unique for each employee throughout the organization? Or is it unique within a branch? In the latter case, a compound key of *employee number#, branch number#* is necessary to establish a unique key, with full dependency of employee attributes now on that compound key.

This attribute-by-attribute cross-check helps us to determine the need to maintain historical data. An employee may have only one salary value at a particular time, his current salary. But over time, with pay rises, the employee will have a range of salaries. It may be appropriate, therefore, to also maintain an EMPLOYEE SALARY HISTORY entity. An employee may report to different managers throughout a period of

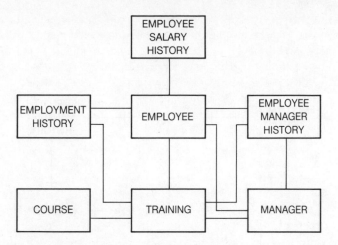

Figure 8.1 Key map of normalized EMPLOYEE entities.

employment with an organization. The first business normal form repeating group cross-check helps us to identify possible historical data which may need to be maintained. The additional third business normal form entities in the case of the entity EMPLOYEE are therefore as follows:

EMPLOYMENT HISTORY   (employee number#, employee start date#, period of employment, salary at termination, title at termination, benefit at termination)

EMPLOYEE MANAGER HISTORY   (employee number#, manager number#, employee start date with manager#, employee title, employee performance evaluation)

EMPLOYEE SALARY HISTORY   (employee number#, salary start date#, salary, (deductions), benefits)

A far more thorough identification of appropriate personnel attributes has come from this detailed cross-check of business normalization. We can now represent these fully business normalized employee entities in a key map, as illustrated in Figure 8.1. This key map has been developed using the steps outlined in Section 7.2.4:

(1) The EMPLOYEE and the COURSE entities are positioned adjacent to the TRAINING (compound key) entity. Similarly, the history entities are positioned close to the primary key entity of EM-PLOYEE.

(2) The MANAGER entity is positioned close to the EMPLOYEE entity, as *manager number#* is a foreign key in EMPLOYEE and is in fact the primary key of MANAGER. Association lines are drawn connecting the entities so related.

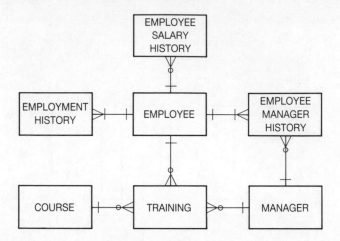

Figure 8.2 Data map for EMPLOYEE, developed from the key map in Figure 8.1.

Figure 8.1 includes, as lines on the key map, all of the potential associations between the entities for an employee. Not all of these associations may be needed. For example, Figure 8.2 shows an EMPLOYEE data map developed from this key map. This defines only those associations required from a business perspective between each of the entities EMPLOYEE, MANAGER and COURSE. The other potential associations have been ignored; if required at a later time, they can be explicitly defined.

We have now covered the first three rules of business normalization. These lead to an equivalent result to that produced by formal normalization. There is a fourth rule of business normalization that we will find particularly useful in identifying additional data and addressing other information needs – fourth business normal form.

8.2 FOURTH BUSINESS NORMAL FORM

With fourth normal form (4NF), business normalization and formal normalization begin to diverge. The formal definition of 4NF is discussed at the end of this chapter. Here, we will use a definition of fourth business normal form (4BNF) which is extremely effective in uncovering business meaning and which identifies subtypes of an entity:

An entity is said to be in fourth business normal form when:

*(1)   It is in third business normal form and its attributes depend not only upon the entire primary (compound key), but also on the **value** of the key, **or***

*(2)   An attribute has been relocated from an entity where it is optional to an entity where it is **wholly** dependent on the key and must exist, and so is **mandatory**.*

The first part of this definition indicates that a 4BNF attribute depends on the value of the key; this is called **value dependence**. The second part indicates that a 4BNF attribute whose existence is optional is moved to an entity where it is mandatory; this is called **existence dependence**. This definition is illustrated by the following examples.

8.2.1   Banking example of 4BNF

In a banking application, we may identify a third business normal form entity called ACCOUNT as follows:

ACCOUNT   (account number#, customer number#, branch number#, account balance, interest rate, maximum overdraft limit, statement date)

There may in fact be many more account attributes that are of interest, but the above will serve our purpose. This 3BNF representation appears reasonable for recording account details. But is it? Let us ask a banker:

'You can't really be serious!' he might say. 'That's not very practical! Where do I keep the data relating to savings accounts? How do I keep that data separate from trading (checking) accounts? They are two totally different things. I can't combine them together in ACCOUNT as you are suggesting!'

To the banker, the suggestion that saving accounts and trading (checking) accounts can be combined is totally unacceptable. These are completely different types of accounts and are generally managed in different parts of the bank. Furthermore, some attributes are relevant only to savings accounts (such as *interest rate*), while other attributes are relevant to trading accounts (such as *maximum overdraft limit* and *statement date*). To distinguish between these two types of banking accounts, they may be allocated a different range of account numbers: one range indicating savings accounts; the other range indicating trading accounts. Alternatively, an account type code may be used to distinguish between them.

   It is apparent that the *interest rate* attribute is dependent not just upon the *account number#* primary key, but also on the account number range or the account type code that relates to savings accounts. (Although many banks now also offer interest on checking accounts.) Similarly, the *maximum overdraft limit* and *statement date* attributes are dependent on the account number range or the account type code that relates to trading (checking) accounts. That is, they are value dependent.

If we differentiate between savings and trading accounts by establishing separate entities for each, we can manage these entities more appropriately. We can satisfy the business requirement for separation of savings and trading account activity.

This is achieved by including with the third business normal form (3BNF) ACCOUNT entity, two additional fourth business normal form (4BNF) entities: SAVINGS ACCOUNT and TRADING ACCOUNT. These are also called **subtype entities**. Each has a primary key of *account number#*. This key may later be physically implemented as a savings account number range, or instead with an *account number#* together with a *savings account type#*, making a compound key.

We will move the *interest rate* attribute into the SAVINGS ACCOUNT entity and explicitly name that attribute *savings account interest rate*. Additionally, we will move the *maximum overdraft limit* and *statement date* attributes to the TRADING ACCOUNT entity, as they apply only to trading accounts. Each has an account balance; therefore, we will define a common *account balance* attribute. We will place this in the ACCOUNT entity, which is in third business normal form, where it can apply to each of the fourth business normal form entities.

We will also define an ACCOUNT TYPE entity, to identify these two account types and any other account types which may be appropriate in the future.

We will assume that a unique primary key of *account number#* is used to distinguish between a savings account and a trading account. The attributes of ACCOUNT are in third business normal form. They are not dependent on the type of account, but are common to all accounts; that is, they are dependent only on *account number#*.

A foreign key of *account type#* is added to ACCOUNT. This indicates if a SAVINGS ACCOUNT entity occurrence or a TRADING ACCOUNT occurrence exists for a particular account number. We can later use *account type#* to reference all 3BNF and 4BNF ACCOUNT entities.

The fourth business normal form entities are now as follows:

ACCOUNT (account number#, account balance, account type#, customer number#, branch number#)

ACCOUNT TYPE (account type#, account type description)

SAVINGS ACCOUNT (account number#, savings account interest rate)

TRADING ACCOUNT (account number#, maximum overdraft limit, statement date)

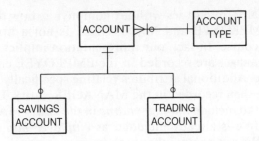

Figure 8.3   A fourth business normal form data map. This format is a characteristic of 4BNF data maps.

ACCOUNT is in third business normal form. A 3BNF entity is also called a **principal entity**. SAVINGS ACCOUNT and TRADING ACCOUNT are in fourth business normal form. A 4BNF entity is also called a **secondary entity**. Furthermore, the relevant *account number#* of these two entities is assumed to be unique, so *account type#* is not required as a compound key of these 4BNF entities. ACCOUNT TYPE is called a **type entity**.

The fourth business normal form entities can be represented in a key map, as shown in Figure 8.3. This key map has been further extended into a data map by defining the degree and nature of each association line. Note also the association joining the 4BNF entities SAVINGS ACCOUNT and TRADING ACCOUNT to the 3BNF entity AC-COUNT. This is an inclusive OR association, as discussed in Chapter 5. It indicates that an account can be either a savings account or a trading account. The data map representation in Figure 8.3 is a characteristic of fourth business normal form entities, with the type entity (ACCOUNT TYPE), the 3BNF entity (ACCOUNT) and the 4BNF entities with the extended association.

The existence of fourth business normal form entities can be difficult for DP analysts and data administrators to identify, but not so for the user. In many cases, a fourth business normal form entity is the only direct way to represent the true data meaning in an organization. For a banker, it was inconceivable that the savings accounts and trading accounts could be merged together. It was just not common sense. In fact, to do otherwise may be a violation of banking regulations in some countries.

8.2.2   4BNF extensions to the employee example

What of other examples? We have already seen one example in our earlier discussion of the EMPLOYEE entity. Referring back to the third business normal form entities without homonyms, how do we interpret the entities EMPLOYEE and MANAGER? Is not a manager also an employee? Of course! In fact, our representation implies that employee details for a manager are recorded in the EMPLOYEE entity as for any other employee. Additional attributes relating specifically to the position as manager are then recorded in the MANAGER entity. Does this mean it was incorrect to include *manager name* in the entity MANAGER? The individual's name is already included as *employee name* in the entity EMPLOYEE. We can now see that *manager name* is probably a synonym (different names referring to the same data) for the attribute *manager title*, rather than the manager's name. Many other specific manager attributes may also be included within MANAGER. They are existence dependent on the key of MANAGER.

What about the primary key of the MANAGER entity? Is *manager number#* a special group of employee numbers? Or would it be more appropriate to consider a compound key for managers, made up of *employee number#* and *manager code#*? In this way, we could identify each manager through *employee number#* and also *manager code#* which may indicate the manager's level in the organization. Some MANAGER attributes may apply to Manager Code 1 (say), while others may be more relevant to Manager Code 2 or to Manager Code 3. MANAGER is obviously a fourth business normal form entity that we may further break down to additional middle management and upper management fourth business normal form entities.

8.2.3   An order entry example

One further example will help us to understand the implications of fourth business normal form entities. Let us consider the acceptance of orders from customers in an order entry application. The order entry entities are as follows:

CUSTOMER
(customer number#, customer name, customer address, customer account balance, customer credit limit)

ORDER HEADER
(order number#, delivery address, order date, customer number#)

ORDER LINE ITEM
(order number#, order line number#, quantity ordered, quantity on backorder, agreed sales price, discount%, product number#)

PRODUCT
(product number#, product name, product quantity on hand, product quantity on order)

These entities are in third business normal form and are illustrated in the key map in Figure 8.4.

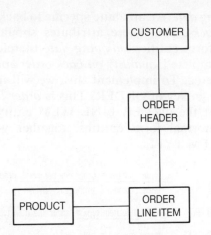

Figure 8.4   A third business normal form key map for order entry entities.

When an order is first accepted from a customer, the order header details are obtained to determine the delivery address and order date. Then the order line items are specified for each product making up the order. These line items indicate the quantity ordered.

On first acceptance, all orders are considered 'outstanding', as none has been processed. As these orders are subsequently processed, the quantity ordered is checked against the quantity on hand for each specific product. If sufficient quantity is available to satisfy the quantity ordered, that line item may be filled. It is therefore prepared for shipment to the customer.

In our example, provision has been made for back-orders (see *quantity on back-order* in ORDER LINE ITEM). If it is not possible to deliver the complete quantity ordered for a specific product, then that remaining quantity is back-ordered, and it is delivered later when received from the supplier. These order line items are not available for complete shipment as the full quantity ordered cannot initially be delivered. These attributes suggest two possible strategies for shipping orders. The first strategy retains the entire line item until the full quantity ordered can be satisfied. However, this may not be satisfactory to the customer. The second strategy is to ship any available quantity immediately. The remaining quantity is then back-ordered and shipped at a later time when the back-order has been satisfied.

To implement these strategies, we need to differentiate between outstanding order line items (which have not been processed at all), shipped order line items (where part of the quantity ordered can be delivered) and back-ordered line items (where the remaining quantity will be delivered at a later time). If a line item is shipped, an additional attribute is *shipping date*. An attribute specific to back-ordered line items is *quantity on back-order*. These attributes should reside in fourth business normal form entities: *shipping date* therefore applies only to orders that are completed; *quantity on back-order* applies only to orders that are back-ordered. To implement this, we will include another key attribute as a foreign key of ORDER. This is *order line item type#*. We can now represent the ORDER LINE ITEM entity as three separate fourth business normal form entities, together with a new entity, ORDER LINE ITEM TYPE:

ORDER LINE ITEM (order number#, order line number#, order line item type#, agreed sale price, discount%, product number#)

ORDER LINE ITEM TYPE (order line item type#, order line item type description)

OUTSTANDING LINE ITEM (order number#, order line number#, product quantity ordered)

BACKORDER LINE ITEM (order number#, order line number#, quantity on back-order)

SHIPPED LINE ITEM (order number#, order line number#, product quantity shipped, shipped date)

The new entity ORDER LINE ITEM TYPE is a characteristic of fourth business normal form entities. It is a type entity, usually implemented as a table. Each separate fourth business normal form (4BNF) entity type comprises a separate table entry. This can be used to allocate a type code to each 4BNF entity and a name to that type. Thus, the ORDER LINE ITEM TYPE entity might contain the entries in Table 8.1. Other line item types (which require special attention) may be added to this table. They can be represented by fourth business normal form entities with unique attributes. These 4BNF entities expand the ORDER LINE ITEM entity and exist together with the other 3BNF entities. ORDER LINE ITEM contains *product number#* as a foreign key. It is therefore associated with PRODUCT.

Figure 8.5 illustrates a complete data map based upon these fourth business normal form entities. Note the representation of the 4BNF entities. Once again, this is typical of a 4BNF data map. ORDER LINE ITEM is in third business normal form and contains attributes common to all line items: *agreed sale price* and *discount%*. ORDER LINE ITEM

Table 8.1 Fourth business normal form types.

Order Line Item Type	Order Line Item Type Name
0	Order line item
1	Outstanding line item
2	Back-ordered line item
3	Shipped line item

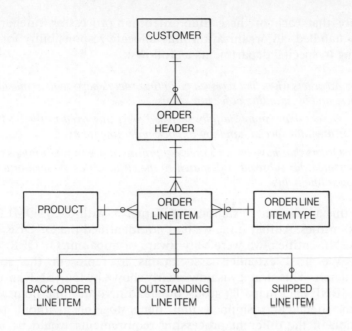

Figure 8.5   A fourth business normal form data map.

TYPE indicates that each line item may have several fourth business normal forms, according to the order line item type table (see Table 8.1). Each 4BNF entity is then related to the 3BNF ORDER LINE ITEM in an inclusive OR association (see Chapter 5). This indicates that an order line item can be outstanding, may be back-ordered or shipped. Once any processing is carried out on it, it is no longer outstanding; so it can either be shipped or it must be back-ordered. By decomposing ORDER LINE ITEM to its component 4BNF entities, we can manage them more effectively. We can exactly identify those products that are to be shipped, those on back-order and those still to be processed.

The data map in Figure 8.5 is in fact a closer representation of real life than the key map in Figure 8.4. With the identification of each of the fourth business normal form entities (OUTSTANDING LINE ITEM, BACK-ORDER LINE ITEM, SHIPPED LINE ITEM), appropriate management attention can be given to handling each specific fourth business normal form line item, as in the following statement of strategy:

> *All outstanding line items must eventually be processed. Those line items that are unable to be satisfied because of back-orders must be specially handled, so that eventually when the back-ordered quantities have been received into inventory the relevant order line items can be reprocessed to satisfy the complete quantity ordered. Only then can the back-ordered line items become shipped line items. Shipped line items, furthermore, must be delivered to the customer and must not be reprocessed.*

To ensure that each of these different order processing categories is correctly handled, an organization may allocate responsibility for their processing to specific departments as follows:

(1) All orders when first received go to the order department, as outstanding orders and outstanding order line items.

(2) Orders that cannot be fully satisfied are transferred to the back-order department for special handling of back-order line items.

(3) Orders that have been completely processed are moved to the shipping department for subsequent despatch to the customer as shipped orders and shipped line items.

We saw this as an earlier example in Chapter 5, with CUSTOMER and ORDER entities. At that time, we had not identified the ORDER LINE ITEM 4BNF entities; we were only aware of apparent ORDER 4BNF entities. We used extended associations to represent the strategy expressed here. This strategy is now clearly shown by the 4BNF entity list and the 4BNF data map. To group outstanding order line items, back-order line items and shipped line items together without proper recognition of the different processing requirements would be totally unacceptable to a distribution organization. Fourth business normal form is a closer representation of real life in business.

8.3 | FOURTH NORMAL FORM

Before we can discuss fourth normal form, we need to define the principle of **multi-valued dependency**. This is a fundamental part of the formal definition of fourth normal form.

Multi-valued dependency is abbreviated to MVD. It is defined by Date as follows [1]:

Given a relation R with attributes A, B and C, the multi-valued dependence (MVD):

$$R.A \rightarrow\!\!\!\rightarrow R.B$$

holds in R if and only if the set of B values matching a given (A value, C value) pair in R depends only on the A value and is independent of the C value. As usual, A, B and C may be composite.

The double arrow is read as **multiple dependent** or 'attribute $R.A$ multidetermines attribute $R.B$'. This definition indicates that MVDs exist only if a relation has at least three attributes. For example, with a relation $R(A,B,C)$ the MVD indicated by $R.A \rightarrow\!\!\!\rightarrow R.B$ holds only if $R.A$

$\to \to R.C$ also applies. We can represent this in a common statement, such as:

$$R.A \to \to R.B | R.C$$

which is read as '$R.A$ multidetermines $R.B$ or $R.C$'.

Date uses an example of COURSE $\to \to$ TEACHER|TEXT. This indicates that a course can be taught by any of the specified teachers, or alternatively uses all of the specified texts as references, or both. We are now ready to define fourth normal form.

Fourth normal form (4NF) decomposes MVDs into functional dependencies (FDs) [2,3]. Date defines 4NF as follows:

> *A relation R is in fourth normal form (4NF) if and only if, whenever there exists an MVD in R, say $A \to \to B$, then all attributes of R are also functionally dependent on A. In other words, the only dependencies (FDs or MVDs) in R are of the form $K \to X$ (that is, a functional dependency from a candidate key K to some other attribute X). Equivalently, R is in 4NF if it is in BCNF and all MVDs are in fact FDs.*

We will apply this rule to the following unnormalized entity:

COURSE   (<u>course#</u>, teacher, text)

The 4NF rule results in the decomposition of this entity into the following entities:

COURSE TEACHER   (<u>course#</u>, <u>teacher</u>)

COURSE TEXT   (<u>course#</u>, <u>text</u>)

This decomposition has achieved a separation of the details relating to teachers of a course (of which there are many) and those relating to the texts of a course (which are also many, but not related in any way to the number of teachers). In this example, a similar 4NF result using business normalization would have been achieved if the unnormalized entity COURSE had been written with its implicit repeating groups, as in the following:

COURSE   (<u>course#</u>, ((teacher)), ((text)))

The decomposition to COURSE TEACHER and COURSE TEXT would have been achieved by applying the 1BNF rule to remove repeating groups, with the repeating group attribute as part of the 1BNF entity compound key, as follows:

COURSE TEACHER	(course#, teacher#)
COURSE TEXT	(course#, text#)

These key-only entities would have encouraged the identification of further attributes, such as (say) the *course tuition fee* paid to the teacher giving a course.

However, business normalization progresses further than 4NF to uncover additional business meaning. It applies the 4BNF rule to determine the dependence of *teacher* and *text* on the value of the key.

Applying the 4BNF rule to the original COURSE entity, we find that we are interested in a more general concept, called (say) COURSE RESOURCE, as well as COURSE (in 3BNF). This introduces the type entity COURSE RESOURCE TYPE, the principal entity COURSE RESOURCE (in 3BNF) and the 4BNF secondary entities COURSE TEACHER and COURSE TEXT, which all have common keys. The fourth business normal form entities are then:

COURSE	(course#,
COURSE RESOURCE TYPE	(course resource type#, course resource type description,
COURSE RESOURCE	(course resource#, course#, course resource type#,
COURSE TEACHER	(course resource#, teacher,
COURSE TEXT	(course resource#, text,

As additional attributes obviously exist for these entities, this is illustrated by terminating each entity with a comma, rather than a right-most closing bracket.

The application of business normalization to 4BNF identifies subtypes. These often exist implicitly with multi-valued dependencies. The 4BNF rule is easy to apply and leads to the identification of additional attributes belonging to those 4BNF entities. The more precise representation of business meaning that emerges in 4BNF implicitly builds business logic into the data model.

References

[1] Date, C. J. (1986). *An Introduction to Database Systems – Volume 1*. 4th edn. Addison-Wesley: Reading, MA.

[2] Fagin, R. (1979). Normal forms and relational database operators. In *Proc. 1979 ACM SIGMOD International Conference on Management of Data*.

[3] Kent, W. (1983). A simple guide to five normal forms in relational database theory. *CACM*, **26**(2).

• Relational mathematical scientific normal form notation.
• Compound keys.
• Multiple candidate keys where values for candidate keys change.
• Null values.

9.1.1   Fourth business normal form hierarchies

Consider a compound fourth business normal form structure (see Fig. 9.1).
Each structure (C, D and E) has an additional fact ... business context
may involve a number of business contexts. See Chapters 7 and 8 (for
SUPPLIER, PRODUCT, STRUCTURE) and the prior chapters 7, 8 ... context
may represent a number (or a subset) of these facts (A, A1, ..., An). This
structure, which may show interrelated facts (C, D, E ... and ... SRA,
PRODUCT, STRUCTURE and COMPANY ...) as is discussed below. These

- Fourth business normal form hierarchies.
- Relationships between fourth business normal form hierarchies.
- Optional foreign keys.
- Multiple fourth business normal form dependencies.
- Circular reference.
- Multiple compound keys.

9.1.1 Fourth business normal form hierarchies

A fourth business normal form (4BNF) entity, related to a third business normal form entity, can also have additional fourth business normal form entities related to it in a multi-tiered form (or hierarchy), as shown in Figure 9.1. This illustrates three 4BNF EMPLOYEE entities: MANAGER, CLERK and SALES PERSON. There are also several types of managers, which are also shown here as 4BNF entities: BRANCH MANAGER, SALES MANAGER and GENERAL MANAGER. Thus, a hierarchy of 4BNF entities is established.

There is no theoretical limit to the number levels in a 4BNF hierarchy. Figure 9.1 shows only two levels. The progression from a strategic model through a tactical model to an operations model (see Part Three) will define only those 4BNF entities of interest to each management level.

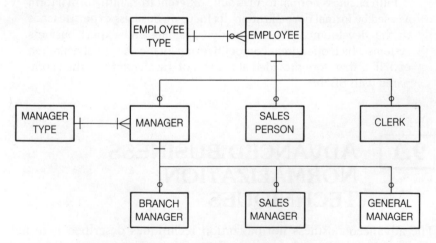

Figure 9.1 Multi-tiered types. A 4BNF entity may have other 4BNF entities below it.

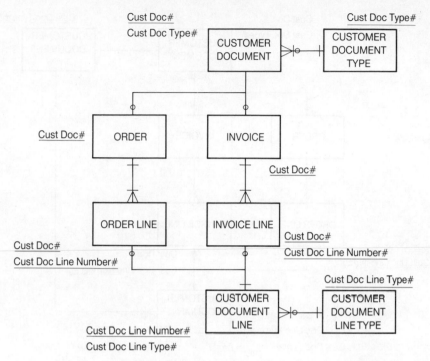

Figure 9.2   4BNF hierarchies with different types.

9.1.2 Relationship between fourth business normal form hierarchies

Figure 9.2 shows two separate type entities: CUSTOMER DOCUMENT TYPE and CUSTOMER DOCUMENT LINE TYPE, with two 4BNF hierarchies interrelated. For clarity, Figure 9.2 illustrates the primary and foreign keys in each entity that establish the associations. If the 4BNF types are identical, one type entity can be used for both of the 4BNF hierarchies CUSTOMER DOCUMENT TYPE and CUSTOMER DOCUMENT LINE TYPE. This still maintains their interrelationship, as shown in Figure 9.3. This figure illustrates that CUSTOMER DOCUMENT TYPE is the dominant type, as the CUSTOMER DOCUMENT entities ORDER and INVOICE are associated with the CUSTOMER DOCUMENT LINE entities ORDER LINE and INVOICE LINE in a mandatory one-to-mandatory many association.

9.1.3 Optional foreign keys

As we briefly discussed in Chapter 7, optional foreign keys indicate the presence of more detailed 4BNF entities. Figure 9.4 illustrates this for an

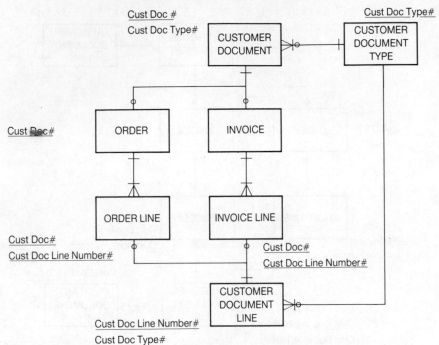

Cust Doc #
Cust Doc Type#

Cust Doc Type#

Cust Doc#

Cust Doc#
Cust Doc Line Number#

Cust Doc#
Cust Doc Line Number#

Cust Doc Line Number#
Cust Doc Type#

Figure 9.3 Relationships between 4BNF similar hierarchies.

optional foreign key of *customer*# in the entity INVOICE. This is represented by the optional nature on the association at CUSTOMER; that is, the association is (apparently) optional one-to-optional many between CUSTOMER and INVOICE. This is resolved as shown in Figure 9.5, where the foreign keys are now all mandatory. As we can see in Figure 9.5, only the entity CREDIT CUSTOMER has an association with the entity INVOICE. This association is now mandatory one-to-optional many. The entity CASH CUSTOMER now has no association at all with INVOICE. The optional one association has disappeared.

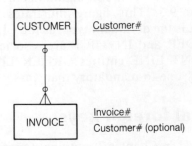

Customer#

Invoice#
Customer# (optional)

Figure 9.4 Optional foreign keys. These indicate the potential existence of more detailed 4BNF entities.

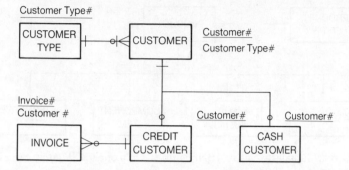

Figure 9.5   Optional foreign keys are now mandatory. This is resolved by 4BNF entities where the foreign key exists only in the entities where it is mandatory.

An optional foreign key, or its data map counterpart (an optional one association), will often emerge during initial modeling. It represents incomplete definition, or worse still, weak audit control. This was highlighted in Chapter 5 in the discussion of sales persons where some received commission and others received none at all. The additional 4BNF entities COMMISSION SALES PERSON and NON COMMISSION SALES PERSON resolve this problem. Figure 5.7, which provides an example of extended associations, is a case in point. As indicated in the discussion of that figure, extended associations provide a design note for more detailed definition later, through business normalization. In its present form, Figure 5.7 indicates weak audit control in the management of a (commission) SALES PERSON and a SALES GROUP (which receives no commission).

Similar comments apply to optional tending to mandatory associations. They indicate underlying conditional logic in a stable (fully business normalized) data model. This can sometimes be replaced by defining two, or more, 4BNF entities where the foreign key is either mandatory or non-existent, as in Figure 9.5. Their real-life representation in a business indicates a need for greater management responsibility and control, or detailed conditional logic to be satisfied.

9.1.4 Multiple fourth business normal form dependencies

Related entities in a 4BNF hierarchy can be either mutually exclusive or mutually inclusive. If they are mutually exclusive, no more than one 4BNF entity can depend on a specific 3BNF entity occurrence at one time. This is illustrated in the manufacturing example of Figure 9.6 which indicates that a product can be an assembly, a subassembly, a component item or an alternative item; that is, it can only be one of these at any one time.

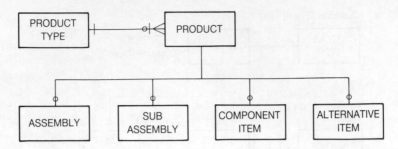

Figure 9.6   Mutually exclusive 4BNF entities. Only one 4BNF entity can exist for a specific 3BNF entity occurrence.

However, in some cases, more than one 4BNF entity can exist for an occurrence of a 3BNF entity. This is illustrated in Figure 9.7 in relation to law enforcement. In this example, a person can be both an offender and a victim, and may also be a witness. Because a person can be more than one type of person at the same time, there is a many-to-many association between PERSON and PERSON TYPE. Figure 9.7 resolves this with the intersecting entity PERSON ROLE (called a 'role' entity) between PERSON and PERSON TYPE. PERSON ROLE has the primary keys *person id#*, *person type#* and a foreign key of *criminal incident id#* which indicates the date and other attributes of a related CRIMINAL INCIDENT. PERSON ROLE is therefore used to indicate each role that a particular person has taken, perhaps at different times and for different incidents – as an offender, or as a victim, or as a witness.

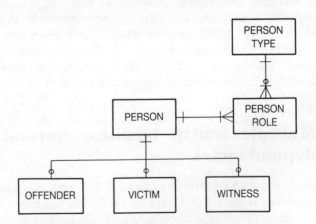

Figure 9.7   Mutually inclusive 4BNF hierarchy. Several 4BNF entities exist for the one 3BNF entity occurrence. The resulting many-to-many association is resolved by an intersecting entity. This is called a 'role' entity.

9.1.5   Circular reference

Several entities may be interrelated in a circular reference, as illustrated
in Figure 9.8. In this example, the entity PERSON belongs to a COST
CENTER; each cost center belongs to a BRANCH OFFICE; and each
branch office is responsible to a manager – that is, a person. Consequently, BRANCH OFFICE is dependent on PERSON, but not every
person is responsible for a branch office (only managers). Hence, the
optional nature at the BRANCH OFFICE end of the association with
PERSON. This results in the circular reference shown in Figure 9.8,
which is also called an **entity cycle**.

The existence of a circular reference makes it difficult to establish
entity ownership, which is needed for automatic derivation of subject
data bases and potential application systems from a data model (see
Chapter 15). There are three situations that can result in a circular
reference:

(1) The implicit existence of 4BNF entities;

(2) Ill-defined management reporting structure;

(3) The incorrect definition of associations.

The first and second situations indicate incomplete business normaliza-
tion. In Figure 9.8, the first situation occurs when using a 3BNF entity
PERSON, rather than the 4BNF entity BRANCH MANAGER which the
BRANCH OFFICE:PERSON association was intended to represent.

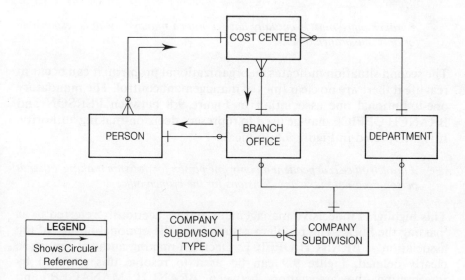

Figure 9.8   A circular reference (also called an entity cycle).

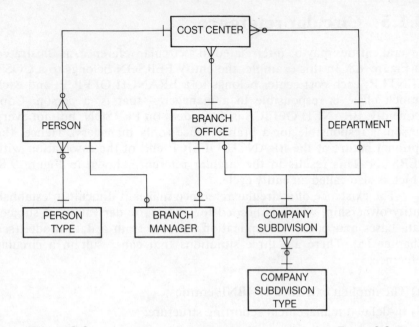

Figure 9.9   Resolution of the circular reference shown in Figure 9.8.

This error is corrected by defining BRANCH MANAGER as a 4BNF entity dependent on PERSON. The association between BRANCH MANAGER and BRANCH OFFICE is then correctly defined as shown in Figure 9.9:

> *A branch office must eventually have a branch manager, who is responsible for only one branch office.*

The second situation indicates an organizational problem: it can occur in real life if there are no clear lines of management control. The mandatory one-to-optional one association in Figure 9.8 between PERSON and BRANCH OFFICE may be used to represent decision-making authority. It is interpreted in Figure 9.8 to mean:

> *A branch office is dependent on only one person for decision making, but that person need not make any decisions for the branch office.*

This highlights indecisive management and is facetiously referred to as 'passing the buck'. The problem results from the optional nature of the association at BRANCH OFFICE. Decision-making authority must be clearly defined. Figure 9.9 can be used to resolve this problem by interpreting the association between BRANCH MANAGER and BRANCH OFFICE as follows.

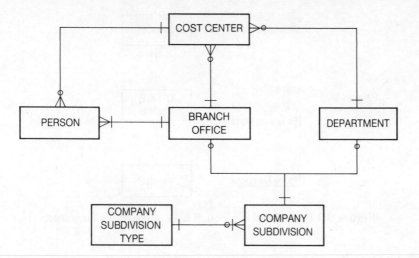

Figure 9.10 Associations for circular reference shown in Figure 9.8.

A decision may not be within the authority of a branch manager (optional tending to mandatory one at BRANCH MANAGER). If it is in his authority, a single clear decision must be made for that branch office (indicated by mandatory one at BRANCH OFFICE).

This is expressed in real-life as 'the buck stops here!' It may require organizational change for full resolution of the problem it highlights.

The third situation, which is generally the more common reason for a circular reference, is due to an error in modeling. The association between PERSON and BRANCH OFFICE in Figure 9.8 is mandatory one to optional one. It may represent the following:

A branch office contains only one person, who may not be assigned to any branch office.

It it corrected in Figure 9.10 with a mandatory many-to-mandatory one association between PERSON and BRANCH OFFICE. Therefore:

A branch office contains many people, but at least one (the branch manager), and each person reports to only one branch office.

9.1.6 Multiple compound keys

During business normalization, multiple compound primary keys may emerge for entities, leading to a high maintenance workload when the

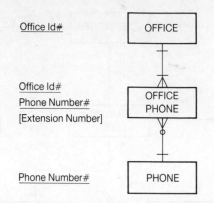

Figure 9.11 Multiple compound keys give high maintenance.

data model is later implemented: if the values of the keys change, all entities in which the primary key(s) exist must each be changed. This is illustrated in Figure 9.11. If an office is later relocated and the office phone numbers are changed, every compound key in the OFFICE PHONE entity must be changed, as well as every PHONE primary key. This problem is resolved in Figure 9.12, where internally allocated primary keys of *office phone key#* in OFFICE PHONE and *phone key#* in PHONE have been used. The compound key of *phone number#* in OFFICE PHONE is now defined in Figure 9.12 as a secondary key in PHONE. The compound key of *office id#* is now defined in OFFICE PHONE as a foreign key. Each of the phone numbers for an office need be changed once only now in PHONE. No changes are necessary in OFFICE PHONE, unless an [*extension number*] (secondary key) is also changed.

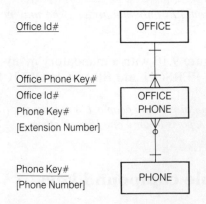

Figure 9.12 Resolution of multiple compound keys.

The internally allocated keys, *phone#* and *office phone#*, establish the associations between the entities in Figure 9.12. These are equivalent to 'surrogate keys', as used in the RM/T model (see Chapter 4). The high processing overhead required in Figure 9.11 to change every primary or foreign key reference for a specific key occurrence is eliminated. Only one change is necessary – now made to the attribute defined as a secondary key, and residing in only one entity.

9.2 | FIFTH BUSINESS NORMAL FORM

Fifth business normal form (5BNF) is particularly relevant to the design of expert business systems as it enables intelligence to be built into the data model. It permits a representation of intrinsic logic, based on the structure that exists between related entity occurrences.

For an information system, the data model represents the logical data base design. The information system is its physical implementation. It is passive; it exhibits no expertise; it is not a knowledge base. It is a repository of data – a well, to be drawn from as needed. With information systems, senior management involvement is largely passive, or even non-existent. With an expert business system, the data model is not the end of the design process. Rather, it is the beginning. The input used for the data model, and the way in which it is used, is the difference. The most essential input is active senior management participation. This provides clear direction for the future.

The data model represents the terminology, the language, of the organization. But a data model also contains inherent logic. Procedures are derived from it to process data, and are expressed as procedure maps: schematic representations of procedures. Expert rules are also derived from the data model. This is an automated generation stage discussed in Chapter 22.

We will introduce the concepts of 5BNF first with an example. Following detailed treatment, we will then cover the formal definition of 5NF and compare its features with 5BNF.

9.2.1 Introduction to fifth business normal form

We will consider a problem that is typical of a manufacturing organization: a bill of material structure. This is used in manufacturing to

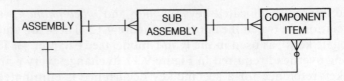

Figure 9.13 A bill of material data map.

represent the component items that are assembled together to manufacture a product. A product may be used, or sold, in its fully assembled, manufactured, form (such as a car) or in a partially assembled form (for example, a carburetor). In the first instance it is called an 'assembly', while in the second instance it is called a 'subassembly'. An assembly is made up of one or many subassemblies, which in turn may be made up of other subassemblies and/or 'component items'. A component item is defined as an elemental piece, or part, that cannot be broken down any further; in other words, its purpose is to be combined with other component items to form subassemblies and/or assemblies. It may also be sold individually, for repair purposes. We can represent assemblies, subassemblies and component items in a data map, as illustrated in Figure 9.13. This tells us that an assembly is made up of one or many subassemblies or component items (but at least one), and a subassembly is made up of one or many component items (but at least one). A component item is designed for use in only one assembly, or in one subassembly, which in turn is designed for use in only one assembly.

In our statement of this problem, we said that a product for sale may be either fully assembled (an assembly) or partially assembled (a subassembly), or a component item may be sold as a product for repair purposes. We therefore have several product types, represented in fourth business normal form in Figure 9.14. Note that Figure 9.14 shows a data map in 4BNF, where the fourth business normal form entities themselves are interrelated: each is a type of product, related to other types of products. This interrelationship should in fact be many to many (rather

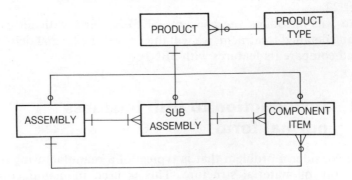

Figure 9.14 Fourth business normal form product entities.

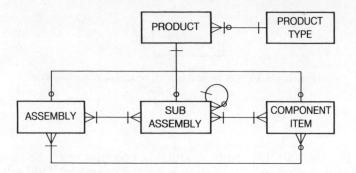

Figure 9.15   Complex fourth business normal form entities.

than the one to many in Figure 9.14) to enable a subassembly to be used in more than one assembly (such as for interchangeable subassemblies) and to enable a component item to be used in more than one subassembly (as interchangeable component items). Furthermore, we were earlier told that a subassembly can also be made up of other subassemblies. The result is the data map shown in Figure 9.15.

Here, we are beginning to see some of the complexity of real life: the complex many-to-many relationships between product types and the recursive association on subassembly, showing an interrelationship between subassemblies.

We can decompose the many-to-many associations as shown in Figure 9.16, but the result is more complex, and we have only considered three interrelated fourth business normal form entities. What if we had

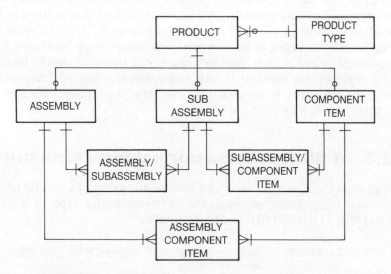

Figure 9.16   Attempted decomposition of 4BNF entities.

Figure 9.17 A typical 5BNF recursive association.

5? Or 10? Or 100? The problem quickly becomes overwhelming. And what about the recursive association on subassembly? This solution is hardly satisfactory. We need to represent these interrelationships another way. The answer is to use fifth business normal form (5BNF).

9.2.2 Recognizing fifth business normal form

A non-technical definition of fifth business normal form is:

> *An entity is in fifth business normal form if its dependencies on occurrences of the same entity or entity type have been moved into a STRUCTURE entity.*

Based on this definition, fifth business normal form is suggested by associations between the entity types (ASSEMBLY, SUBASSEMBLY and COMPONENT ITEM) in Figure 9.15, and also by the recursive association on SUBASSEMBLY. In fact, it is often the recursive association that first alerts us to a possible 5BNF entity. For example, in the early stages of data modeling, we may have established a strategy that a 'product is made up of one or many other products'. This is a valid, but not sufficiently detailed definition which is represented by Figure 9.17. Of course, we have already seen in Figure 9.15 how this should be more clearly represented. But this is still not adequate. Let us define a new STRUCTURE entity as suggested by our definition above, called in this case PRODUCT STRUCTURE.

9.2.3 A fifth business normal form structure

In entity list form, we can show the interrelationship of a product entity with other occurrences of the same entity or entity type in a 5BNF PRODUCT STRUCTURE entity, as follows:

PRODUCT STRUCTURE (Product no#, product type#, sequence#, product no#, product type#, quantity for assembly)

Table 9.1 Tabular representation of 5BNF product structure.

(1) *Product No#*	*(2)* *Product Type#*	*(3)* *Sequence No#*	*(4)* *Product No#*	*(5)* *Product Type#*	*(6)* *Quantity for Assembly*
123	ASSEM	1	418	SUB	6
		2	413	SUB	3
		3	812	ITEM	4
		4	893	ITEM	10
413	SUB	1	506	SUB	2
		2	893	ITEM	6
		3	813	ITEM	4
418	SUB	1	517	SUB	3
		2	581	SUB	3
		3	813	ITEM	10
506	SUB	1	893	ITEM	4
		2	813	ITEM	5
618	ASSEM	1	506	SUB	5
		2	418	SUB	10
		3	413	SUB	4

The logic inherent in the 5BNF structure above can be best illustrated by examining a typical bill of material table based on this structure, as shown in Table 9.1. The first two numbered columns (*Product No#* (1) and *Product Type#* (2)) are keys that identify the particular product number to be assembled and the level of assembly – either an assembly product type (ASSEM) or a subassembly product type (SUB). The third column (*Sequence No#* (3)) defines the sequence in which assembly is to take place. The 5BNF recursive association with other products is defined by the fourth and fifth columns (*Product No#* (4) and *Product Type#* (5)). These identify the product number and type to be used for each part of the assembly of a product – either subassemblies (SUB) or component items (ITEM) – and the quantity of each required for assembly (see column 6). We can clearly see that product 123 is assembled from six of subassembly 418, followed by three of subassembly 413, and then four of item 812 and ten of item 893. Furthermore, subassembly 413 is itself assembled from two of subassembly 506, followed by six of item 893 and four of item 813. Table 9.1 also indicates the assembly of subassemblies 418 and 506, and assembly 618.

Table 9.1 is a bill of material explosion for products. The term 'explosion' in manufacturing refers to the progressive decomposition of an assembly into all of its subassemblies and component items, and then

Table 9.2 A bill of material 'where used' list.

(4) Product No#	*(5)* Product Type#	*(1)* Product No#	*(2)* Product Type#	*(3)* Sequence No#	*(6)* Quantity for Assembly
413	SUB	123	ASSEM	2	3
		618	ASSEM	3	4
418	SUB	123	ASSEM	1	6
		618	ASSEM	2	10
506	SUB	413	SUB	1	2
		618	ASSEM	1	5
517	SUB	418	SUB	1	3
581	SUB	418	SUB	2	3
812	ITEM	123	ASSEM	3	4
813	ITEM	413	SUB	3	4
		506	SUB	2	5
893	ITEM	123	ASSEM	4	10
		413	SUB	2	6
		506	SUB	1	4

the progressive decomposition of those subassemblies until only elemental component items are left.

But what about a bill of material 'where used' list? This is used to allocate a specific component item quantity across a number of subassemblies and assemblies using that item. Table 9.2 provides the basis. We will use the fourth and fifth columns for selection as now shown in Table 9.2. This is not to suggest that two versions of the table are needed. Two tables have only been used here to illustrate 5BNF concepts. With appropriate software, the same table may be accessed (referenced) either as in Table 9.1 or in Table 9.2. We are now able to identify, for each component item or subassembly, all of the subassemblies or assemblies in which it is used, the quantity required for assembly and the point (or sequence) when it is needed for assembly.

We can represent the complexity of Figure 9.15 with a very simple data map, which includes our PRODUCT STRUCTURE entity. This is shown in Figure 9.18. The data map is clear. The complexity has been removed, being now included as occurrences in the PRODUCT STRUCTURE entity as illustrated in Tables 9.1 and 9.2.

We will now use the suffix 'STRUCTURE' as part of the entity name to indicate a 5BNF entity throughout this book. A 5BNF entity is also called a **structure entity**.

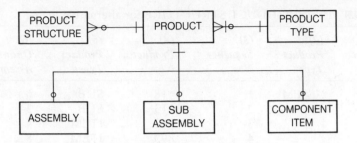

Figure 9.18   Bill of material data map, with a 5BNF structure.

9.2.4   The power of fifth business normal form

As indicated earlier, fifth business normal form is extremely powerful. It is used to implement a high level of expertise in the data model and is used as a dynamic knowledge base of expert rules. An example will illustrate the potential of this technique.

Consider the problem of unavailability of specific component items or subassemblies needed for manufacture of particular assembled products. This may be due to the warehouse waiting a new shipment of those items from suppliers – but there is a transport strike, or the required subassemblies have to be manufactured from other items which are out of stock. In such a situation, a manufacturer may use alternative items for manufacture in place of the unavailable items. This can be addressed by adding another product type to the data map (ALTERNATIVE ITEM), as shown in Figure 9.19. The items that can be used as alternatives (*product type#* = ALT) are defined in the PRODUCT STRUCTURE entity in Table 9.3. This shows part of Table 9.1, but now with alternative items for selected component items (812 and 893). However, the third column (*Sequence No#*) is now interpreted for alternatives to mean

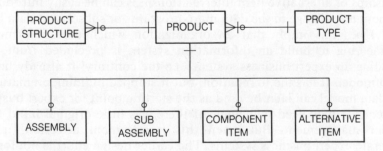

Figure 9.19   The 5BNF data map, with alternative items.

Table 9.3 Use of PRODUCT STRUCTURE for alternative items.

(1) Product No#	(2) Product Type#	(3) Sequence No#	(4) Product No#	(5) Product Type#	(6) Quantity for Assembly
123	ASSEM	1	418	SUB	6
		2	413	SUB	3
		3	812	ITEM	4
		4	893	ITEM	8
812	ALT	1	212	ITEM	0
		2	203	ITEM	0
		3	401	ITEM	0
893	ALT	1	141	ITEM	0

Alternative Priority#, for selection of the best alternative based on this priority.

Table 9.3 indicates that product 123 is assembled first using six of subassembly 418, then three of subassembly 413. Next, four of item 812 is used. However, if item 812 is not available, then item 212 may be used in its place, as an alternative. If item 212 is also unavailable, then item 203 can be used in place of item 812. Failing that, item 401 is the third alternative for item 812. Finally, product 123 is assembled using eight of item 893, or its alternative, item 141. In the case of alternatives, the quantity is zero in Table 9.3. The original quantity for item 812 – namely 4 – is used for each alternative.

The PRODUCT STRUCTURE entity comprises a number of entity occurrences, with each occurrence representing a row in the product structure table. Thus, bills of material, as well as alternative items, can be easily defined and dynamically changed as required. The introduction of alternatives allows substantial intelligence to be built into bills of material, using alternative items from different suppliers, and their relative availability. Furthermore, future bill of material interrelationships or alternative item interrelationships can be easily introduced, without any change to the data map, programs or subsequent data base.

Does this imply that an organization which used information engineering to build an information system is precluded from later building an expert business system? To the contrary! It already has its data model. It has the foundation, but it stopped building prematurely. Its data model can later be used as the starting point for expert business systems. It may need refinement if there was little original input from senior management. But given this management direction, it can generate expert business systems. The earlier design effort is not lost.

Because of the tabular representation, a 5BNF entity can be used as a dynamic repository of expert rules – able to be changed as easily as changing a product description, for example. The changing of expert rules can be initiated by a person or, if expert rules for changing expert rules (called meta-rules) are defined, by a machine. This enables an expert business system to learn from experience.

This representation of 5BNF can be implemented by most DBMSs available today – whether third or fourth generation. However, it is most flexible when implemented as tables using a relational DBMS, or with 5GLs such as PROLOG or LISP.

9.2.5   Examples of fifth business normal form

Many examples of fifth business normal form exist in real life. The following is a small list of some of the possible applications of this representation:

- Grouping of otherwise unrelated insurance claims dynamically, to identify an insurance 'catastrophe' in an expert reinsurance system.
- Definition of technical substitutes or supersessions in an expert inventory management system.
- Interrelationship between criminals and crimes based on modus operandi, physical description, and so on, in an expert criminal investigation system.
- Expert profit optimization through interrelated income and expense analysis, with goal seeking.
- Land feature interrelationships, such as roads, rivers, and so on, in an expert land information system.
- Symptom interrelationships in an expert medical diagnostic system.
- Geological structure interdependence in an expert minerals exploration system.
- Analysis of interrelated buying patterns in an expert retail information system, or an expert marketing information system.
- Route optimization for deliveries in an expert distribution system.
- Customer-oriented expert systems in banking, insurance, retail and distribution based on total value to the organization of a customer across all products and services.

However, use of fifth business normal form alone does not constitute an expert business system. The problem is not that simple. It requires far more analysis and representation than is suggested by the foregoing discussion of 5BNF. It requires a method for progressive discovery and refinement of the standard terminology of the business, and identification of its expert rules. This is achieved by capturing data terminology and expert rules in an expert design dictionary for development of expert business systems. This is discussed later, in Parts Three and Four.

Chapters 7–9 have introduced the concepts of business normalization. They have shown how this powerful technique can be used to clarify the true meaning of data. The rules of business normalization, as applied by information engineering, are summarized in Box 9.1.

9.3 FIFTH NORMAL FORM

There is a substantial difference between the formal definition of 5NF and the business definition of 5BNF. Fifth normal form is based on the concept of join dependency. Date defines **join dependency** as follow [1]:

> *Relation R satisfies the join dependency (JD)* (x, y, . . . , z) if and only if R is equal to the join of its projections X, Y, . . . , Z, where X, Y, . . . , Z are subsets of the set of attributes of R.*

The decomposition of a relation (entity) into other relations is called **projection**. These projected (or decomposed) relations can be combined together based on common keys. This is called a **join**. Join dependency therefore means that a relation, after projection into three or more subset relations, must be capable of being joined again on common keys to form the original relation. A relation that can be projected to three or more relations is called ***n*-decomposable**: this is a characteristic of join dependency.

We can now define fifth normal form in terms of join dependencies. In fact, 5NF is sometimes called projection – join normal form, or PJ/NF. According to Date:

> *A relation R is in fifth normal form (5NF) if and only if every join dependency in R is a consequence of the candidate keys of R.*

Thus, 5NF is dependent on projection based not only on the primary keys, but also on candidate keys. For example, consider SUPPLIER now with two candidate keys *supplier#* and *sname*:

SUPPLIER (supplier#, sname, status, city)

Applying the 5NF rule, we project this into several relations, as follows:

SUPPLIER NAME (supplier#, sname)

SUPPLIER STATUS (supplier#, status)

SUPPLIER CITY (sname, city)

Box 9.1
The rules of business normalization

First business normal form

Identify and remove repeating group attributes to another entity. The primary key of this other entity is made up of a compound key, comprising the primary key of the entity in which the repeating group originally resided, together with the repeating group key itself, or instead another unique key based on the business needs. The name of the new entity may initially be based on a combination of the name of the repeating group and the name of the entity in which the repeating group originally resided. It may be later renamed according to its final attribute content after business normalization is completed.

Second business normal form

Identify and remove those attributes into another entity which are only partially dependent on the primary key and also dependent on one or more other key attributes, or which are dependent on only part of the compound key and possibly one or more other key attributes.

Third business normal form

Identify and remove into another entity those attributes which are dependent on a key other than the primary (or compound) key.

Fourth business normal form

An entity is said to be in fourth business normal form when: (1) it is in third business normal form and its attributes depend not only upon the entire primary (compound key), but also on the value of the key; or (2) when an attribute has been relocated from an entity where it is optional to an entity where it is wholly dependent on the key and must exist, and so is mandatory.

Fifth business normal form

An entity is in fifth business normal form if its dependencies on occurrences of the same entity or entity type have been moved into a STRUCTURE entity.

BOX 9.2
The rules of formal normalization

First normal form

Take projections of the unnormalized relation to eliminate any domains containing non-atomic values. This step will produce a collection of 1NF relations.

Second normal form

Take projections of the original 1NF relations to eliminate any non-full functional dependencies. This step will produce a collection of 2NF relations.

Third normal form

Take projections of those 2NF relations to eliminate any transitive functional dependencies. This step will produce a collection of 3NF relations.

Boyce/Codd normal form

Take projections of those 3NF relations to eliminate any remaining functional dependencies in which the determinant is not a candidate key. This step will produce a collection of BCNF relations.

Note: The above rules can be condensed into the single normalization guideline: '*Take projections of the original relation to eliminate all FDs in which the determinant is not a candidate key.*'

Fourth normal form

Take projections of those BCNF relations to eliminate any MVDs that are not also functional dependencies. This step will produce a collection of 4NF relations.

Note: In practice it is usual to eliminate such MVDs *before* applying the 1NF, 2NF and 3NF rules.

Fifth normal form

Take projections of those 4NF relations to eliminate any join dependencies that are not implied by the candidate keys. This step will produce a collection of 5NF relations.

The rules of formal normalization that were described in Chapters 7–9 have been summarized in Box 9.2. This is based on Date's definitions. Date provides additional references at the end of his Chapter 17 on *Further Normalization*.

In formal normalization, the definition of 5NF is based on the ability to project a relation into its component relations, which can then be rejoined (called projection–join) to form the original relation without any loss of data. This is completely different to the definition of 5BNF (see Section 9.2.2). 5NF focuses on projected relations from candidate keys, with the ability to join those projected relations together – interrelated by common keys (candidate or primary). In contrast, 5BNF is based on interrelated entity or entity type occurrences, to establish associations dynamically. The dynamic nature of 5BNF arises from the duplicate keys and types used in 4BNF, on which 5BNF is based. As we have seen, 5BNF is extremely powerful, enabling a dynamic repository of expert rules to be established.

On normalization generally, Date remarks:

'The notions of dependency and normalization are semantic (Date's emphasis) in nature. . . . In other words, those notions are concerned with what the data means. By contrast, the relational algebra and relational calculus, and languages such as SQL that are based on these formalisms, are concerned only with data values; any interpretation of those values is imposed from the outside (by the human user). . . . The normalization guidelines should be regarded as a discipline to help the data base designer – a discipline by which the designer can capture a part, albeit a small part, of the semantics of the real world in a straightforward and simple manner.'

The rules of business normalization used by information engineering have evolved to capture these real-world semantics, using simple definitions that can be easily applied by users and which draw on the expert knowledge of those users to define the meaning of the data. We have seen, in Chapters 7–9, the power of business normalization to achieve this objective. We also saw, in Chapters 3–5, the clarity of data meaning that results when business normalization is applied in conjunction with data mapping conventions also used by information engineering. We will draw on these concepts many times in this book as we cover the various steps of information engineering for the design and development of information systems and expert business systems. The basic principles covered in this part will now be applied, in Part Three, to the planning and execution of information engineering projects.

Reference

[1] Date, C. J. (1986). *An Introduction to Database Systems – Volume 1*. 4th edn. Addison-Wesley: Reading, MA.

PART THREE

Information Engineering Projects

CHAPTER 10

Strategic Planning: Defining the Future, Today

Information engineering encompasses strategic planning as well as analysis and design and implementation support for the generation of data bases and development of computer applications. This chapter introduces some of the initial concepts of strategic planning. It discusses strategic implementation and strategic management. An understanding of these concepts is vital to ensure the successful introduction of a strategic plan into an organization. Strategic planning has evolved into a discipline that can be used by any organization, large or small, government or commercial. Although it is normally applied at the highest level, it is progressively applied throughout all management levels of the best run organizations.

10.1 INTRODUCTION

It is not the purpose of this book to discuss strategic planning in detail. There is much excellent literature on the subject. However, we will draw on two specific authors: Peter Drucker and Michael Porter. Drucker [1] describes many fundamental principles while Porter [2] addresses more recent perspectives.

10.2 THE NEED FOR STRATEGIC MANAGEMENT

Strategic planning in itself is not enough. To be effective, plans must be implemented. This is called **strategic implementation.** Success lies in communication, execution and management of strategic planning. This is called **strategic management.** When strategic planning has been used and has failed, the fault has invariably been in implementation and management. Developing this further, Gray [3] indicates that:

> *'Strategic planning as many text books describe it may not be around for much longer but not for the reasons most critics give. If formal strategic planning vanishes in a few years, it will be because wherever it is undertaken it either gets better or it gets worse, depending on how well it's done: if you do it poorly, either you drop out or you rattle around in its mechanics; if you do it well, you evolve beyond strategic planning into strategic management.'*

We will distinguish between two main forms of strategic planning in this book:

- Corporate strategic planning (also called corporate planning).
- Systems strategic planning (also called systems planning).

Corporate strategic planning is very much a management activity, whereas systems strategic planning relates generally to data processing. We will use the terms **corporate planning** or **strategic planning** for the management focus on planning, and **systems planning** for the DP emphasis. As an organization becomes more reliant upon computers, its data processing hardware and software resources need to be closely aligned to its corporate plan. This has been difficult to achieve for several reasons.

Corporate planning is carried out at the highest levels of an organization, while most DP departments are much lower in the organizational hierarchy. To align systems planning closely with corporate planning, some organizations have established a systems planning function in the corporate planning department.

Corporate planning is still an inexact judgmental science; systems planning is also imprecise. The impact that different corporate planning alternatives have on the systems plan (the hardware and software resources needed to support the corporate plan) has been difficult to determine. Part of the reason is due to the lack of early strategic planning feedback. The failure of strategic planning is due to lack of strategic management. Planning is difficult, but strategic management is harder. Close management of the implementation of strategic plans is one of the emphases of strategic management.

While planning, alternative approaches are not always obvious. Furthermore, problems may not be apparent due to insufficiently detailed plans, with implications or alternatives not being thought out and inadequate attention being given to implementation. The planning process itself is all that is important. But the plan may be wrong.

Managers must ensure that the plan is as accurate as possible so that it can be implemented correctly. They must plan to evaluate the plan. The traditional evaluation method, based on a pilot introduction of the plan using part of the organization, may not give feedback for 6–12 months, which is too long. Clear, early feedback mechanisms must be defined, so that deficiencies can be detected and corrected early. If not, these deficiencies will in time become problems; and if not solved, these problems may lead to failure.

The other emphasis of strategic management is the approach that managers take towards strategic planning itself. Traditional strategic planning has a long feedback cycle, often 3–5 years. As a result, it is a start – stop process. It should not be. With strategic management, planning is a continuing process. It is a planned, progressive evolution into the future.

Traditional strategic planning may bring with it substantial change. The impact of that change may not have been fully evaluated. If change is not well managed, chaos is the result. Strategic management avoids this chaos by uncovering implications and problems of change. But more than just avoiding chaos, strategic management focuses on the planning process and on its implementation. Strategic management establishes an environment for planning. It recognizes that a manager's job is first and foremost to determine whether change is needed. If needed, change must be managed so it is made correctly. Anyone can control a car, a plane or a boat – if no change is made in its direction. The skill is in deciding that the present direction must be changed; in determining what the new direction should be; when to change direction and how fast or how slow the change should be made; whether the change has been effective or whether further change is necessary. For this to be possible, early feedback is essential. When the right change is decided, its implementation must then be closely managed.

10.2.1 Strategic modeling leads to strategic management

Strategic planning is the starting point: strategic plans form the initial catalyst. Strategic implementation is achieved through strategic modeling and tactical modeling. These provide feedback for strategic management, leading to refinement of the strategic plans, as illustrated in Figure 10.1. Problems are identified early, adjustments are made where necessary, and alternatives are tested easily and quickly. Strategic and

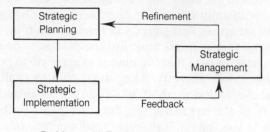

Problems with Traditional Strategic Planning

Strategic Planning	Limited strategic alternatives
Strategic Implementation	Ineffective communication
	Misinterpretation
Strategic Management	Long feedback cycle (3–5 years)
	Ineffective performance monitoring

Figure 10.1 The problems of traditional strategic planning. Strategic plans can be defined through modeling, for strategic implementation. Modeling provides rapid feedback to strategic management for refinement of the plan.

tactical modeling lead to firm implementation of the strategic plans. They lead to an environment of small, planned adjustments, as the organization moves into the future.

A strategic plan may have been fully defined, or it may only be broadly expressed. Either way, strategic and tactical modeling use the plan to identify data and information needed to support its achievement. In so doing, they lead to early feedback and refinement of the plan where necessary.

Where an organization has already developed a formal strategic plan, a clear expression of the plan exists with management commitment. However, the content of the plan, and the format of its presentation, may not provide all of the detail needed for strategic modeling. The documented plans may need to be restructured, presented in a slightly different form or expanded in certain areas to ensure that the essential strategic input to a strategic modeling project is clearly expressed. Changes to existing strategic plans will of course vary from organization to organization. The following chapters indicate the degree to which those plans may need to change.

Where an organization has not previously undertaken any strategic planning, or where the strategic plan is perceived to be substantially out of date, two approaches can be used. These are:

- Formal strategic planning.
- Informal strategic planning.

This and the following chapters discuss each of these strategic planning approaches. Once plans have been defined, whether formally or informally, the strategic statements embodied in those plans are used to define the data needed by management to achieve their objectives. Strategic and tactical modeling help to identify the information needed at different management levels throughout an organization. Operations modeling identifies the underlying detailed data from which that information is derived.

As described in Part Two, the data and information so identified are documented in a data model. This comprises a schematic data map and its supporting entity list. Tools such as business normalization and software, which automates information engineering (see Part Four), are used to progressively define and clarify this data. The data model provides feedback to management for refinement, enhancement or extension to their strategic plans. This feedback is essential for effective strategic management.

A productive, interactive strategic planning environment is established: the feedback from strategic modeling is rapid and precise, and strategic alternatives are identified and evaluated. Computer-aided strategic planning carried out by expert systems leads to rapid evolution of strategic planning thought by management. A clear expression of strategic direction emerges in the data model and supporting narrative documentation. This indicates data and areas of the enterprise that support achievement of the strategic plan. Managers at lower levels in the organization then define the necessary underlying detail in the form of tactical models, through tactical modeling. In so doing, they apply their knowledge of the business to implement the strategic model, reflecting the strategic plans. Problems are identified and new opportunities become apparent. The resulting tactical and operations models, and their detailed documentation, provide further feedback to management for resolution or refinement of the strategic plans.

In this chapter, we will review formal strategic planning as used by information engineering. Formal strategic planning is optional: if it is not undertaken prior to the project, the informal strategic planning approach described in Chapter 11 can be used instead. The data model produced by the informal strategic planning approach can then be used as a catalyst for later introduction of formal strategic planning.

10.3 | STRATEGIC PLANNING TERMINOLOGY

Formal strategic planning in information engineering is based on years of research. The material presented here provides a brief overview drawn from publications and workshops on strategic planning [4]. These are used to train management throughout an organization.

Strategic planning applies not just to commercial enterprises who operate competitively in the private sector for profit, but also to public sector organizations who operate in a non-competitive environment with funding from government revenue. This includes government agencies, as well as statutory authorities such as utilities. The terminology used for strategic planning is related to the type of organization in the following.

The private sector measure of *profit* has a public sector equivalent of *cost effectiveness*. While competition can lead to both *opportunities* and *threats* for a private sector organization, different political parties can have a similar impact for a government agency or statutory authority. One party may present different opportunities to another party, because of different political platforms or policies.

A private sector organization evaluates *threats* presented by competitors, while a government agency or authority considers *constraints* that apply depending on relevant legislation relating to its operation and the political party in power. The private sector interest in *markets* (that is, customers) for different *products* or *services* compares to the public sector focus on *clients* or *population segments* who use different services supplied by government agencies.

Both types of organization must evaluate the impact of either competition or change of government and legislation, or both, on their strategic plans. These factors must be addressed in their plans.

10.4 | THE STEPS OF FORMAL STRATEGIC PLANNING

The steps of formal strategic planning are illustrated in Figure 10.2.

10.4.1 Identification of current strategy

The current strategies applied at the corporate level, and at each relevant program and business unit level, must first be identified. They may be defined in documented corporate plans – if not, they must be determined by interview with management – in publications provided for the benefit of customers and shareholders of the organization, in an annual report or in the legislation for a government department that establishes its purpose and the various functions it carries out. Additional internal documentation may provide further insight into the current strategy. Internal, confidential reports discussing existing policies, issues and

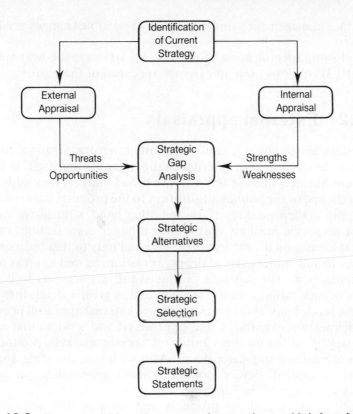

Figure 10.2   The stages of formal strategic planning that establish firm directions for the future.

directions may be valuable input. Forecasts, plans and budgets developed by management for both the short and long term also provide insight. These indicate management thinking, relating to the current strategy and to possible future strategies.

These documents generally provide a narrative description of the current organizational environment, its markets (or population segments for government), its products and services, and the channels of distribution for delivery of those products and services to the markets. They may identify anticipated future changes in markets, and possible future products and services to satisfy those changes. New technology to support different channels of distribution may also be addressed.

Existing documents may have differing degrees of usefulness, depending on the purpose for which they were originally generated. However, they all act as a catalyst for discussion and expansion by management. They are a starting point for a focus on possible strategic directions. They define the organization as it exists today and provide an insight into management's thinking today of possible changes needed for tomorrow.

Following identification of the current strategy, the next step (see Figure 10.2) is to carry out an external appraisal of the business.

10.4.2   External appraisal

Where strategic planning is applied for an entire organization, this step examines the environment external to the organization itself. It focuses on various business units in terms of the broad markets they address (its users or clients, or the public), in addition to the products or services that they supply to their markets. If, on the other hand, strategic planning is used for a specific business unit within a larger organization, external appraisal focuses on the environment external only to that business unit. This may include other parts of the organization, as well as areas outside the organization. The separate products and services, as well as the markets of each business unit, are evaluated in greater detail than at the corporate level. Thus, at the corporate level, external appraisal provides a broad delineation of markets, and of products and services that address those markets. At the business unit level, specific markets, products and services are defined in greater detail. At both levels, the same appraisal approach is applied. Before looking at these approaches, we need to discuss the concept of the life cycle.

Both markets, and the products and services that address those markets, move through a number of life cycle stages. These stages are defined as:

- Development.
- Growth.
- Shakeout.
- Maturity.
- Saturation.
- Decline.

These stages are used to assess the status of each related group of markets, and of products and services, during the external appraisal step, as described in the following subsections. The first task is to evaluate external factors at the business unit level. This is illustrated in Figure 10.3.

External business unit appraisal

Threats/constraints and opportunities   The position of each product or service in its market is defined in terms of the life cycle illustrated in

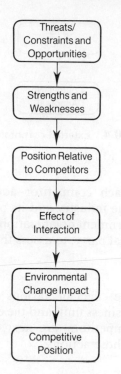

Figure 10.3 External business unit appraisal.

Figure 10.3. Environmental considerations such as demographic, economic, social, legal, legislative, availability and uncertainty factors are used to identify potential threats for commercial organizations, or constraints for government agencies. They may also indicate opportunities for each market and product/service segment.

Strengths and weaknesses   An assessment of the life cycle position of the business unit within its industry, and the position of that industry within the market, indicates the potential for competition from other organizations operating in that market.

This step also assesses the likelihood of legislative change and its potential impact on the organization. Under- or over-utilized capacity in the industry, growth rates, market shares, competition for resources and overall profitability or cost effectiveness of the business unit are evaluated to identify strengths and weaknesses. Freedom from, or dependence on, the policies of different political parties is a further measure of the strengths and weaknesses of a government agency.

Position relative to competitors   The business unit is next compared with each of its immediate competitors, using the approach just described: in

Figure 10.4   External corporate appraisal.

terms of the markets each competitor addresses, its products and services, its position in the industry and its perceived relative strengths and weaknesses. For government organizations, this evaluation is carried out for each major political party, to assess the impact different political philosophies may have.

Effect of interaction   The effect of various actions by competitors or political parties on the business unit, and the effects of various actions by the business unit on competitors, are next determined, together with their likely responses to those actions.

Environmental change impact   The effect of environmental changes on the industry, the business unit and its competitors is further evaluated to identify potential threats and opportunities for the business unit, the competitors and the industry as a whole. For government organizations, this focuses on constraints rather than threats.

Competitive position   The result of this analysis defines the competitive position of each business unit, together with relevant threats or constraints and opportunities associated with that position for both private sector and public sector organizations.

This external appraisal is carried out for each business unit in terms of the markets in which it operates. The external appraisal is then applied again at the corporate level (see Figure 10.4).

External corporate appraisal

An organization's business units may operate in different industries. These industries are evaluated for relative 'attractiveness' by applying the product life cycle appraisal, just described, to each separate industry. Each business unit is then evaluated in terms of its position in the industry relative to its competitors, and to sensitivity to different government policies.

Current portfolio   Based on this evaluation, a current portfolio position for each business unit is established in terms of the markets and industries in which it operates.

Competitive appraisal   The organization is then compared with its major competitors (or other political parties) by undertaking a similar analysis for each known business unit of the competitors. For each competitor, this identifies its possible actions in the market and industry as a whole. The competitors' actions are then compared with the organization's likely actions in the same industries or markets, to clarify potential threats/constraints or opportunities, and possible competition for the same financial or other resources.

The external corporate appraisal outlines the position of the organization and its business units in terms of factors external to the organization. It clarifies threats or constraints and opportunities relevant to the organization during corporate analysis, and then for each business unit in turn. Following this external appraisal, a more detailed internal appraisal is undertaken.

10.4.3   Internal appraisal

These threats and opportunities must now be evaluated in terms of the relevant strengths and weaknesses of the organization itself. This is carried out by an internal appraisal (see Figures 10.5 and 10.6), which provides an audit of the current situation for each relevant business unit, as well as for the organization.

Internal business unit appraisal

Strengths and weaknesses   An internal appraisal identifies areas of strength and weakness for a number of factors in each business unit. For example, the production areas of a manufacturing organization or business unit are evaluated in terms of plant modernization, plant flexibility and plant productivity. Financial areas of the organization are evaluated in terms of profitability, low use of credit and cash flow. Management itself may be evaluated for each business unit in terms of innovative capability, establishment of performance indicators for staff,

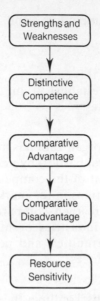

Figure 10.5   Internal business unit appraisal.

performance against own performance indicators and depth of experience. Other factors may be identified for each business unit, which may include marketing, purchasing, personnel and public relations.

Distinctive competence   By breaking each business unit down into specific areas or functions, and by evaluating each area in turn, areas or functions of distinctive competence can be identified.

Comparative advantage   Areas of distinctive competence indicate areas of strength in the organization. For example, these may include marketing, production or finance. Areas that exhibit distinctive competence are grouped together to emphasize those characteristics providing a comparative advantage over its competitors, or with a strength to survive political or legislative change for government agencies.

Comparative disadvantage   Similarly, factors in each business unit that exhibit average or weak performance are grouped together. These identify disadvantages that may impede attainment of objectives. They may give the organization a comparative disadvantage in relation to its competitors, or they may bring about political or legislative change. Possible remedies to help improve areas of average or weak performance in certain factors may be identified.

Figure 10.6   Internal corporate appraisal.

Resource sensitivity   Areas of distinctive competence, which indicate strengths, as well as areas that indicate weaknesses must be evaluated in terms of their sensitivity to resource variations. For example, a manufacturing organization may exhibit competence in its production capability and its productivity, but may be wholly dependent upon a single supplier of key raw materials, and so may be sensitive to the performance of that supplier. The production strength thus may need to be offset by a resource dependency weakness. An organization that is strong financially, but whose financial strength is obtained in an area that is vulnerable to industrial disputes or strike action, may find that its strength becomes a weakness because of its dependency on factors outside its control. A government agency that is totally dependent on the present political party in power for its survival also exhibits resource sensitivity. This is particularly true where opposition parties adopt policies that target its dismantling or privatization. With a change of government, its funding may be stopped, severely curtailed or it may be completely demolished!

Following the internal appraisal of each relevant business unit, a similar approach is applied to the organization itself. This is the internal corporate appraisal, as illustrated in Figure 10.6.

Internal corporate appraisal

At the corporate level, senior management face the problem of generating financial resources and deciding on their allocation to particular business units in the organization's portfolio of activity.

Business unit performance   Performance data on each business unit is defined in terms of attainment of objectives, success in carrying out defined strategies, financial condition and potential for generating surplus financial resources. The strengths and weaknesses of each business unit, determined from the business unit internal appraisal, are established for the organization as a whole. Particular emphasis is placed on areas where distinctive competence or comparative advantage has been determined.

Organization performance   Performance data on the organization itself, its financial condition overall, its potential for generating surplus financial resources and its corporate management capability is then evaluated.

Performance indicators   These factors are used to identify performance indicators. Performance is ranked against each indicator in terms of strong, average or weak. Performance indicators assessed as strong in various business units are used to evaluate the organization as a whole. They identify particular areas of distinctive competence or comparative advantage over competitors. Similarly, performance indicators assessed as average or weak are evaluated across all business units to identify any comparative disadvantages when compared with competitors.

The result of this internal appraisal is a clear definition of:

- Strengths and weaknesses of each business unit.
- Business units with comparative advantage over competitors, and political stability.
- Strengths and weaknesses of the organization as a whole.
- Comparative advantage of the organization over competitors, and political stability.

10.4.4   Strategic gap analysis

The external appraisal identifies threats/constraints and opportunities to the organization, and to individual business units. The internal appraisal then identifies strengths and weaknesses, and areas of comparative advantage against competitors, exhibited by individual business units and the organization as a whole. These are used in strategic gap analysis to evaluate the effectiveness of the organization's current strategy, as determined in the first stage (see Figure 10.7).

Specific comparative advantage   Strategic gap analysis is carried out first at the business unit level, then the corporate level. Areas of distinctive

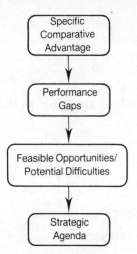

Figure 10.7   Strategic gap analysis.

competence identified through the internal appraisal are compared with the competitive position of those areas as determined through the external appraisal. This identifies specific comparative advantages for a particular business unit, or for the organization itself.

Performance gaps   The effect of current strategies on the identified threats and weaknesses is then evaluated, and likely performance gaps are identified.

Feasible opportunities and potential difficulties   Areas of comparative advantage and distinctive competence are compared with identified opportunities, to determine feasible opportunities. Similarly, strengths and weaknesses are compared to identify potential difficulties.

Strategic agenda   Performance gaps, together with identified feasible opportunities and potential difficulties, then form the strategic agenda that the organization must consider for the future. This provides input to an identification and evaluation of the strategic alternatives open to management.

10.4.5   Strategic alternatives

Following the strategic gap analysis, various strategic alternatives are identified and evaluated. Each strategic agenda item identified from the strategic gap analysis is grouped into:

- Performance gaps.

- Potential difficulties.

- Feasible opportunities.

Each agenda item within these groupings is then evaluated in terms of:

- Indicated alternatives.

- Strategic directions.

- Assumptions.

- Alternative assumptions.

- Likely threats or weaknesses.

- Evaluation.

The emphasis at this stage is to identify and evaluate those strategic alternatives that build on strengths and take advantage of opportunities. The natural tendency is to concentrate first on weaknesses, while avoiding threats or constraints. However, this should be resisted. By emphasizing strengths and opportunities instead, the organization moves to a position of comparative advantage over its competitors. It draws on its strengths such that it makes its weaknesses or threats/constraints insignificant.

10.4.6   Strategic selection

Following identification and evaluation of strategical alternatives, the most appropriate strategies to be followed are selected. Each of the identified strategic alternatives is evaluated in terms of the following factors:

- The extent to which a strategic alternative contributes to objectives.

- Confidence in the analytic process through which alternatives were generated.

- Political emphasis and relative power within a business unit.

- Constraints or prescriptions imposed at corporate, legislative or political levels.

- The relevant strategic emphasis of proactive or reactive, adaptive or entrepreneurial, risk or caution.

10.5 CONCLUDING REMARKS

This brief discussion has outlined the formal strategic planning approach used in information engineering. It is comprehensive, examining in detail significant business units in an organization and the organization itself. It leads to a clear positioning of the organization and component business units within their markets, and in terms of their competitors or political philosophies for government. It identifies specific strengths and weaknesses, and indicates those strategic directions that emphasize strengths and minimize weaknesses. Such a clear definition of strategic directions provides a firm foundation on which strategic modeling and tactical modeling may be based. It allows these techniques to be used to identify data and information needed by management to help the organization achieve its strategic plan. It allows ready identification of information needed by management as the organization moves into the future according to its strategic directions.

With this strategic analysis, a clear definition emerges of relevant markets, of products and services, of channels and of objectives for the organization in the future. These statements provide input to strategic and tactical modeling, and, through these techniques, early feedback is provided for management to refine strategic directions during implementation. Strategic management then becomes not just another management buzzword, but is fully integrated into the organization. It becomes a corporate culture.

However, in many organizations, such a formal approach to strategic planning may not be appropriate. It requires management commitment and time, as well as support at all levels of management. Such commitment and support may only be obtained over time, and so it may not be appropriate to use a formal approach initially. This brings us to the second, alternative, approach used by information engineering, informal strategic planning, which is discussed in the next chapter.

References

[1] Drucker, P. (1974). *Management: Tasks, Responsibilities, Practices*. Harper & Row. New York.

[2] Porter, M. E. (1980). *Competitive Strategy*. The Free Press, MacMillan Publishing: New York.

[3] Gray, D. H. (1986). Uses and misuses of strategic planning. *Harvard Business Review*.

[4] Birkett, W. (1983). *Practical Strategic Planning*. Information Engineering Press: Sydney.

CHAPTER 11

Informal Planning: Strategic Stage

Where it is not possible to introduce formal strategic planning, the informal strategic planning approach is used. This is called 'informal' as it can be used by all management levels: it reflects their perception of appropriate strategic directions based on their knowledge of the organization. It provides useful input to senior management and corporate planning staff. Although it may not reflect a senior management perspective initially, it can evolve to satisfy their viewpoint later.

11.1 STRATEGIC PLANNING FEEDBACK

When used in conjunction with the development of a data model, the informal strategic planning approach can provide valuable feedback to senior management for identification of alternative strategies that may not have been immediately apparent. Informal strategic planning used in conjunction with strategic and tactical modeling provides rapid feedback to management which may later lead to a formal strategic planning study being undertaken.

For decision making to be possible, management must have all the information necessary and it must be accurate. With a data model, we can represent an organization – its business, products, services and markets – in terms of its data – its key resource – and use this to develop data bases for information systems or knowledge bases for expert business systems. The data model allows management to experiment with and evaluate the impact of strategic alternatives; the data model is a blueprint of the data resource and so represents the organization. As an architect's plan of a building can be used to evaluate alternative external and internal designs of that building, so also a data model allows the impact of alternative organization structures to be evaluated.

The data model is developed from strategic and tactical statements. These are narrative documents, produced prior to, and during, the informal strategic planning process. They describe business units of the organization in terms of:

Strategic statements
- Mission and purpose.
- Concerns and issues.
- Goals and objectives.
- Policies.
- Strategies and tactics.

Tactical statements
- Markets.
- Products and services.
- Channels.

We will shortly describe the content and development of each of these strategic and tactical statements. The strategic statements are discussed in this chapter, while the tactical statements are discussed in Chapter 12. Both are documented in a narrative form and they are used in a modeling example in Chapter 16.

It is often difficult to obtain direct input from senior management for the initial creation of these statements. However, input can be obtained from the participants of a strategic modeling study through a questionnaire, as described in Chapter 13. The strategic statements prepared from this questionnaire by the project team are then reviewed by senior management, when they may be accepted or changed to reflect a different emphasis. Whatever the decision of management, their input is obtained.

The questionnaire approach to developing the strategic statements achieves three objectives.

(1) It incorporates the perspective of the actual participants of the strategic modeling study.

(2)   Through senior management review, their insights are included in those statements.

(3)   It opens up the opportunity for subsequent review by senior managers of the evolving data model. They see how the data model provides a useful feedback tool for identifying and evaluating alternative strategic approaches.

The power of the data model as a management planning tool becomes apparent. Its use for management feedback applies to increasingly higher levels of management. This can later lead to the initiation of a formal strategic planning project, using the data model both as an input catalyst and as an evaluation mechanism.

11.2   DEVELOPING THE STRATEGIC STATEMENTS

Figure 11.1 shows the first stage of informal strategic planning: developing the strategic statements. These steps are highly iterative. We will start the strategic stage with the mission and purpose.

11.2.1   Determine mission and purpose

The mission and purpose statement outlines the broad directions to be taken by the organization both now and in the future. It is essentially timeless. It defines the business or industry of the organization as a whole, as well as the part of the organization that is to be the focus of a strategic modeling and tactical modeling study. We will refer to this study focus as the **project area**. The project area may comprise the entire organization or it may be one business unit of a large enterprise. A business unit may be one agency of a government department or it may be a subsidiary company or a profit center of a private sector organization. A business unit may include many functional areas. A **functional area** may be referred to as a division, department, section, branch or some other term.

The mission and purpose statement first addresses the organization as a whole. It then focuses on the project area. Where the project area addresses only one business unit, or a functional area of a business unit, the mission and purpose considers the 'markets' of the project area, and the products and services provided by the project area to other parts of the organization itself, as well as to areas external to the organization. This establishes the overall project scope in terms of the business units or

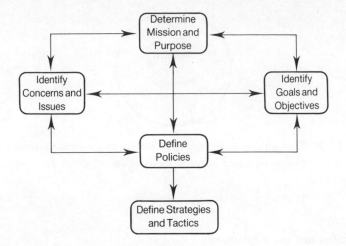

Figure 11.1 The strategic stage of informal strategic planning. This is iterative. It defines the strategic statements: the catalyst for strategic modeling.

functional areas to be examined. Thus, a project area that just addresses the personnel department of a larger organization might develop a mission and purpose such as:

> '*The provision of services for the recruitment, support, staffing, management and well-being of managers and employees of the XYZ Company.*'

Markets that are outside the business unit, but still within the organization, are referred to as **internal markets**. Markets that are outside the organization entirely are referred to as **external markets**. Thus, the employees and managers of the XYZ Company represent the internal market of the personnel department. Taxation authorities, health funds or banks who receive tax deductions, health insurance premiums or savings deducted from employees' salaries represent external markets.

Content of the mission and purpose statement

The mission and purpose is a brief and agreed description of the prime objective of the project area. It is used to maintain a focus on the specific part of the organization identified, as described in later chapters. It is central to the project area, as illustrated in Figure 11.2. We will develop this figure progressively, as we discuss the steps involved in informal strategic planning.

According to Drucker [1], the mission and purpose statement should address three questions:

Figure 11.2 The mission and purpose is central to the organization, and to the business unit or functional area that is the focus of the project area. It represents the prime objective.

(1) What is our business now?

This defines the present emphasis of the business: its industry, the market areas it addresses, its broad products and services, its overall philosophy.

(2) What will our business be in the future?

This examines the direction the organization is presently taking and reflects its focus if no change is made in that direction. It may emphasize the impact that competitors or legislation may have on the organization if it does not change.

(3) What should our business be in the future?

This clearly defines the directional changes needed in markets, or products and services, or in the industry the organization operates within, to respond to anticipated competitive or legislative changes.

For many organizations, the third question is the hardest of all to answer. An appropriate future direction may only emerge as an outcome of the strategic and tactical modeling study. This will become apparent in later chapters. For the time being, we will concentrate mainly on the first two questions.

A number of examples of typical mission and purpose statements, initially based only on the first of the three questions, follow for government and commercial organizations:

Children's hospital

'*The provision of health services and associated facilities specifically directed to the care and well being of children.*'

Distribution company

'*The purchase of goods from local and overseas suppliers and the distribution of those goods to retailers across the country.*'

Custom manufacturer

'*The manufacture of goods or equipment designed to satisfy the unique needs of our customers.*'

Police department

'*Preservation of the peace, protection of life and property, and the prevention and detection of crime.*'

Drucker's second and third questions establish broad directions for the future. The mission and purpose statement defines factors that should be taken into account when considering changes in those directions. The statement broadly defines *what* the customers (clients or users) of the organization require: it describes the needs of both internal markets and external markets, including anticipated changes that may occur in those markets over time. It discusses possible opportunities that may emerge, to open up potential future markets to the organization.

The statement also focuses on the evaluation of future markets and business opportunities. It defines the broad factors that management should consider in selecting future markets or business opportunities. Rather than discussing specific future markets – which may be impossible today – the statement instead identifies the criteria that should be used to select future markets.

Organizations change and opportunities emerge based not only on new markets but also on new technologies. Consequently, the mission and purpose should ideally define criteria for the selection of relevant technology – to serve markets, both now and in the future. New technologies may open up new channels for delivery of products and services to the markets. The changes in banking due to automated teller machines is one example of this. New computer and communications technology opened up a new channel of self-service banking, with significant competitive and cost-saving benefits for banks and other financial institutions.

We will illustrate the application of Drucker's second and third questions to the mission and purpose statements listed earlier. These are expanded by criteria for the selection of new markets and/or technology, as shown below in bold:

Children's hospital

'*The provision of health services and associated facilities specifically directed to the care and well being of children **or other dependent members of the public – to ensure their speedy return to society**.*' (New market and technology criteria)

Distribution company

'*The purchase of goods from local and overseas suppliers and the distribution of those goods to retailers* **or other organizations across the country, in areas and with goods or services that can be delivered with better customer service than our competitors.**' (New market and technology criteria)

Custom manufacturer

'*The manufacture of goods or equipment designed to satisfy the unique needs of our customers,* **in markets where we can offer significantly greater added value or manufacture at a lower cost than our competitors. Manufacturing will be undertaken by us or will be contracted out to enable us to achieve a profit after tax at least 10% greater than the inflation rate.**' (New market, profitability and technology criteria)

Police department

'*Preservation of the peace, protection of life and property, and the prevention and detection of crime,* **for improved security of all members of the public – based on effective utilization of available resources and new technology. This will be carried out while observing the rights of the individual at all times.**' (New cost effectiveness and technology criteria)

In summary, the mission and purpose defines both the present and future direction at the philosophical and strategic level. It is a top management perspective. It remains stable until there is a fundamental change in the type of business conducted. It is typically less than one page although it may only be one or two sentences. It can be found in the annual report of a publicly listed company or a government organization, or from other corporate documentation for a privately held company. It may be clearly stated or it may require some discussion and clarification by management. It is included as part of the questionnaire distributed to participants of a strategic modeling study (see in Chapter 13).

We will now discuss the remaining strategic steps used in informal strategic planning. These are: concerns and issues, goals and objectives, policies, and strategies and tactics, as illustrated in Figure 11.1. The interrelationship of these statements is shown in Figure 11.3. As can be seen in Figure 11.3, goals and objectives expand on the mission and purpose. However, these may be influenced by concerns and issues, which may bring about changes in the ideal goals and objectives. Policies also reflect the mission and purpose. They are affected by, and define boundaries for, goals and objectives based on concerns and issues. These all interact iteratively. They lead to the establishment of appropriate strategies and tactics.

Because of the interrelated nature of these strategic steps, we will start by examining concerns and issues. Next, we will define goals and objectives. Finally, we will establish policies. However, these steps are all iterative and can be applied in any order, as illustrated earlier in Figure 11.1.

Figure 11.3 Goals, objectives, policies are based on mission and purpose, and on identified concerns and issues. These lead to the definition of appropriate policies, and also of strategies and tactics.

11.2.2 Identify concerns and issues

An organization may not have a formal corporate planning process or clear objectives, although the concerns and issues that need resolution are well known by management. Management establishes policies, and sets goals and objectives to resolve them, as shown in Figure 11.3. The concerns and issues may well have been the initial catalyst for informal strategic planning.

By identifying issues, a focus can be placed on particular areas of weakness or threat. These may be expressed as constraints for a public sector organization. Strengths or opportunities may also be emphasized. Issues are readily identified: they represent problems known to management. They may be the catalyst for initiation of the project itself. Examples of perceived weaknesses which may be expressed as issues are:

- Inability of the organization to change rapidly in times of competitive threat.

- Inadequacy of information available for management decision making.

- Dependency on markets, products or services that are approaching the end of their life cycle.

- A dependency on outmoded technology.
- A need for reorganization to address some of the weaknesses, and an inability to identify the optimum organization structure.
- A need to establish alternative strategies for organizational change.

From the examination of concerns and issues, a better understanding of appropriate directions, or instead constraints, emerges. These lead to the establishment of goals and objectives.

11.2.3 Identify goals and objectives

Goals and objectives define the results to be achieved by the organization and its personnel. They ensure that the directions set for the future are achieved. Goals are set for the long term; objectives are short term. In many organizations, goals may also be called **corporate objectives**. Policies are also sometimes referred to as **corporate objectives**. We will be more precise in this book. We will distinguish clearly between policies, goals and objectives.

From the statement of issues, appropriate policies may emerge. Policy statements are generally expressed in qualitative, rather than quantitative, terms. As we will see shortly, policies establish the boundaries for selection of solutions to concerns and issues, and setting of appropriate goals and objectives.

Although the terms *policies*, *goals* and *corporate objectives* are used interchangeably in many businesses, we will define them precisely as follows:

- **Policies** describe broad directions which are *qualitative* in nature.
- **Goals** and **objectives** identify specific achievements that are *quantitative* and can be precisely measured. Goals define *long-term* quantifiable targets, while objectives establish *short-term* quantifiable achievements.

Policies establish qualitative guidelines. In contrast, goals and objectives are both quantitative. They define *what* is to be achieved, as well as the amount of achievement. They reflect the expectations of management and define levels of performance achievement for staff. They lead to management objectives at various levels throughout the organization.

From an examination of the mission and purpose, and of concerns and issues, a picture emerges of those specific areas that management wishes to emphasize. Based upon these areas of emphasis, particular long-term and short-term achievements can be defined. These achievements are expressed in quantitative terms, clearly and unambiguously.

Goals are broad in scope, long term, and identify specific targets for achievement. On the other hand, objectives are short term: they are defined in detailed statements as achievable values. Both are sometimes called **performance indicators**. They may also be called **critical success factors**. They are measurable: they decompose into work and are therefore actionable. They should be defined so that they require effort to achieve.

To be clearly defined and quantifiable, a goal or an objective must have three characteristics:

- Measure.
- Level.
- Time.

The **measure** should clearly indicate the specific performance indicator to be quantified. This should equate to an attribute (or attributes) that represents the particular performance indicator. For example, an operational objective set for the sales department may be:

'*Orders must be delivered to the orders department within two hours.*'

The performance indicator for this objective therefore is the *sales processing time* (an operational attribute). The time when the sales person receives the order from the customer and the time when the order details are received by the orders department should both be captured. These are also attributes. The recording of these times by the sales and orders departments allows the sales processing time to be derived. Sales processing performance can therefore be measured. Similarly, an operational objective set for the orders department may be:

'*Orders must be processed within one hour.*'

This objective addresses the *order processing time* (also a derived, operational attribute). It uses the time of receipt of the order from the sales department, as just described. The time when the order is completed by the orders department is also recorded; this is when the warehouse picking list has been prepared and sent to the warehouse department. The order processing time can thus be derived. Order processing performance can be measured.

The **level** of an objective identifies the actual performance value that is to be achieved. In the sales department and orders department examples, *all* orders are to be processed within the sales processing and order processing times. The level is thus 100% achievement: no orders must exceed the specified processing times. If they do, the objective has not been achieved.

The **time** component of the objective statement may be used to indicate when the level should be achieved. For example:

'*Within three months, all orders will be processed within the defined sales processing and order processing times.*'

The time component of the objective is the three months grace period before all orders must be completed within the defined processing times, which are the measures of the objective.

Level and time can be combined, as in:

'*Over the next two months, 90% of confirmed orders shall be delivered by the sales department to the orders department within one hour of receipt, with 100% of all confirmed orders delivered within a maximum time of two hours of receipt. After two months, all confirmed orders must be delivered within a maximum time of two hours of receipt.*'

The percentages and delivery times are the *level* components of the objective statement, indicating particular performance values to be achieved. The period indicates when that achievement is to be reached (two months): it is the *time* component of the objective.

The use of objectives for exception reporting

In effect, the level and time components of an objective set a threshold of acceptable performance defined by management. This threshold indicates whether the objective is achieved or not. It may be a single value or, alternatively, it may be two values specifying upper and lower bounds of achievement. Acceptable performance may fall within a defined range or it may be three values, specifying a range and also a target value within that range. Regardless of whether a single threshold is defined, or a threshold range and a target, these values indicate points that management wish to track closely. When the threshold is crossed and performance falls outside the defined range, management wish to be notified by an exception report. They want to identify and correct the cause of unacceptable performance. This is reactive, and they may need to take immediate action.

By defining objectives at this level of detail, the relevant threshold values or ranges can be incorporated into the subsequent data model. Information systems or expert business systems developed from the data model can automatically produce exception reports for management. The objective statements and defined threshold ranges or values are used to control the production of those exception reports.

By varying threshold values or ranges, a manager can directly control the sensitivity of exception reporting. For example, performance indicators may need to change over time or different levels of perform-

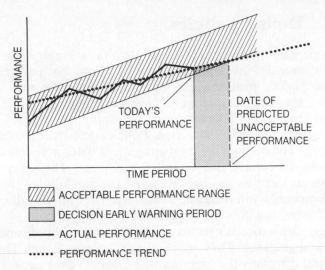

Figure 11.4 A decision early warning trend analysis graph. The performance indicator on the Y axis may be any defined objective. The shaded band represents a range of acceptable performance. Actual objective achievement, measured over several time periods, allows trends to be detected for early warning to management.

ance may apply in certain circumstances. A one-hour sales processing time may be feasible for metropolitan orders, while two hours may be the best that can be achieved for country orders. Defined in this way, management objectives become a very active and precise control mechanism for exception reporting to management.

As well as being immediately notified in an exception report of objectives that have fallen outside acceptable performance, managers also like to see emerging trends. This may enable them to take action when a *trend* towards unacceptable performance is detected, *before* the performance actually becomes unacceptable. They may make changes to correct the trend. Management then becomes proactive, rather than reactive. This leads to the development of a decision early warning system, as shown in Figure 11.4. We will examine the establishment of ranges of acceptable performance for objectives to be used in a decision early warning system in later chapters.

From an examination of the mission and purpose, and of concerns and issues, goals and objectives can be set as discussed here. These define performance achievements, indicating the reports or information that management need. Several alternative approaches may be available to address these identified areas, but not all may be feasible or allowed. Guidelines or policies are needed: to define boundaries of responsibility; to allow or restrict certain avenues open to management; to manage the overall direction of the organization into the future.

11.2.4 Define policies

The strategic stage of informal strategic planning is highly iterative as we discussed earlier. For example, Figure 11.3 shows that policies may be established directly from the mission and purpose. But they may also reflect concerns and issues, as well as goals and objectives, as shown by these areas abutting the policies area.

An organization needs direction. Policies define the conduct of the organization. The policies set by management determine the corporate environment, its culture and its ability to change. They may focus on certain concerns and issues. They establish the capability of the organization to compete, to innovate and to survive. They provide direction for staff. They provide a plan for future action.

Policies bring together related areas of an organization, and provide direction and guidance. They are analogous to a road map. They define *what* general direction the organization will take as it moves into the future. They help set targets, which are expressed as goals and then objectives. They help decide more detailed directions, which define *how* the targets are to be reached. These are expressed as strategies and tactics, as we will see shortly. Policies allow management to decide what is important and what is irrelevant. They limit, or instead open up, alternative courses of action.

Properly formulated, expressed and communicated, policies act as the automatic pilot of an organization. They are analogous to the flight plan of an aeroplane. Decision early warning systems then ensure the policy is followed correctly. They track policies, in terms of achievement of goals and objectives based on those policies. They immediately report unacceptable performance in exception reports – for reactive attention of management. As illustrated in Figure 11.4, they also identify trends – for proactive management of the organization as it moves into the future.

We saw earlier that goals and objectives are quantitative. *They identify specific data attributes which measure their achievement.* Policies, on the other hand, are qualitative. *They help identify related groups of data entities, rather than attributes.* They do not have specific measures; instead, they emphasize areas of responsibility as reflected in groups of data entities.

The foregoing paragraph states two fundamental principles which we will use in this book to develop data models directly from strategic plans. We will also use these principles to help refine strategic plans from the resulting data models. But expressed as they are, they are incomplete. We need one other component: a definition of strategies and tactics, developed from policies and their supporting goals and objectives, as illustrated in Figure 11.1. At the end of this chapter, we will state these principles as explicit strategic planning rules.

11.2.5   Define strategies and tactics

While goals and objectives define what is to be achieved, they may be achieved in many ways. These alternatives, called strategies, detail *how* the objective can be reached. The detailed tasks, or steps, in carrying out those strategies can then be defined. These steps are the tactics, or tasks. Tactics are the detailed implementation of the strategy. They provide a step-by-step approach for carrying out the strategy and achieving the objective. It is a manager's job to select the most appropriate strategies and tactics to achieve each objective. These subsequently lead to the definition of procedures that detail the sequence of steps to be carried out.

As discussed earlier, policies reflect related groups of entities. These entities are interrelated by associations, as described in Part Two. The associations indicate *how* the entities are to be managed. We saw that associations are expressed both schematically in a data map, as well as in text. This text provides a narrative purpose description. It also includes narrative strategies that detail required management and audit controls, and which describe how the associations are to be used and managed.

Based on strategies developed from specific policies, those strategies may in turn lead to a definition of specific objectives to be achieved. These objectives must be quantified. They will be subsequently implemented as specific attributes within entities. Similarly, objectives may lead to a definition of further strategies that outline how the level of performance is to be achieved. The strategy focuses on how the required performance defined by the objective can be reached. For example, part of the objective described earlier:

> *'90% of orders to be received by the orders department within one hour and all orders within two hours.'*

This may lead to a definition of one strategy, such as:

> *'All sales persons will telephone orders to the orders department immediately on receipt from the customer, using the customer's telephone and reimbursing him for the call.'*

On the other hand, if sales people do not have ready access to customers' telephones, such as in the country, then an alternative strategy may be to install telephones or two-way radios in sales persons' cars. The strategy now becomes:

> *'All sales persons will telephone or radio orders directly to the orders department immediately on receipt from the customer. This communication will be carried out using your installed car telephone or two-way radio.'*

We have now completed the strategic stage of informal strategic planning, which is summarized in Box 11.1 at the end of this chapter. We have also examined several fundamental principles used to relate strategic statements to data. We will now consolidate these principles in a set of rules which will be used throughout this book.

11.3 STRATEGIC PLANNING RULES

In this chapter we have learned that policies, goals and objectives, and also strategies and tactics can be used to identify data and information needed by management. The mission and purpose, as well as concerns and issues, can also be used. These are fundamental principles that establish strategic planning rules. These rules are used extensively in strategic modeling, and also in tactical modeling. They relate strategic statements to data.

11.3.1 Relating strategic statements to data

There are three information engineering rules that relate strategic statements to data and information (see Box 11.2).

Relating policies and issues to data

The mission and purpose, concerns and issues, and also policies establish boundaries (or the scope) of business activity defined by management. For convenience, throughout the book, we will refer to all of these statements generically as policies and issues. They lead to the first rule to connect strategic plans to data. This is stated as:

Rule 1
Policies and issues relate directly to entities.

Several interrelated entities will be needed to represent the mission and purpose, or implement an established policy, or address an identified concern or issue when a data model is developed from strategic statements. Alternatively, a data model can be used to define relevant strategic statements. A group of related entities may suggest the need for an appropriate policy to be defined. This provides feedback for refinement of the mission and purpose, or policies, or concerns and issues.

Relating goals and objectives to data

Goals are set for the long term; objectives are short term. Both should be measurable as discussed earlier: an objective (or a goal) should have a level (or target) for achievement; it should have a time for achievement of the level. This brings us to the following rule:

Rule 2
Goals and objectives relate directly to attributes.

The measure of the objective identifies one, or several, attribute(s) which record specific achievement. For example, to implement an objective for payment by customers of their accounts, we may use the measure 'average payment period'. To record this, we would define an attribute called (say) *customer average payment time*. We may also define other attributes, such as *customer maximum payment time* and *customer minimum payment time*. These allow a range of payment times to be recorded for each customer, for exception reporting and trend analysis purposes.

Relating strategies and tactics to data

Whereas goals and objectives indicate *what* is to be achieved, strategies define *how* they will be reached. Strategies define the procedures to achieve the goals or objectives. Tactics detail the steps to carry out a strategy. This leads to the following rule:

Rule 3
Strategies and tactics relate directly to associations.

The associations, established between entities, define *how* the organization goes about its business. These are linked to the text of strategies or tactics which describe how the association is used to carry out a particular procedure, or, step by step, how to implement specific tactics. Each functional area may have its own strategies and tactics, all linked to the same, or many, associations.

Reference

[1] Drucker, P. (1974). *Management: Tasks, Responsibilities, Practices.* Harper & Row: New York.

Box 11.1
Strategic stage of informal strategic planning

Determine mission and purpose

The mission and purpose statement outlines broad directions to be taken by the organization both now and in the future. It is essentially timeless. It defines criteria for changing those directions. It answers the questions:

- What is our business now?
- What will our business be in the future?
- What should our business be in the future?

The mission and purpose statement identifies the customers, clients or users of the business which represent its markets. It then focuses on the criteria to be used to select current and future markets and technology.

Identify concerns and issues

Concerns and issues indicate areas of weakness or threat, or constraint. They may also indicate strengths or opportunities. Examples are:

- An inability of the organization to change rapidly in times of competitive threat.
- Inadequacy of information available for management decision making.
- Dependency on markets, products or services approaching the end of their life cycle.
- A dependency on outmoded technology.
- A need for reorganization to address some of the weaknesses.
- An inability to identify the optimum organization structure.
- A need to establish alternative strategies for organizational change.

Box 11.1 (cont.)
Strategic stage of informal strategic planning

Identify goals and objectives

Goals and objectives are *quantitative*. They define *what* is to be achieved, as well as the amount of achievement. **Goals** define *long-term* quantifiable targets; **objectives** establish *short-term* quantifiable achievements. They define levels of performance achievement for staff. They lead to management objectives at various levels throughout the organization.

Both may be called **performance indicators**, or **critical success factors**. They are measurable and actionable, requiring effort to achieve. A goal or an objective must have three characteristics. These are:

- Measure.
- Level.
- Time.

The **measure** indicates the specific performance indicator to be quantified; the **level** identifies the actual performance value to be achieved; the **time** indicates when that level should be reached.

Define policies

Policies bring together related areas of an organization. They provide direction and guidance. They help set targets, which are expressed as goals and objectives. They help management decide what is important and what is irrelevant. They limit, or open up, alternative courses of action.

Define strategies and tactics

Goals and objectives define what is to be achieved. Strategies detail *how* the objectives can be reached. They provide a procedural description of how to reach the objective. They lead to tactics and to procedures that detail the sequence of steps to be carried out.

Box 11.2
Strategic planning rules

Relating policies and issues to data

The mission and purpose, concerns and issues, and policies establish boundaries (the scope) of business activity defined by management. These are generically referred to as policies and issues. They connect strategic plans to data entities in Rule 1:

Policies and issues relate directly to entities.

Several interrelated entities represent the mission and purpose, policies, or concerns or issues when a strategic model is developed from strategic statements.

Relating goals and objectives to data

Goals are long term; objectives are short term. Both are measurable: an objective (or a goal) has a level and time for achievement. They indicate *what* is to be achieved. The measure is related to one or several attributes in Rule 2:

Goals and objectives relate directly to attributes.

The relevant attributes record achievement of the objective or goal.

Relating strategies and tactics to data

Goals and objectives indicate *what* is to be achieved. Strategies define *how* they will be reached: the procedures to achieve the goals or objectives. Tactics detail the steps to carry out a strategy. They relate to associations in Rule 3:

Strategies and tactics relate directly to associations.

Associations define *how* the organization goes about its business. They are linked to strategies or tactics which describe how the association is used to implement a particular procedure, or, step by step, how to implement specific tactics.

CHAPTER 12

Informal Planning: Tactical Stage

The strategic statements discussed in Chapter 11 define the long-term directions of an organization. They indicate broad markets to be addressed. The specific market segments, appropriate products and services, and the organization structure implement those directions. These were previously strategic decisions, which changed only over a long period. However, in today's environment, these decisions may change frequently. The objective of the tactical stage is to help an organization respond rapidly to environmental changes.

12.1 DEVELOPING THE TACTICAL STATEMENTS

As we live in a world of rapid technological change and intense competition, the environment in which an organization operates rarely remains static. Figure 12.1 illustrates some environmental factors that impinge upon the strategic directions.

Market segments, products or services and organization structure may need to change over time to ensure strategic directions continue to be observed. A business must respond rapidly under competitive, legislative or political pressure. To achieve this, many previously defined strategic decisions have to be made at a level lower in the organization than was done in the past. The strategic statements provide the overall direction, and the criteria for selection of appropriate markets and technology; that is, they provide a long-term focus. The tactical statements use this guidance to implement specific directions for the short

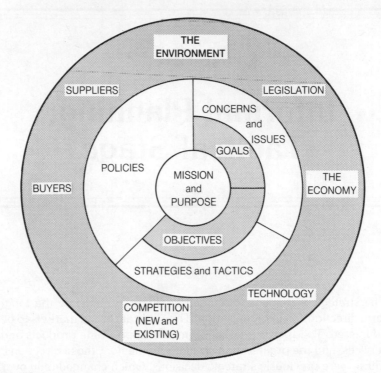

Figure 12.1 Strategic directions, developed from the mission and purpose, provide tactical guidance. They allow an organization to respond rapidly to environmental changes.

term. They allow the organization to structure itself for rapid change in its environment, the economy, legislation, competition, technology, and in relation to buyers and suppliers. This tactical focus surrounds the strategic emphasis, as illustrated in Figure 12.1.

The tactical statements are developed from the perspectives and directions established by the strategic statements. The steps involved are illustrated in Figure 12.2 and summarized in Box 12.1 at the end of the chapter.

12.1.1 Identify relevant strategic statements

The first step of the tactical stage is to identify those strategic statements that relate to the area of the organization being considered at the tactical level. We will call this the **tactical area**. As illustrated in Figure 12.2, these steps are carried out as follows:

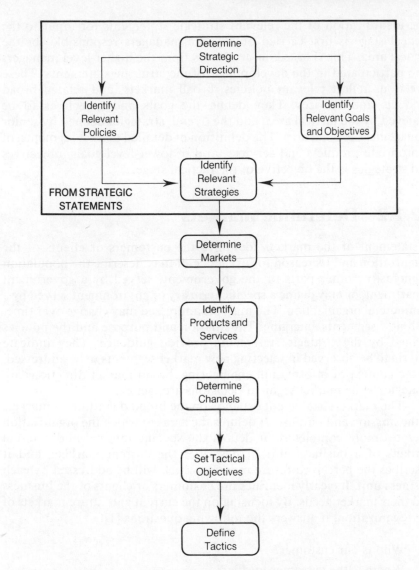

Figure 12.2   The tactical stage of informal strategic planning. This uses the central strategic statements (see Figure 12.1) and defines tactical statements for tactical modeling.

- Determine relevant strategic direction.
- Identify relevant policies.
- Identify relevant goals and objectives.
- Identify relevant strategies.

The identification of the relevant strategic statements for input to the tactical stage is first carried out by the managers responsible for the tactical area. This is based on directions from the higher-level managers who participated in the development of the strategic statements. These directions reflect relevant policies, broad markets, and related broad products and services. They define the goals and objectives to be achieved by the tactical area, and the overall strategies defined by senior management for that area. The definition of detailed market segments, of appropriate products and services, and of lower-level goals, objectives and strategies is the objective of the tactical stage.

12.1.2 Determine markets

A statement of the markets identifies the customers or clients of the organization and its reason for existence. It may describe the population segments, or other parts of the government, served by a government department, or may define a specific industry or environment served by a commercial organization. The markets addressed may change over time, with new segments emerging. The mission and purpose and the policies defined by the strategic statements provide guidance. They indicate criteria to be observed in selecting new market segments to be addressed. In the context of information engineering, broad market directions are strategic, while market segment decisions are tactical.

The markets' statement expands on the broad definition of markets in the mission and purpose. It defines the areas in which the organization operates more completely: it details the specific internal and external markets of a business unit; it describes the current markets; and it describes the perceived future markets which will be addressed by each business unit. It clearly identifies the customers or clients of the business and their market needs. By focusing on the current and future markets of the organization, it answers the following questions [1]:

- Who is our customer?
- Where is the customer located?
- What does the customer require?
- What is the customer prepared to pay?
- What does the customer consider value?

The market statement should begin by defining each of the internal and external market segments, then, for each of those market segments, it describes that market in terms of these questions.

Perceived market trends brought about by changes in technology, by competitive pressures or by legislation are used to examine how the markets – and the needs of the customers represented by those markets – may change over time. Together with criteria from the mission and purpose statement for selection of appropriate future markets, a clear understanding emerges of possible future changes in internal and external market segments of the organization.

12.1.3 Identify products and services

These are the outputs of the organization, produced to satisfy its market segments. For a manufacturer or a distributor, the products are easy to identify. For a government department, university or hospital, their identification is more difficult. Consequently, the term **service** is also used. A university provides educational services; a hospital offers health care services; a government department provides specific services for various population segments; a manufacturer or distributor may also provide services – such as warranty or repair services, or delivery services. Increasingly today, product planning is market driven: products and services are developed to satisfy market needs.

Following definition of the markets of the organization, products and services addressing those markets are then identified. For each internal and external market segment, the relevant products and services are detailed. The products and services should address the defined market needs now. They should also be capable of changing to satisfy market needs in the future. These future products and services may not be defined precisely; rather, they may be expressed in terms of criteria that outline factors to be used for the selection of future products and services for emerging markets.

For external markets, the products and services are generally easy to identify. These are the goods that are produced or the services that are provided by the organization. These are sold to satisfy the needs of their markets. For internal markets, however, the products and services are not so immediately obvious. For example, for the production department of a manufacturer, the manufactured products are delivered to the distribution warehouses used by the sales or orders department. These are the internal markets of the production department. In turn, these departments then deliver the products to the external market – the customers of the organization. For the payroll department, the market is wholly internal: employees of the organization itself. Its products are salaries and wages, paid weekly, fortnightly or monthly. Other services may include automatic deductions from salaries and wages for health insurance, savings, stock purchase, and so on. For the marketing support department, the market is also internal: the sales department. It provides services based on market surveys. It tracks the penetration of various products in the external markets of the organization, and the actions and likely activities of competitors. It prepares sales material for the sales department, advertising programs, and so on. Similarly, the products and services provided by the sales department are orders – delivered to its internal market: the orders department. Based on these orders, the orders department provides services to the warehouse, such as warehouse picking lists of products needed to satisfy the orders. The outputs of the warehouse department are its products: the completed orders, once all requested products have been selected (picked) from inventory. The product or service of the shipping department is the physical delivery of completed orders to the customer. Thus, by defining markets, both internal and external, the products and services that address those markets can be clearly identified.

Not only are current products and services detailed. The mission and purpose statement may indicate possible market changes. It may define criteria for the selection of likely products and services to address future market needs.

12.1.4   Determine channels

An organization needs structure and resources to deliver its products and services to its markets. It needs people, money, machines, components – to build its products or provide its services. The channels statement describes these resources. It defines how the organization is structured to satisfy the needs of its customers or clients, and how it achieves its objectives. It details how resources are acquired; how they are utilized to make the product; the support services required; the distribution mechanisms; the operational procedures of the organization. The channels statement is readily available. In fact, most people first think of an organization in terms of its channels, and not in terms of its markets or mission.

So far, we have defined internal and external markets, and identified outputs – the products and services that address those markets. The channels statement details ways in which those products and services are delivered to the markets. It also identifies the inputs required to produce the relevant products or services. Thus, the orders produced by the sales department and provided to the orders department, become its inputs. Similarly, the warehouse picking slips from the orders department become the inputs to the warehouse department. The earlier tactical statements focussed on *what* market segments to address, and *what* products and services were needed. The channels statement defines *how* those inputs and outputs are delivered to their markets today, and *how* they may be delivered in the future.

Many factors will affect the future channels. These are due to changes in the markets themselves; changes in the products and services to be produced in the future; changes due to new technologies. For example, orders may be currently delivered as order forms to the orders department; they may be verbally phoned in by sales people; they may be physically delivered by mail or by courier. But technology may suggest new feasible future channels. To illustrate, briefcase or laptop computers may be used by the sales person to capture orders directly from the customer. Now, the verbal phone or posted mail channels need not be used. The order details can be transmitted automatically from the sales person's computer to the orders department computer, or to a central computer.

The channels statement thus describes the inputs of the organization and its business units today. It defines how inputs are processed to produce outputs. It details how those outputs are delivered to their relevant internal and external markets. It addresses possible emerging new markets, new products and services, and new technologies. It broadly outlines anticipated organization changes that may be required. It considers the effects of those possible future organization changes on the operation of today's channels.

The channels statement is *procedural*: the emphasis is on *how* these channels are used, as well as identifying what channels apply, both now and in the future. In many ways, the channels statement is often the easiest of all to produce. It describes the way in which the organization is structured, and how each business unit operates to deliver its products or services to its relevant internal and external markets.

12.1.5   Set tactical objectives

Based on the increasingly detailed tactical description of the organization, its markets, products and services, and channels – now and in the future – a picture emerges of specific areas that management wish to emphasize. Based on these areas of emphasis, specific objectives can be defined.

When we discussed the strategic statements in Chapter 11, we considered long-term goals and short-term objectives. They apply to higher-level managers and so are called strategic objectives. In the tactical statements, other objectives emerge which apply to lower-level managers. These are called **tactical objectives**. They apply to the operational end of the organization. As for strategic objectives, tactical objectives are also called performance indicators. They must be measurable and actionable. They should be defined so that they require effort to achieve.

Tactical objectives are expressed in quantitative terms, clearly and unambiguously. As we saw earlier with strategic objectives, a tactical objective must also have three characteristics if it is to be clearly defined and quantifiable. These are: a measure; a level; and a time. The *measure* clearly indicates the specific data attribute or attributes that are to be used to represent the particular performance indicator. The discussion of strategic objectives in Chapter 11 used sales and order processing times to illustrate the concept of measures. In fact, those measures related more to tactical objectives, as they apply at the operational, tactical end of the business. The *level* of a tactical objective identifies the actual performance value that is to be achieved, while the *time* component indicates when the level should be achieved. The level and time components of the objective statement define the performance values to attain and when that achievement is to be reached.

As for strategic objectives, the level and time components of a tactical objective define a threshold of acceptable performance set by management. This threshold indicates whether the objective was achieved or not. It may be a single value or two values, specifying an upper and lower level of achievement. Acceptable performance may fall within a defined range. When the performance falls outside the defined range, the threshold is crossed. Tactical managers can be notified by an exception report.

The relevant threshold values or ranges of tactical objectives can also be incorporated in the data model. Information systems or expert business systems, developed from the data model, can automatically produce exception reports for tactical management. The objective statements and defined threshold ranges or values are used to control the production of those exception reports.

As we saw for strategic objectives, by varying threshold values or ranges, the manager can directly control the sensitivity of exception reporting: performance indicators may need to change over time; different levels of performance may apply in certain circumstances; or specific areas may need to be tracked more closely, while other areas can be tracked broadly. Chapter 11 described how decision early warning systems provide proactive guidance of unacceptable performance trends to strategic management (see Figure 11.4). Similarly, they can also be used to track tactical objectives for early warning of tactical decisions to be made.

12.1.6 Define tactics

In Chapter 11, we saw that strategies define how strategic objectives are achieved. So, also, tactics define how tactical objectives will be achieved. They define the detailed steps to be carried out to reach the defined tactical objective.

We also saw in Chapter 11 that strategies relate to associations. The associations detail how the related entities will be managed. Tactics also relate to associations. They provide more detail of *how* the relevant associations are used. As described in Part Two, associations are expressed in the form of strategies or tactics that detail management controls.

Tactics also represent procedures. They may be documented, step by step, in procedure manuals or they may be expressed as a series of computer program instructions to be executed. As we progress through this book, we will see how strategic statements are used to develop strategic models. Tactical statements then expand the strategic models into tactical models and then operations models. Box 12.1 summarizes the tactical stage of informal strategic planning.

BOX 12.1
Tactical stage of informal strategic planning

Identify relevant strategic statements

This identifies the strategic statements that relate to the tactical area, as follows:

- Determine relevant strategic direction.
- Identify relevant policies.
- Identify relevant goals and objectives.
- Identify relevant strategies.

The identification of relevant strategic statements for the tactical stage is first carried out by the managers responsible for the tactical area.

Determine markets

The markets statement details the specific internal and external markets of business units and the organization. It describes the current markets and the perceived future markets that will be addressed by each business unit. It answers the following questions:

- Who is our customer?
- Where is the customer located?
- What does the customer require?
- What is the customer prepared to pay?
- What does the customer consider value?

(cont'd)

BOX 12.1 (cont.)
Tactical stage of informal strategic planning

Identify products and services

The products and services statement defines the outputs of the organization, produced to satisfy its market segments. This statement addresses the defined market needs now. It should be capable of changing to satisfy future market needs.

Determine channels

The channels statement describes how the organization is structured today. It defines how it produces its products and services, and how it delivers them to its relevant internal and external markets. It describes the operational procedures of the organization, which may change dramatically as technology changes.

Set tactical objectives

Tactical objectives apply to the operational end of the organization. As for strategic objectives, tactical objectives are also called performance indicators. They must be measurable and decompose into work, requiring effort to achieve. A tactical objective must also have a measure, a level and a time. The measure indicates the specific performance indicator; the level identifies the actual performance value to be achieved; the time indicates when the level should be achieved.

Define tactics

Tactics define how tactical objectives will be achieved. They define the detailed steps to be carried out to reach the defined tactical objective. Tactics also represent procedures. They may be documented, step by step, in procedure manuals or they may be expressed as a series of computer program instructions to be executed.

12.2 DEFINITION OF STRATEGIC, TACTICAL AND OPERATIONS MODELS

A definition of strategic, tactical and operations models is now appropriate:

> A **strategic model** comprises high-level **strategic entities** of interest to senior management of a project area. These strategic entities are so called because they contain primary and foreign key attributes to establish associations between related entities. Strategic entities may also contain high-level, non-key attributes (called **strategic attributes**) which generally represent aggregates derived from lower-level tactical entities. These strategic attributes may also measure achievement of long-term goals.

> A **tactical model** comprises lower-level **tactical entities** of interest mainly to middle management of a project area. These tactical entities contain non-key attributes (called **tactical attributes**) which provide detailed data of interest to these middle managers. Tactical attributes may include aggregates derived from lower-level operations entities or may measure achievement of short-term tactical objectives.

> An **operations model** comprises day-to-day operational level entities (called **operations entities**) containing detailed non-key attributes of interest to staff at the operational level of an organization. These are referred to as **operations attributes**. They may include attributes to measure achievement of day-to-day operational objectives.

At this point, we have discussed two approaches to strategic planning: the formal approach and the informal approach. We now need to put these in perspective. We need to cover how the strategic statements are used. This is addressed in the next chapter.

Reference

[1] Drucker, P. (1974) *Management: Tasks, Responsibilities, Practices*. Harper & Row: New York.

CHAPTER 13

Using the Strategic Statements

Where senior management are actively involved, the formal strategic planning process described in Chapter 10 can be applied. A clear understanding of the factors that influence the organization now and the directions that it should take in the future emerges. Formal strategic planning provides senior management input to the project.

In many organizations, the catalyst for a strategic or tactical modeling project may emerge much lower in the management hierarchy. In this case, senior management are unlikely to become involved initially, so informal strategic planning is the only option.

13.1 | DEVELOPING STRATEGIC AND TACTICAL STATEMENTS

Strategic directions are expressed in terms of strategic and tactical statements, defined through either the formal or the informal strategic planning approach, as described in the previous chapters. These statements define, and are used to implement, the strategic plan throughout the organization. They form the input to both strategic and tactical modeling. They lead to the design of manual systems, and the design and generation of computer-based information systems and also expert business systems.

With formal strategic planning, senior management are directly involved in producing and reviewing the statements. This is their input to the project. With informal strategic planning, lower-level managers (or even the project team) produce the statements, or they may be directly obtained from the project participants as described in *The Management Questionnaire*. These statements therefore reflect only what they *think* senior management want. Their statements provide input to the project, but they are not senior management input.

The output from the project comprises strategic and tactical models, together with suggested management statements of policies, objectives and strategies developed from those models. The development of strategic models and relevant supporting statements is discussed in later chapters. They are presented to senior management for review throughout the project. Management accept these statements as is, or change them.

Regardless of whether formal or informal strategic planning is used, this project output can be used by management to test alternatives. The data model provides immediate feedback. An interactive strategic planning environment emerges, as summarized in Box 13.1 and developed further in this book.

Senior management input is thus obtained either during or after the project, through this review process – rather than prior to the start of the project as with formal strategic planning. If the management statements suggested by the data model are not acceptable, senior managers will change them. These changes can then be reflected in the strategic and tactical models; the project team and lower-level management change the data maps and entity lists accordingly. Alternatives are directly tested against the strategic and tactical models, rather than by using part of the organization as a guinea pig. Consequently, strategic planning progresses faster, with fewer false starts, fewer reorganizations, and at less cost and disruption. Strategic management is achieved as a bonus. This is discussed in the final section of this chapter.

For easy reference to the approaches and steps discussed so far, a number of summary boxes have been provided in the chapters. Box 11.1 summarizes the strategic stage of informal strategic planning; Box 12.1 then summarizes the tactical stage of informal strategic planning; Box 13.1 discusses formal and informal strategic planning and their interrelationship. These establish firm approaches, used to develop the strategic and tactical statements to be later used as catalysts for strategic and tactical modeling. However, as with any task, the hardest part is often knowing where to start. This is achieved with a questionnaire, as discussed in the next section.

13.2 THE MANAGEMENT QUESTIONNAIRE

The managers involved in an information engineering project have much experience and wisdom to offer. The strategic planning approaches

---

Box 13.1
Development and refinement of strategic and tactical statements

---

Project initiation

(1) The strategic and tactical statements, developed either formally or informally, or through a questionnaire, provide input to the project.

Strategic modeling and refinement

(2) Strategic models are developed based on the strategic statements.

(3) These models are used to refine or develop additional strategic statements.

(4) Senior managers review the refined strategic statements. They accept or change them as appropriate.

(5) These changes are incorporated in the strategic models.

Tactical modeling and refinement

(6) The strategic models and tactical statements then provide input for development of tactical models.

(7) Tactical models provide feedback which may highlight alternatives at a tactical level as a consequence of the strategic statements.

(8) Tactical alternatives are expressed as tactical statements. Tactical management may refine or add to the tactical statements.

(9) These refined tactical statements are further reviewed by both strategic and tactical management for both strategic and tactical impact.

Final review and refinement

(10) The most appropriate alternatives are selected, or the strategic or tactical statements are further refined as a consequence of this feedback.

(11) Final recommendations are presented to senior management for review.

discussed in Part Three focus that expertise to define appropriate strategic and tactical directions. Many managers participate at all levels of the organization.

All staff also use strategic planning, either explicitly or implicitly. It may not be necessarily called a strategic plan at the lowest parts of the organization. But all areas, and all individuals, work to strategic plans – either formally or informally expressed. They may be called targets or directions, or they may be embodied in the job description applying to the position occupied by an individual. For the manager of an area, this job description is a *de facto* strategic plan for the area to be managed. And, of course, each job description is a strategic plan for the individual.

To capture each person's perspective, free from the constraints or inhibitions that may be created in a meeting of managers at different levels, a questionnaire is useful. This requests detailed input from each participating manager. The questions asked address factors that apply to the manager's specific responsibilities, and also to the organization. The questionnaire is distributed to all participants in a strategic planning study, or a strategic modeling project, prior to the first meeting, to enable each person to complete the questions asked. The responses are then returned to a central point, where they are collated in a document and presented to all participants at the first meeting. The questionnaire is documented in Box 13.2, at the end of this chapter. It is presented here as a guideline only. It must be tailored to each organization: terminology adjusted, extra questions added as necessary, questions modified, where appropriate. However, all questions should be asked as they request input that applies to the stages and steps discussed in this Part – particularly the informal strategic and tactical planning approaches.

At the end of the questionnaire, each respondent is asked for name, title and department or section. When questionnaires are consolidated, statements extracted from different responses are *not* attributed to their specific source, to encourage free comment. However, a knowledge of the source may be appropriate to the central coordinating group if expansion of certain points is required at a later date.

The questionnaire provides input to strategic modeling sessions. An example of the use of part of this input, the mission statement, is illustrated in Chapter 16.

13.2.1   Benefits of the questionnaire

By using the questionnaire approach, several objectives are achieved:

- It provides early input to plan the best approach to be used for a strategic planning study prior to a strategic modeling project.
- It helps to identify people who have been omitted and who can contribute.

- It obtains different perspectives free from constraints imposed by management hierarchies: some managers may not be prepared to express certain statements verbally, or may not want to make other statements in the presence of their managers or their subordinates.

- It allows a consolidation of different perspectives – as a catalyst to the study.

- Each manager has a clear appreciation of the type of information needed for the study and can prepare accordingly.

- Each manager, at all levels of participation, is involved and directly contributes.

- It provides direct input to the strategic and tactical modeling stages of a project.

13.3 | GOAL ANALYSIS

Where a strategic plan already exists, the management questionnaire is accompanied by that plan. Staff who were not directly involved in developing the plan can thus consider its implications from their perspective. This is essential communication. It is the first step in the strategic implementation process, as discussed earlier in connection with Figure 10.1.

Where an organization has not previously established a strategic plan, the management questionnaire is first distributed to senior management for their input. Their responses are consolidated and are examined in **goal analysis**, sometimes also called **critical success factor analysis**. This section briefly introduces the steps of goal analysis. These steps are illustrated in Figure 13.1 and are discussed in more detail in Chapter 15.

Analyze mission and purpose

The mission and purpose statement, with its comments from the management questionnaire, are used as a starting point. These are analyzed to identify major data subjects. Typically, only four to six subjects will initially emerge. These are represented in a broad data map, showing interrelationships between those data subjects generally as many-to-many associations. This data map is thus a schematic representation of the mission and purpose, and its associated comments. It is called the **mission model**.

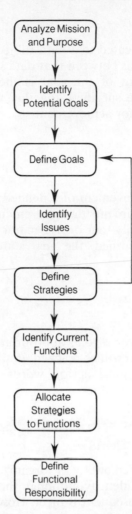

Figure 13.1 The steps of goal analysis.

Identify potential goals

Potential goals are identified, expressed in terms of one or two descriptive words. These represent critical factors that influence the ability of the organization to obtain business and grow in its identified markets. They are vital for the success and the survival of the business. They are therefore termed **critical success factors (CSFs)**. Potential goals or CSFs include: customer satisfaction, product quality, market share, revenue growth, net income, asset growth, staff turnover, staff productivity.

Define goals

Each potential goal is allocated to a data subject in the mission model, and to relevant associations between that data subject and other related data subjects. A statement of the goal is then defined. Appropriate measures for that goal are specified, together with quantifiable targets (that is, levels) and times for achievement.

Identify issues

Issues that may affect achievement of a defined goal are next identified. These may indicate impediments to achievement or catalysts for greater achievement. Typically, only four or five major issues are identified per goal. As issues are determined, the goal statement may need to be modified.

Define strategies

For each issue identified for a goal, appropriate strategies are defined. These indicate how the goal will be reached, in the context of the relevant issue. They start with typical action words such as: establish and maintain, ensure, guide and direct.

Identify current functions

The current functions carried out by the organization are detailed. These are generally very easy to identify, although they may later change as a result of the study and subsequent project. However, at this point, they will enable us initially to allocate functional responsibility for each strategy defined in support of each goal. They are documented in a matrix that lists the strategies carried out by the function. This is called the **function–strategy matrix**, as illustrated in Figure 13.2.

Allocate strategies to functions

Each strategy is allocated to the function that will have major responsibility for carrying out that strategy – it is listed under that function in Figure 13.2. If a strategy appears to apply to more than one function, it generally indicates a level of detail appropriate to a lower management level. In such a case, a more general strategy should be defined which can be allocated to only one responsible function. The detailed strategies are

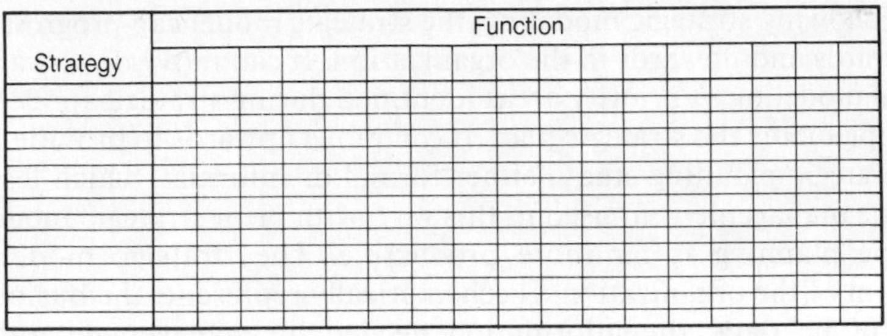

Figure 13.2 The function–strategy matrix. This allocates strategies to functions.

later allocated when the goal analysis process is applied to a lower management level.

Develop functional responsibility

The strategies allocated to each vertical function column in Figure 13.2 are extracted and documented in full for each function, to provide a statement of functional responsibility. This forms the foundation of a job description for the manager responsible for the function.

This completes goal analysis at the relevant management level. Each strategy is next examined to define lower-level objectives to be achieved, which will ensure that the strategy is carried out. Issues relating to those objectives are determined, then strategies, similar to the approach just described for goals. Functional responsibility is allocated for these lower-level objectives and function descriptions are prepared for each lower-level position.

Goal analysis thus refines the input obtained from the management questionnaire. It results in the informal development of goals, issues and strategies from the mission and purpose statement. These form the initial strategic statements for input to a strategic modeling project.

13.4 A CATALYST FOR STRATEGIC MANAGEMENT

From the questionnaire responses and subsequent goal analysis, a picture emerges of appropriate organizational emphases, which provides clear input for a more detailed strategic planning study. But it also provides another benefit: it can be used immediately to initiate a strategic modeling project. This is discussed in Chapter 14.

Following strategic modeling, the strategic model can progress both downwards and upwards in the organization. It can move downwards to tactical modeling in priority areas identified during strategic modeling – this implements the strategic plan. It can move upwards to provide input to a strategic planning study, either formal or informal, which leads to strategic management. If used in this way, with prior strategic modeling, strategic planning is far more productive. The strategic model is a blueprint of the organization. It schematically represents the business in terms of its data, the information needed by management and the strategies used to manage different parts of the business. The data map illustrates these graphically, as discussed in Part Two.

Strategic alternatives can be applied to the strategic model as associations and entities. A clear picture emerges of the impact of alternatives, thereby providing managers with immediate feedback. Many different approaches can be tested, adopted, adjusted or discarded – at no cost other than meeting time! Managers can progress through several evolutions of strategic planning thought. The result is an unambiguous, precisely expressed direction for the future. But even more than this, managers begin to adopt a strategic approach to the business at all levels in the organization. Strategic planning becomes a normal way of management life. The directed approach to strategic thought introduced by information engineering becomes a tool used by all managers on a day-to-day basis. It becomes a corporate culture. Managers use strategic and tactical models to test new options. As the business changes, they use data modeling and business normalization as management and business techniques to plan for the future. Strategic plans are communicated fully and implemented exactly. Following the direction set by Gray [1], *the organization moves beyond strategic planning to strategic management!*

Reference

[1] Gray, D. H. (1986). Uses and misuses of strategic planning. *Harvard Business Review*.

Box 13.2
Management questionnaire

The management questionnaire that follows provides a catalyst for the project. It is completed based on the perspective of each individual's responsibilities and environment. It is *not* intended to be completed by committee; rather, by each manager independently of all others. It allows each person to provide maximum input to the project, free from any political or hierarchical constraints.

It is not intended to be a final, correct document – it is a preliminary draft. It may be accompanied by an existing strategic plan or form the basis for the development of a strategic plan. It outlines the mission of the individual's area, and documents associated concerns, issues, strengths and weaknesses. It details any policies, objectives and strategies that apply to the area and prioritizes them from the individual's perspective. It also identifies the products and services produced by the area, and the markets (customers, clients or users) who use those products and services. It details the channels for delivery or provision of the products and services to the markets.

On receipt of the responses, they are analyzed and all relevant responses are consolidated under each question. These consolidated responses are distributed to all project participants, maintaining anonymity of all individual responses. They form a catalyst for subsequent modeling and refinement sessions in the project. Complete, candid replies to each question are therefore very important.

Strategic and tactical statements

General

In developing information systems and decision-support systems to assist management decision making, it is important that they be based on our organization's needs for the future as well as today. To help in identifying those needs, please take a few moments to complete the following questionnaire from your perspective. Unless otherwise indicated, you should answer the questions as they relate to your area of responsibility.

(cont'd)

Box 13.2 (cont.)
Management questionnaire

Mission and purpose

As an example, it could be said that our mission and purpose is:

NOTE: *Include the agreed mission and purpose of your organiz-ation or the project area here, before distributing the questionnaire.*

Please comment on this statement.

What *should* our mission and purpose be?

Mission and purpose of your area

Please write what you feel is the mission and purpose of your area or section in achieving our overall mission and purpose. As a guide, it should address the questions:

What is the business (that is, main purpose) of your area now?

What will it be in the future?

What *should* it be in the future?

Box 13.2 (cont.)
Management questionnaire

Concerns and issues

Please indicate the major concerns and issues in achieving the mission and purpose and serving the market. What are our strengths and weaknesses?

Concerns

Issues

Strengths

Weaknesses

(cont'd)

Box 13.2 (cont.)
Management questionnaire

Policies, objectives and strategies

Please list what policies, plans or objectives should be in place in your area to achieve your mission and purpose.

(1)

(2)

(3)

(4)

(5)

(6)

(7)

(8)

(9)

(10)

Box 13.2 (cont.)
Management questionnaire

Priorities

Please rate your objectives in terms of their importance in achieving your mission and purpose. Please indicate their relative position by giving them a priority rating from 1 to 10 (1 for the most important).

Objective No.   **Priority Rating**

(1)

(2)

(3)

(4)

(5)

(6)

(7)

(8)

(9)

(10)

(cont'd)

Box 13.2 (cont.)
Management questionnaire

Markets

Who are our existing customers (or users or clients) – that is, the users of our products and services?

Where are they located?

What do they need?

What do they consider value?

What are they prepared to pay?

Box 13.2 (cont.)
Management questionnaire

Products and services

Please give a brief description of our present products and services and,
if relevant, any products or services that should or may be developed in
the near future.

Present products/services

Future products/services

Channels

**How are our products and services provided or distributed to their
markets?**

**How should they and possible new products and services be
distributed to present and future markets?**

(cont'd)

Box 13.2 (cont.)
Management questionnaire

Questionnaire respondent

Organization _____

Name _____

Title _____

Dept/Section _____

Phone _____

Date _____

CHAPTER 14

Phases of Information Engineering

As indicated in Chapter 10, information engineering encompasses strategic planning as well as analysis, design and implementation support for the generation of data bases and development of computer applications. This chapter gives an overview of these phases of information engineering – analysis, design and generation – before discussing them in more detail in the following chapters, with specific examples illustrating the application of these phases.

14.1 INTRODUCTION

Information engineering comprises three broad phases – analysis, design and generation – each of which comprises a number of formal steps or stages, as illustrated in Figure 14.1

The **analysis phase** uses the strategic and tactical statements to identify data needed to support the organization. This is the responsibility of the users, who use their expert knowledge. They use the information engineering techniques of strategic and tactical modeling. They use expert systems to automate the analysis process. There is expansion of detail as this phase progresses and further data is discovered. Much of the data may exist redundantly throughout the organization.

The **design phase** identifies redundant data and achieves data consolidation, or integration, throughout the organization. All parts of

221

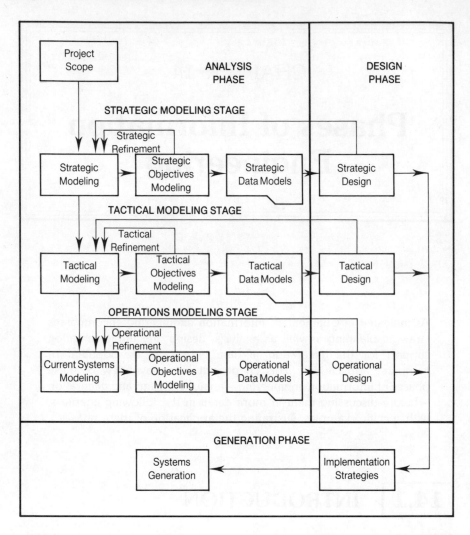

Figure 14.1 The overall process of information engineering, showing the separate stages in each of the three phases of analysis, design and generation.

the organization can refer to specific, authorized data of interest. This is not based on separate personal copies of data held within their own areas, but on common access to a single copy of the data. Design is an automated phase, based on the expert systems software described in Part Four.

Expert systems software extracts separately implementable sub-models from the integrated data models generated during the design phase. These submodels are known as subject data bases. Potential applications for information systems or for expert business systems are identified by the software for management evaluation, and implementation priorities are identified. These can be varied based on management priorities. An implementation plan is then automatically developed for progressive delivery of those systems. Application systems, menus, screens and reports are designed.

The **generation phase** is also automated. Data bases are automatically generated for information systems guided by the implementation plan. They can be manually coded using third or fourth generation languages and DBMS products, or they can be automatically generated from data models (see Part Four). Alternatively, other software can be used to develop expert business systems. Expert rules are derived from strategies defined by the users, ready for development as expert business systems. A knowledge base is automatically built. The designed expert business systems may then be developed. Part Four discusses a number of software tools that automate much of the information engineering methodology.

14.2 | ANALYSIS PHASE

The analysis phase of information engineering progressively defines data and the information derived from the data required at the strategic and at the tactical management levels of an organization. It involves the following stages and steps:

(1) **Project scope stage.**

(2) **Strategic modeling stage:**

- Strategic modeling.
- Strategic objectives modeling.
- Strategic refinement.

(3) **Tactical modeling stage:**

- Tactical modeling.
- Tactical objectives modeling.
- Tactical refinement.

(4) Operations modeling stage:

- Current systems modeling.

These stages are summarized in Boxes 14.1, 14.2 and 14.3.

14.2.1 Project scope stage

In the project scope stage (see Chapter 15), formal preparations are made for an information engineering study (see Box 14.1). This is a critical step. The project can succeed or fail here, before it even starts. For example, if management support and sponsorship are not obtained, experienced users may not be available to the project. Their expert knowledge is vital: without them, relevant data and expert rules cannot be defined accurately.

14.2.2 Strategic modeling stage

This stage and its component steps examine the strategic statements discussed earlier. The mission and purpose statements for the organization and the project area provide the starting point for strategic modeling (see Chapters 16 and 17). Identified goals and objectives, policies, and concerns and issues are used as catalysts to identify strategic data fundamental to the organization and the project in achieving the mission.

With management input, performance criteria are defined from policies, goals and objectives. This is **strategic objectives modeling**. If senior management are not actively involved here, the eventual return to the organization is severely diminished.

Strategic data identified in strategic modeling and strategic objectives modeling is progressively refined. This is **strategic refinement**. It also provides feedback for refinement of the strategic statements, and, in the process, some tactical data may also be identified. These broad tactical data represent a strategic view of the organization's markets, its products, services and channels.

Strategic modeling

The strategic data is represented in a strategic model, which provides a broad perspective of the organization in terms of its data – not its procedures, for they may change. It focuses on the entire organization, or specific divisions, departments or functional areas, according to the project scope established in the previous stage.

Strategic modeling produces the strategic data model using a management-oriented and business-directed application of normalization (see Chapters 7–9).

Strategic objectives modeling

This ensures that relevant data has been identified to measure the achievement of goals and objectives. Some of this data may need to be

Box 14.1
Strategic modeling stage

Project scope

- Identifies the project area for the information engineering study.
- Identifies personnel to be involved in the project, and obtains authorization and sponsorship from responsible management.
- Establishes project plans, tasks, milestones and funding.
- Identifies available documentation to be used as input to the project (the strategic statements and the tactical statements).
- Trains project personnel in strategic modeling (for senior management) and tactical modeling (for operational management).

Strategic modeling

- Sets strategic directions with management responsible for the project area.
- Analyzes the strategic statements and directions set for the future.
- Identifies broad strategic data of interest to management and identifies operational parts of the organization that generate tactical data on which the strategic data is based.

Strategic objectives modeling

- Reviews goals and objectives, policies, and concerns and issues.
- Determines performance criteria for performance monitoring.
- Identifies strategic data for measurement of performance criteria.
- Establishes performance ranges and controls for decision early warning.

Strategic refinement

- Progressively refines strategic data using a formal approach.
- Identifies standard terminology and expert rules at the strategic level.
- Produces strategic data models that represent a strategic blueprint for management and a basis for applying tactical modeling.

aggregated from detailed tactical data, processed further and provided to management as measured performance criteria. This information may be presented in a variety of ways, such as with the decision early warning system discussed earlier.

At this point, the strategic data model typically comprises a high-level grouping of data and details of some strategic data items – the strategic attributes. A clarification process, based on strategic refinement, is necessary, leading to further strategic modeling and strategic objectives modeling.

Strategic refinement

This uses business-oriented normalization to further clarify the definition of strategic attributes that emerge during strategic modeling and strategic objectives modeling. It applies business normalization to these data, with reference to policies, goals and objectives set for the future. Strategic refinement identifies business alternatives and challenges management to evaluate those alternatives. Through this process, it provides feedback for refinement of the strategic statements. As a business technique, it identifies key factors essential to the enterprise; that is, it helps to define performance criteria – the expert rules used by management to chart a path into the future. In other words, it establishes the rules necessary to manage the business and change in the business.

The strategic modeling stage is carried out with the responsible senior managers of the project area. When information engineering is applied to an entire organization, this stage involves the chief executive officer and senior staff. When it is applied to a division, department or branch, the responsible manager of that part of the organization is involved, with the immediate staff and line managers in that area. Where management do not provide their strategic input, strategic modeling is not applied at all – only the tactical modeling stage is used. At this level, little planning can be done for the future, since the people who set the future by their decisions today are not involved. Consequently, only a passive information system results, which is reactive, not proactive.

The strategic data model is used to plan the detailed tactical modeling stage. Strategic data submodels are used to identify tactical data relevant to specific areas of the organization – referred to as functional areas – and this is used in the tactical modeling stage.

14.2.3   Tactical modeling stage

The steps used to define tactical data in the project area are **tactical modeling**, **tactical objectives modeling** and **tactical refinement**. These steps are user driven (see Box 14.2).

Box 14.2
Tactical modeling stage

Tactical modeling

- Identifies the tactical environment with middle and operational management.
- Expands strategic data models based on detailed analysis of markets, products, services and channels in key functional areas of the project area.
- Identifies detailed tactical data of interest to middle and operational management, and data used to derive strategic data of interest to senior management.

Tactical objectives modeling

- Examines management objectives at various levels in the project area.
- Progressively refines objectives, strategies and tactics.
- Further refines strategies for later detailed definition of expert rules.
- Identifies data necessary to manage achievement of objectives.
- Identifies exception reports and decision triggers at the tactical level.

Tactical refinement

- Progressively refines tactical data using a formal approach applied against each functional area separately.
- Establishes standard terminology and expert rules at the tactical level.
- Produces tactical data models which are a detailed blueprint of the organization.

Tactical modeling

The tactical statements (markets, products and services, and channels) are used in this step to identify tactical data for each functional area. Much of the detail of the project area's data resource is defined in this step, with each functional area giving rise to a separate tactical data model. These are expanded by tactical objectives modeling and by tactical refinement.

Tactical objectives modeling

Tactical objectives indicate the expected performance achievements at each management level – that is, the data that measures the achievement of objectives is identified, establishing performance controls. Tactical objectives modeling identifies many of the exception reports needed by middle and operational managers. It identifies criteria for decision making at the tactical level. These criteria are sometimes also called decision triggers.

Tactical refinement

It is during tactical refinement that the detailed standard terminology of the business is clarified. This step also uses normalization, but applied with a different emphasis. Different interpretations across functional areas of tactical data are identified and related data may be grouped together. A distinction between CONSUMER MARKET and CORPORATE MARKET may require a similar emphasis between CONSUMER CUSTOMER and CORPORATE CUSTOMER at the tactical level. The tactical data for these two types of customers may be quite different, and such differences are uncovered by tactical refinement.

14.2.4   Operations modeling stage

As discussed earlier, the foregoing steps are iterative. Depending on the organizational environment, current systems modeling may also be used. This examines the systems or packages (manual or automated) currently in use and defines interfaces to those systems or packages that will be maintained.

Current systems modeling

This step does not require the same level of business knowledge as the previous steps. It is a formal cross-check of strategic and tactical data against the existing data used by the organization. This is reflected in various source documents, reports, enquiries, ledgers and computer files. It is a step that can ideally be carried out by analysts or data administrators. Because of its formality, it cross-checks data identified during the previous strategic and tactical steps.

Current systems modeling is mainly a DP-driven step. It uncovers factors for consideration by management. For example:

- Data that exists today and is also needed for the future must migrate to that future. What data priorities apply for conversion from existing systems?

- Data that does not exist today but is required for the future may be essential to new directions for the organization. Where are the sources of such data? When are they needed? What are their relative priorities?

- Data that exists today, but is not required for the future may well be data essential for yesterday. Is it not used now? Or has it been overlooked by the users? Were insufficient (or inexperienced) users involved in the strategic and tactical modeling stages? Who should review the apparently obsolete data? If it is not needed for the future, it should be discarded. Or it may indicate that there is a strategic gap: the data is required for the future but its purpose has not yet been identified.

The focus on separate functional areas during tactical modeling and operations modeling is continued through tactical objectives modeling, tactical refinement and current systems modeling. The data required for the effective operation of each functional area is thus identified. The operations modeling stage is summarized in Box 14.3.

The analysis phase of information engineering results in the progressive definition of the data resource. Later steps force the review and refinement of data defined in prior steps. Some of the identified data may be unique to a functional area, while some may be common across several functional areas. This common data may exist in redundant versions throughout the enterprise. The design phase of information engineering identifies this common data, which is made available in a knowledge base, to be shared by all interested and authorized users.

14.3 DESIGN PHASE

This is an automated phase that uses an expert design dictionary. It comprises **strategic design**, **tactical design** and **operational design** (see

> **Box 14.3**
> Operations modeling stage

Current systems modeling

- Optionally used with tactical modeling for current manual or automated systems, or packages, needed for the future.

- Formally cross-checks data presently used in existing source documents, reports, enquiries, ledgers and computer files against tactical data models.

- Discards current data not needed for the future.

- Includes data for the future which was overlooked in the previous stages.

Operational objectives modeling

- Examines operational objectives in the project area.

- Identifies data necessary to manage achievement of objectives.

- Identifies exception reports and decision triggers at the operational level.

Operational refinement

- Progressively refines operational data for each functional area separately.

- Establishes standard terminology and expert rules at the operational level.

- Produces operational data models for day-to-day operation of the organization.

Figure 14.1). Although it may be applied after the analysis phase, it is most productive when applied concurrently with analysis. Software is discussed briefly in this section in relation to the design phase, and in more detail in Part Four.

14.3.1 Strategic design

Strategic data identified in the analysis phase is entered into an expert design dictionary, which is itself an expert system. It fully automates the information engineering process. It checks strategic data for consistency and completeness of definition. Where several strategic data models exist, arising from separate information engineering studies carried out in different divisions or departments of a large enterprise, it identifies strategic data that may be common across those several data models. It automatically combines common data into an *integrated* strategic model.

14.3.2 Tactical and operations design

As tactical modeling, tactical objectives modeling and tactical refinement progress through each relevant functional area during analysis, tactical data is also entered into the expert design dictionary. This tactical data may have been further extended to operational data in the operations modeling stage. The dictionary checks the consistency and completeness of the definition of tactical and operational data. Analogous to strategic design, tactical and operational data models for each functional area are analyzed and common data is combined into integrated tactical and operational models.

14.4 | GENERATION PHASE

Following strategic, tactical and operations design, the resulting integrated data models are used as the design blueprint for generation. Generation may commence for high-priority areas while analysis and design are still underway in low-priority areas.

Information engineering is technology independent: it focuses only on the data needed to run the business. The generation phase defines implementation strategies appropriate to each part of the integrated strategic and tactical models. It determines the hardware, software and communication facilities, and the physical design and development of defined information systems and expert business systems. The analysis and design phases, up to this point, have been logical – physical design has been left aside. Only now is it appropriate to define how data, reports or systems might be implemented physically. This is covered in systems generation.

14.4.1 Implementation strategies

Part of the integrated models may represent manual systems while another part may represent automated systems. The data and systems may be centralized or geographically dispersed. The data may be implemented using DBMS products, conventional files, 3GLs or 4GLs or as expert business systems in their own right, using expert systems generation software. Expert systems software decomposes the data models in the expert design dictionary into separately implementable submodels during the analysis phase. These submodels may represent potential applications for development in information systems, using 3GLs or 4GLs, or they may represent complete expert business systems. They are prioritized for progressive development. This is an automated stage, based both on data model dependencies and on business priorities set by management.

14.4.2 Systems generation

Data models may be strategic, tactical or operational, and at this point will have been decomposed into separately implementable submodels. There is much logic implicit in the strategies represented in the submodels, and expert systems software analyzes this implicit logic, requesting additional clarification and refinement where necessary. Data models provide a DBMS-independent interface to data bases and knowledge bases.

The data models developed and refined in this way provide input for the development of expert business systems and information systems as described in this book. These systems are tailored, based on the organization's defined expert rules and standard terminology. Part Four describes this software in more detail.

Data models provide input for manual coding using either 3GLs or 4GLs, and manual data base design of information systems. Alternatively, the data models may be translated automatically to data base definitions for relevant DBMS products. This is carried out by translation expert systems, also described in Part Four.

Any maintenance changes are made by the users against the data models, as relevant. From these models, changed data bases and

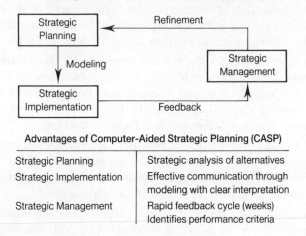

Figure 14.2   Advantages of computer-aided strategic planning.

knowledge bases are regenerated. The maintenance workload of traditional development methods is dramatically reduced, and the application backlog shrinks. The advantages of computer-aided strategic planning (CASP) are illustrated in Figure 14.2, as applied by information engineering.

14.5 | BENEFITS OF INFORMATION ENGINEERING

As we have seen, information engineering leads to the development of a data model (a blueprint) of the organization. This blueprint offers the following benefits:

- It is data oriented: Information engineering identifies data that is fundamental to the organization: data that supports management decision making. This defines the standard terminology essential for common information systems or tailored expert business systems.

- It is objectives driven: Information engineering may start at the top of an organization, based on its corporate goals and objectives. It projects objectives through all management levels. Alternatively, it may start at any point within the organization based upon lower-lever objectives, and then project down, and up.

- It uses modeling techniques: Simple graphics are used to represent data, illustrating strategies for the management of the data and the organization itself. This is represented in a schematic data model. These strategies are the expert rules needed to run the business.

- It is user driven: Information engineering draws on the expert knowledge of users throughout the organization. They actively develop the data model themselves, based on the information engineering steps. They identify the data and information at all management levels needed for decision making.

- It is evolutionary: Information engineering uses formal steps that progressively expand and enrich the definition of the data model, and its strategies and expert rules, as the process extends through various management levels in the organization.

- It achieves data consolidation: Information engineering includes cross-checking steps, both manual and automated, to identify redundant versions of data. The result is an integrated data model, able to be shared by all authorized parties who use the same data.

- It provides rapid feedback: Information engineering draws on strategic statements from corporate plans. These statements represent data needed to support the corporate plan. This data is documented in a schematic data model which allows management to evaluate the implications of strategic alternatives.

- It uses *what-if* strategic planning: Management can consider the implications of alternative strategies and evaluate the significance of those alternatives. As the architect can make a design change to his blueprint, so also management can introduce an alternative strategy, represent that in the data model, determine its effect and modify it immediately if required.

- It is highly automated: Both strategic and tactical plans and data are captured by expert systems in an expert design dictionary. This is user driven. Common data is automatically integrated and separately implementable submodels and implementation plans are derived. Data bases are automatically translated to target third or fourth generation DBMS products. Knowledge bases are automatically generated. Subsequent maintenance is automated: changes to the data models result in regenerated data bases and knowledge bases.

CHAPTER 15

Defining the Project Scope

The formal or informal approaches to strategic planning described in Chapters 10–12 are carried out prior to starting the project. In effect, they form its charter. The strategic plans become the catalyst for the project: they are its input. We will now use those plans for strategic modeling. The resulting strategic models provide highly effective feedback to management, for evaluation of strategic alternatives.

Regardless of whether strategic planning is undertaken prior to the project or is introduced later, many tasks must be carried out. They are involved in starting the project, and relate to the project scope. This chapter describes these tasks.

Before looking at these tasks, however, we first need to discuss the principles involved in automated project analysis. The software that provides this capability is discussed in more detail in Part Four. Automated project analysis is used for the development of an implementation plan and for project planning. It provides input for the development of the project scope.

15.1 AUTOMATED PROJECT ANALYSIS

As data is defined during the analysis phase (see Chapter 14), common data used by different functional areas is automatically identified by software and consolidated in integrated strategic and tactical models.

235

Software also analyzes the defined associations for implementation validity, grouping related entities into subject data bases and implementation clusters. A **subject data base** contains a group of related entities that are implemented together. To distinguish a subject data base from an entity, we will write its name in italicized capitals. (An entity name is written in plain capitals.) An **implementation cluster** is a group of related subject data bases that are implemented in a defined sequence. It generally represents a specific application system or part of an information system. (An example of an implementation cluster is shown in Figure 15.2.)

The following sections describe how subject data bases, implementation clusters and an implementation plan are derived from a data model. This is automated project analysis. The concepts introduced here will be drawn on later in Chapter 16. As a foundation for this discussion, we will use Figure 15.1, which is a data map of an organization and its personnel.

As we saw in Part Two, a data map allows the clear representation of business strategies. For example, the line joining PERSON and PERSON SKILL in Figure 15.1 may be interpreted to indicate:

Association between PERSON and SKILL

'A person may have one or many skills, but may have none. Each person skill provides skill details (such as skill level or date trained) relating to one person, and relates only to that one person.'

The entity ORGANIZATION in Figure 15.1 is called a **principal entity**: it is in third business normal form (3BNF). The entity ORGANIZATION TYPE is used to define different parts of the organization. This is a **type entity**. Different organizational parts are shown as fourth business normal form (4BNF) entities: a 4BNF entity is called a **secondary entity**. Figure 15.1 shows one 4BNF entity HEAD OFFICE. Other 4BNF entities may also be required: MARKETING DEPARTMENT, ACCOUNTS DEPARTMENT, BRANCH OFFICE, and so on. However, they are not included in this data map for the sake of simplicity. 4BNF entities may also be interrelated. For example, the accounts department and the marketing department are part of head office. 4BNF interrelationships are represented in a 5BNF entity: this is ORGANIZATION STRUCTURE. A 5BNF entity is called a **structure entity**. It captures expert knowledge (the experience of key individuals) that may be held external to the data model.

Similarly, PERSON TYPE indicates several types of PERSON (3BNF). Figure 15.1 shows two 4BNF (secondary) entities of SALES PERSON and SALES MANAGER.

Finally, SKILL is a 3BNF (principal) entity. Each person in the organization may have many skills. Similarly, a particular skill may be held by many personnel. This is indicated by the entity PERSON SKILL: this is called an **intersecting entity**.

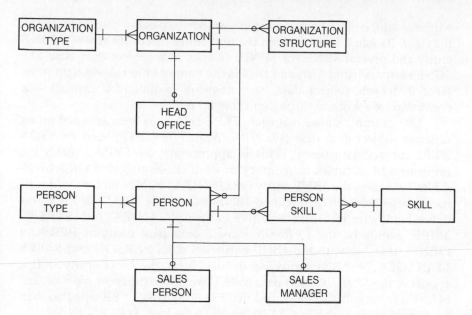

Figure 15.1   A simple data map of an organization.

Automated project analysis produces a **subject data bases report** to indicate how related entities are grouped together into subject data bases. The following example indicates the format of such a report:

ORGANIZATION TYPE
    ORGANIZATION TYPE

ORGANIZATION
    ORGANIZATION
    HEAD OFFICE
    ORGANIZATION STRUCTURE

PERSON TYPE
    PERSON TYPE

PERSON
    PERSON
    SALES PERSON
    SALES MANAGER

SKILL
    SKILL

PERSON SKILL
    PERSON SKILL

The subject data bases listed here were derived in conjunction with the data map in Figure 15.1. Each subject data base is listed. The entities within a subject data base are listed immediately below and indented to the right. Its name is taken from the first entity listed. If there is a 3BNF entity and several 4BNF (or 5BNF) entities in a subject data base, the 3BNF entity is listed first, and thus is the name of the subject data base. Note that each subject data base name is in italicized capitals – a convention we will use throughout this book.

Our example shows that each TYPE entity has been grouped into a separate subject data base (see *ORGANIZATION TYPE* and *PERSON TYPE* subject data bases). This is appropriate, as TYPE entities are implemented as tables in memory or on disk. Notice that *ORGANIZATION* contains the 3BNF entity ORGANIZATION (which provides its name), together with each related 4BNF entity (only HEAD OFFICE was defined in Figure 15.1) and the 5BNF entity ORGANIZATION STRUCTURE. Similarly, the *PERSON* subject data base contains PERSON (3BNF), together with the 4BNF entities SALES PERSON and SALES MANAGER. No 5BNF entity was defined. Next, the 3BNF entity SKILL resides in the *SKILL* subject data base. If we define different types of skill (4BNF), these will also be placed in *SKILL*. SKILL TYPE will also then be defined as an additional TYPE entity. Now look at PERSON SKILL. This has been placed in a separate subject data base, *PERSON SKILL*, rather than being grouped in *PERSON* or *SKILL*. As we discussed earlier, this is an intersecting entity. Volume processing in information systems or expert business systems generally centers around intersecting entities. It has therefore been implemented in its own subject data base: offering maximum performance tuning flexibility for physical implementation on a computer later.

We will now use these subject data bases to illustrate the automated derivation of implementation clusters and an implementation plan from a data model. An implementation cluster indicates the phase in which each subject data base is implemented. A report of all clusters derived from a data model is called an **application systems report**. If sufficient development resources are available, separate clusters may be implemented concurrently. Furthermore, priority systems can be scheduled as concurrent implementation projects, for early delivery of systems to management based on available resources. Implementation clusters are used to develop an implementation plan. An example of a cluster derived from the data map in Figure 15.1 and based on our example subject data bases, is as follows:

ORGANIZATION TYPE
    (1) *ORGANIZATION*
PERSON TYPE
    (2) *PERSON*
SKILL
      (3) *PERSON SKILL*

This lists the six subject data bases as an implementation cluster, with the allocated implementation phase indicated in brackets. There are four phases for this cluster: phase 0–phase 3. Any subject data base that is not preceded by a phase number in brackets is in phase 0. Each subject data base is dependent on those listed above it, in a lower phase, and they must be implemented first. This cluster is interpreted as follows:

- *ORGANIZATION TYPE* is implemented in the initial phase (phase 0). This must be before the subject data bases in other phases, as they are dependent upon it.

- *PERSON TYPE* is also in phase 0. It may also be implemented concurrently with *ORGANIZATION TYPE*, as it does not depend on any other data.

- *ORGANIZATION* is implemented in phase 1. It is grouped below *ORGANIZATION TYPE* and so is dependent on it. It is indented one position to the right for phase 1. It is not dependent on *PERSON TYPE*, which is below it.

- *PERSON* is implemented in phase 2. It is dependent on *PERSON TYPE*, and *ORGANIZATION* (and hence on *ORGANIZATION TYPE*), as it is grouped with these subject data bases but below them, indented one further position to the right in a higher-phase number (phase 2).

- *SKILL* is also in phase 0. It is not dependent on any other subject data base and may be implemented concurrently with *ORGANIZATION TYPE* and *PERSON TYPE*.

- *PERSON SKILL* is implemented in phase 3. It is dependent on *SKILL* and *PERSON* (and hence is also dependent on *PERSON TYPE*, *ORGANIZATION* and *ORGANIZATION TYPE*) as it is grouped with these subject data bases but below them and in a later phase (phase 3) indented another position to the right.

An implementation plan can be developed from the implementation cluster either manually or automatically (using software).

15.1.2 Automated implementation plans

Separate implementation clusters are plotted in implementation priority sequence as an **implementation phase data map**. This is both a data map and an implementation plan. It illustrates concurrent implementation potentials for subject data bases, and permits progressive implementation and early delivery of priority systems to management.

Figure 15.2 illustrates the format of an implementation phase data map that has been derived automatically by software, although this is not

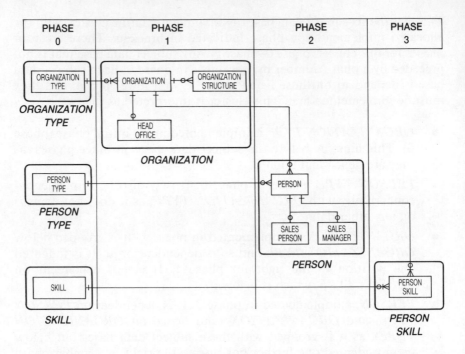

Figure 15.2   Implementation phase data map format. Subject data bases are highlighted as boxed groups of entities in this figure.

an actual plotted data map. It shows entities in each subject data base plotted together as a group, which have been boxed in for illustrative purposes only with the name of the relevant subject data base in italicized capitals beneath it. Chapter 21 shows more detailed examples of automatically derived data maps.

Notice that each subject data base is positioned vertically by implementation phase. This allows concurrent implementation opportunities to be clearly identified. For example, the subject data bases in phase 0 (*ORGANIZATION TYPE, PERSON TYPE* and *SKILL*) can all be implemented concurrently, if sufficient development resources are available.

The implementation sequence for all subject data bases is now clearly apparent. Contrast this with the data map in Figure 15.1. The *ORGANIZATION* subject data base is dependent only on *ORGANIZATION TYPE*; it is implemented in phase 1. In this figure, the *PERSON* subject data base is dependent on ORGANIZATION and *PERSON TYPE*; it is therefore implemented in phase 2. Finally, *PERSON SKILL* is dependent both on *PERSON* and *SKILL*; it is implemented in phase 3.

An implementation phase data map indicates potential concurrent project activity over many implementation phases. For a strategic model, this usually includes 4–6 phases; for a tactical model, this may extend to 8–10 phases; for a detailed operations model, 12–14 phases may be plotted. Implementation phase data maps can be plotted for each separate cluster, or for any combination of, or all, clusters.

Figures 15.1 and 15.2 only include 10 entities. However, an organization may typically have 600–800 entities. The analysis of a data model, manually, for implementation phases has been estimated to take 420 person days for only 200 entities by one organization. If the data model changed, this analysis would have to be repeated each time, which is clearly impractical. Software took only 22 minutes for the same analysis on a micro.

We will use the principles of automated project analysis and automated implementation plans for project planning in the following sections, as we discuss the project scope.

15.2 PROJECT SCOPE

The steps of the project scope stage are illustrated in Figure 15.3. These steps are:

- Identify project area.
- Select project software.
- Establish initial project plan.
- Establish project teams.
- Set project budget and funding.
- Schedule information engineering workshops.

15.2.1 Identify project area

The first task is to select the project area. This delineates the boundaries of the project, clearly identifying the business units to be examined and those to be excluded. It defines the project scope. Unless this scoping is done, the project will expand to cover areas that are not relevant at this time, which can jeopardize eventual project success.

Within the project scope, management must set specific business priorities. These may be defined from the policies, goals, objectives, concerns and issues identified during the strategic planning stage, or from the management questionnaire (see Box 13.2). Major policies, goals or issues will dictate the emphasis or priorities to be taken by the project. From these defined priorities, specific project objectives will be set by management. These objectives relate to the project itself, its deliverables

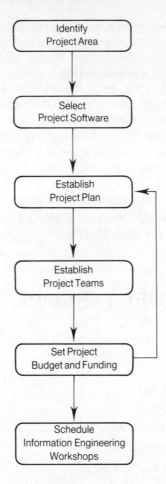

Figure 15.3 The project scope stage, prior to strategic modeling. This defines the project area. It ensures software, people and funding resources are allocated. There may be several iterations until a project plan is defined within acceptable budgets.

and its time for completion. They detail specific project achievements which management require, thereby leading to firm project management.

The project scope, priorities and objectives may be defined for the entire organization, or they may be defined for selected business units where management have identified a need for change as an outcome of the strategic planning exercise.

15.2.2 Select software tools

Appropriate software tools for strategic and tactical modeling are selected to be used later in the project. This includes data dictionaries or design dictionaries with automated data modeling capability. The factors that should be taken into account in the selection of this software are described in Chapter 18.

In particular, this step determines whether automatic plotting of data maps from defined data is supported by the software being considered, and whether text strategic plans can be automatically linked to the data supporting those plans. If this capability is *not* provided by the software, it will have to be additionally developed in the project. Software to interface a computer-aided design system and a word processing package to a data dictionary will be required. This is a major development effort, which will divert people and funding resources from the project itself.

Regardless of whether a manual dictionary is used for small projects (less than 50 entities – see Chapter 6), or whether software products provide documentation support, documentation tools are *vital* to the project; documentation is essential for subsequent systems development. The documentation produced during an information engineering project is extensive, even for small projects.

Appropriate software and the relevant hardware must be selected and installed during the project scope period, ready for immediate use as the project gets under way.

15.2.3   Establish initial project plan

An initial project plan for strategic modeling is developed based on project durations described in this section. This plan establishes broad milestones, and indicates the elapsed duration for strategic, tactical and operations modeling and implementation.

A detailed project plan is developed later, based on the strategic data identified during the strategic modeling workshop. This is conducted at the end of the project scope stage (see Chapter 16). During the workshop, the knowledge held by the project team members is drawn upon to develop an initial strategic model. The instructor acts as both a teacher and a catalyst. The project scope is used initially to focus on priority areas, in sufficient detail only to identify strategic entities.

During the strategic modeling workshop, strategic data is identified by the project team and processed by the software selected. An initial implementation plan can be automatically derived as discussed earlier in this chapter. This implementation plan is used to develop a detailed tactical modeling project plan.

A number of priority areas are selected to progress to the tactical modeling stage. If enough resources are available, these areas can be addressed as concurrent tactical modeling projects. Figure 15.4 illustrates the progression of a typical project through strategic modeling to tactical modeling, operations modeling, strategic management and then to implementation. It shows training for each phase, and concurrent activity of modeling and refinement in each strategic, tactical and operations project area. By establishing concurrent project teams, a high degree of control over project duration can be achieved.

As the project progresses and additional data is defined, this data can be used for more detailed refinement of the project plan and for estimating the duration of later stages. Automated project analysis is carried out against the evolving strategic model as discussed earlier. This analysis is first conducted in the strategic modeling workshop. Data maps

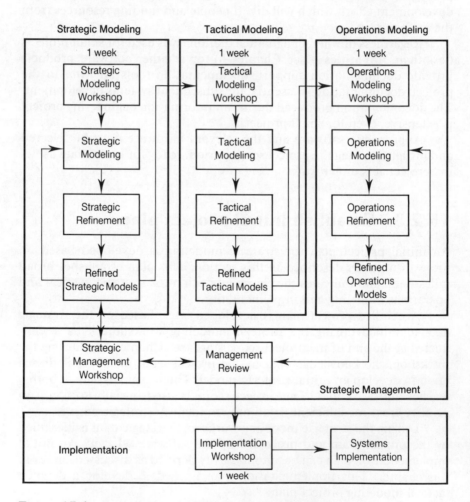

Figure 15.4 Project flow for strategic, tactical and operations modeling to strategic management and then to implementation. There may be multiple concurrent strategic, tactical and operations areas, with iteration between modeling and refinement in each area.

are automatically plotted in implementation sequence as implementation phase data maps, used to develop detailed project plans. Implementation phase data maps clearly illustrate concurrent project opportunities. They may represent only one implementation cluster, as in Figure 15.2, or they can be used to plot many clusters. They provide a clear direction of the implementation sequence for project planning and other purposes, as demonstrated in the following discussion.

We saw that each vertical group of subject data bases in Figure 15.2 represents a phase for implementation, from phase 0 at the left-hand edge of the data map through later phases moving to the right-hand edge. For example, Figure 15.2 shows a single cluster with four phases, phase 0–phase 3. The entities in each phase are summarized as follows:

Phase	Entities implemented in this phase
0	ORGANIZATION TYPE, PERSON TYPE, SKILL
1	ORGANIZATION, HEAD OFFICE, ORGANIZATION STRUCTURE
2	PERSON, SALES PERSON, SALES MANAGER
3	PERSON SKILL

Given sufficient staff resources, the potential exists for many concurrent project teams. Each team focuses on a project area, concentrating on one or several implementation clusters. They address each entity in implementation phase sequence.

A strategic or tactical project area is normally defined as one or several implementation clusters, each comprising up to 30–40 entities. Any more entities than this will result in an area that is too complex. Each project area is so defined to focus on a related grouping of entities and/or clusters to support a specific application or function in the organization. Project areas are therefore also referred to as functional areas.

As each entity in a project area is examined during strategic modeling, more entities may emerge. Additional project areas may then be identified, based on related groups of implementation clusters from the latest application systems report and observing the limit of 30–40 entities per area.

Similarly, each tactical project area is defined to contain no more than 30–40 entities. As each entity is examined during tactical modeling, more detailed tactical entities will emerge. Additional tactical project areas are defined, which are then taken to operational detail.

Figure 15.5 shows the progressive expansion of a strategic project area to a number of tactical areas, and then to operational areas through tactical modeling and operations modeling. Operations modeling is carried out following tactical modeling: it models the existing systems in the organization. It is also referred to as current systems modeling, as discussed in Chapter 14.

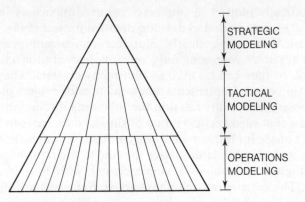

Figure 15.5   Expansion of a strategic area into tactical and operational areas, when moving from strategic modeling to tactical and operations modeling.

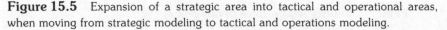

Table 15.1 shows that a typical strategic model may comprise 50–90 strategic entities in a strategic area. Each entity has an average of two attributes – these are mainly keys. There are typically around 20 tactical models per strategic model, with 10–20 tactical entities per tactical model. Each tactical entity has an average of five attributes, comprising keys and non-key attributes. At this level of definition, the strategic model will have expanded to include a total of 250–700 strategic and tactical entities. But this is not the end of the story. Each tactical model (tactical area) comprises an average of three operational systems. Each operations entity now has an average of 10 attributes, with operational

Table 15.1   Entities and project areas in a strategic model.

No. of Models	No. of Entities	Entity/Attribute Ratio
One strategic model for each strategic area	50–90 entities per strategic model	1:2
Approximately 20 tactical models for each strategic model	10 – 20 entities per tactical model	1:5
	250–700 entities per strategic model	
Approximately three operational systems for each tactical model	2–5 entities per operational system	1:10
	400–1000 entities per strategic model	

data included. An operational system may contain 2–5 entities. At this level of operational detail, a total of 400–1000 strategic, tactical and operational entities will have been identified. This represents approximately 60 operational systems per strategic model. Table 15.2 provides broad project durations for each stage. This table can be used in conjunction with Table 15.1 as a guide for the initial project plan. Note that the quoted durations are *elapsed times* for each strategic or tactical area. As the number of concurrent project areas increases, the amount of project area interaction also increases. Because of this interaction, the elapsed durations in Table 15.2 will vary according to the project complexity.

As strategic and tactical modeling progress, the amount of data in each area, and the number of areas, increases. Implementation phase data maps help to manage this data growth and allow firm project management. This data growth begins with the strategic modeling workshop, discussed in Chapter 16. Until that time, Table 15.2 helps to establish the initial project plan.

Table 15.2   Broad estimates for the initial project plan.

Project Stage	Description	Duration
Formal strategic planning	Uses formal strategic planning to set strategic directions and define the strategic statements to be used as input to later stages	3–6 months
	or	
Informal strategic planning	Uses informal strategic planning (or the management questionnaire) to define the strategic statements to be used as input to later stages	1 month
Strategic modeling	Establishes and refines strategic models in priority project areas	1–2 months per strategic area
Tactical modeling	Develops tactical models from priority tactical areas in each strategic model	1–2 months per tactical area
Operations modeling	Develops operations models from priority tactical areas in each strategic model	1–2 months per operations area
Implementation	Develops operational systems in priority areas, using third or fourth generation DBMS products and languages	1–2 months per system

The number of person months at each stage, and hence the cost, is of course directly proportional to the size of each project team. This includes both full-time and part-time members. The total project elapsed time is affected by the number of project teams, the degree of concurrency that can be achieved and the extent to which these concurrent project areas interact.

A typical organization will have around 50–90 strategic entities and 500–700 tactical entities. This describes 80% of organizations, regardless of their size or turnover. The estimates in Table 15.2 address this *typical* environment: each strategic, tactical and operations project area will typically take one to two months. This assumes that at least three modeling sessions, each of three hours (see Chapter 16), are conducted per week, with processing of defined entities and attributes carried out between each meeting.

Because of management commitments, most organizations are only able to establish one strategic project team. In this case, a typical organization may break its strategic model into three strategic project areas – of high, medium and low priority – rather than one strategic area, as suggested in Table 15.1. This allows work to start on tactical modeling of high-priority areas before all strategic modeling has been completed. In this case, each strategic area will comprise only 20–30 strategic entities. The strategic project team addresses these strategic areas serially, with the highest priority area first. In this serial fashion the three areas take an elapsed time of three to six months, depending on the number of entities, and provided at least three modeling sessions per week are scheduled. Figure 15.6 illustrates a project of three strategic areas, with overlapped strategic modeling extending over only four months.

After the first strategic project area has completed strategic modeling, it can move to tactical modeling. If concurrent tactical project teams are formed for each tactical area, they can overlap tactical modeling of strategic project area 1, while the strategic team addresses strategic area 2. Tactical modeling will then progress to strategic area 2, while strategic modeling moves on to area 3. This is illustrated in Figure 15.6, where four tactical project teams work on a total of 12 tactical areas concurrently with one strategic team working on three strategic areas. This approach overlaps strategic and tactical modeling for a total project duration of six months for the example in Figure 15.6. However, if concurrent strategic and tactical project teams cannot be allocated, or if computer access is inadequate, strategic modeling must be completed *before* tactical modeling starts. Furthermore, if there is only one tactical project team, each tactical area must then be addressed in turn. This represents a project duration of four months for strategic modeling, and most likely 18–24 months for tactical modeling, with a total project duration of 22–28 months.

INITIAL PROJECT PLAN

Business Unit: _____   Date: _____

Strategic Areas: 3 Strategic Teams: 1   Tactical Areas: 12 Tactical Teams: 4

Team	Task	Month 1	Month 2	Month 3	Month 4	Month 5	Month 6
S1	Strategic Modeling Workshop	▪					
S1	Strategic Area 1	▭					
S1	Strategic Area 2		▭				
S1	Strategic Area 3			▭			
	Tactical Modeling Workshops	▬▬					
	Strategic Area 1						
T1	Tactical Area 1.1		▭				
T2	Tactical Area 1.2		▭▭				
T3	Tactical Area 1.3		▭				
T4	Tactical Area 1.4		▭				
	Strategic Area 2						
T1	Tactical Area 2.1				▭		
T2	Tactical Area 2.2				▭		
T3	Tactical Area 2.3			▭			
T4	Tactical Area 2.4				▭		
	Strategic Area 3						
T1	Tactical Area 3.1					▭▭	
T2	Tactical Area 3.2					▭	
T3	Tactical Area 3.3					▭▭	
T4	Tactical Area 3.4					▭▭	

■ Workshop   ▭ Project Team Activity

Figure 15.6 Gantt chart of a typical project with multiple project teams, overlapping between strategic, tactical and operations modeling for the shortest possible project duration.

Figure 15.6 assumes four tactical modeling workshops are scheduled to train each of the four tactical project teams, and also assumes the maximum availability of staff for scheduling of tactical teams based on required business expertise in each area. It also assumes that all required processing of defined data can be completed between each modeling session. It assumes the availability of sufficient microcomputers or terminals, with associated computing power for concurrent processing as appropriate. This computer processing includes the capture of data definitions after each modeling session as they are progressively identified. It also includes analysis of those definitions to identify implementation cluster and project plan changes as further detailed data definitions emerge.

This example relates to a typical project. In contrast, a *simple* project involves only specific business units, or a small organization that operates in a specific industry niche. This may represent only 50–80 strategic entities and 300–400 tactical entities. It represents two strategic areas and generally three potentially concurrent tactical areas for each strategic area. Furthermore, the project duration for each tactical area is correspondingly less; usually 80% of the typical estimates given in Table 15.1 because of the reduced interaction between project areas. With one strategic team and only two tactical teams, for example, this project would take approximately 12 months.

A *complex* project is one involving an organization with several businesses and markets, or products and services, which are quite diverse, such as banking and insurance. The total model will contain perhaps 200 strategic entities and more than 1200 tactical entities. This may represent a number of unrelated businesses, combined only at the corporate level for financial reporting purposes. A complex project must be broken down into typical or simple projects. For example, a complex project may be defined as two concurrent typical projects, with two strategic teams and three concurrent tactical teams per strategic team. Project area interaction will be greater and so project duration will be longer. Depending on the amount of the organization to be addressed concurrently and the number of concurrent teams, the estimates in Table 15.2 will need to be increased by a factor of 1.5–2 for each project area, to allow for this greater project area interaction.

Let us consider this example of two typical projects, running concurrently. Assume there is some interaction between strategic areas and that each strategic team has five tactical teams. Even though both groups of teams are working concurrently in their project areas, with an overall total of 10 tactical teams, the resulting project interaction factor will extend the total duration to around 12 months. This assumes that each team has its own hardware and software facilities, with no limitation of staff resources. Establishment of concurrent typical projects is essential in this complex environment. This allows overlap of strategic and tactical modeling in each concurrent project, but total project duration is constrained by the overall project interaction and complexity.

Figure 15.6 has been extended in Figure 15.7 to show a typical project plan. This covers only six months, focusing on priority areas. It provides an overall project plan that addresses the initial training of: a strategic team in strategic modeling and strategic management; a tactical team in tactical modeling and operations modeling; and an implementation team. It addresses only priority areas. It includes consulting support for quality assurance as each team becomes more proficient through experience while working on the priority areas. Based on this experience, each team then moves subsequently to lower priority areas until the project is completed.

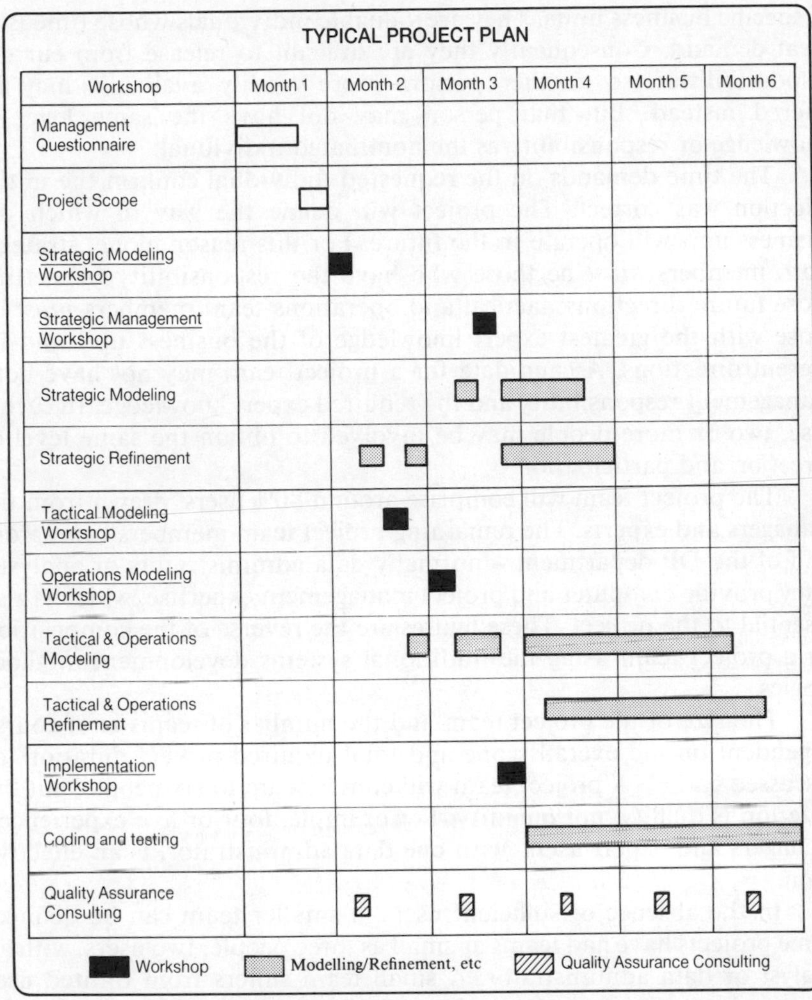

Workshop	Month 1	Month 2	Month 3	Month 4	Month 5	Month 6
Management Questionnaire						
Project Scope						
Strategic Modeling Workshop						
Strategic Management Workshop						
Strategic Modeling						
Strategic Refinement						
Tactical Modeling Workshop						
Operations Modeling Workshop						
Tactical & Operations Modeling						
Tactical & Operations Refinement						
Implementation Workshop						
Coding and testing						
Quality Assurance Consulting						

TYPICAL PROJECT PLAN

■ Workshop   ▨ Modelling/Refinement, etc   ▨ Quality Assurance Consulting

Figure 15.7   A typical project plan, which shows the overlap of strategic modeling, tactical modeling, operations modeling, strategic management and implementation.

15.2.4   Establish project teams

Information engineering requires a knowledge of the business, rather than of computers. The majority of the project team (both full-time and part-time members) is therefore comprised of managers and experienced staff from the business units defined in the project scope. This section covers factors to be considered in setting up these teams. The composition of project teams is discussed in more detail in Chapter 16.

Project team members are selected based on their expert knowledge of specific business units. They are valuable individuals whose time is in great demand. Consequently they are difficult to release from current responsibilities, so another person, more readily available, may be offered instead. But that person may not have the same level of knowledge or responsibility as the nominated individual.

The time demands on the requested individual confirm the initial selection was correct. The project will define the way in which the business unit will operate in the future. For this reason alone, strategic team members *must* be those who have the responsibility for setting those future directions; tactical and operations team members *must* be those with the greatest expert knowledge of the business unit and its present directions. A candidate for a project team may not have both management responsibility and the required expert knowledge. In such a case, two or more people may be involved to obtain the same level of direction and participation.

The project team will comprise around 80% users, drawn from the managers and experts. The remaining project team members come from staff of the DP department – normally data administrators or analysts. They provide computer and project management expertise, which is also essential to the project. These figures are the reverse of the composition for a project team using the traditional systems development methodologies.

The size of the project team and the number of teams is of course dependent on the overall scope and total required project duration, as discussed earlier. A project team will comprise up to six people, but the criterion is quality, not quantity. For example, four or five experienced managers and expert users, with one data administrator, is an effective team.

In the absence of sufficient users, a smaller team can be defined. Some projects have had teams as small as three people: two users, with an analyst or data administrator. A small team suffers from limited user input and interaction, and loss of quality. Don't give in to temptation and substitute extra DP staff for users. Their experience is likely to be at the tactical or operational end of the business and may be limited. Most analysts and data administrators do not have the expert business knowledge of the users; rather, their experience is in project management and systems development.

The team should not exceed six people. If the project is complex, it should be broken down into smaller projects with several smaller project teams, as discussed earlier. A large project can be separated into several smaller, concurrent strategic, tactical and operations subprojects. The separate teams come together at defined project milestones, to integrate the results of their subproject activities.

For very large projects, where the project scope encompasses several business units or an entire organization, multiple project teams are essential, as discussed earlier. This enables separate teams to work concurrently on different business units, and on different areas within those business units. These teams come together at milestones, for progressive integration and completion of the larger project. This achieves a high degree of parallel activity. It draws on the expertise of managers and users throughout the organization: separately in each of the project teams, and then collectively as the project teams combine their models and integrate the project areas.

The output of each team is the development of strategic, tactical and operations models, in the form described in Part Two. Software automatically combines them to produce a single integrated model for the entire project area or organization.

15.2.5   Set project budget and funding

Based on the project scope, number and size of project teams, hardware and software project support, and the project plan as described earlier, project budgets and funding can be developed. This may require changes in the size, composition and concurrency of project teams to achieve a reasonable trade-off between project cost and total project duration. Figure 15.3 illustrates this iteration.

The budget covers the personnel resources involved. This includes both full-time and part-time project team members, as well as administrative and clerical staff. It covers hardware and software support to the project, and the number and cost of training workshops for all full-time and part-time project team members (see Section 15.2.6). It includes funding for consulting support, which is essential for the first project, to help project team members consolidate their understanding of the design techniques used. While project teams are formally trained in strategic, tactical and operations modeling as appropriate, they must also be able to recognize emerging real-life problems. They must know which techniques are used to resolve problems; such knowledge is based on experience, gained from initial projects. Consultant support is essential to build that experience. Without it, the cost of lost project time can be very high. In addition, errors in the defined systems may have a higher cost.

As a guideline, assuming the project team is trained as follows, each separate team will require an average of five days' consulting support per month, over four to six months. This focuses on quality assurance: it ensures that the project teams develop the necessary expertise to become self-supporting as soon as possible. Figure 15.6 shows quality assurance consulting following training for strategic, tactical and operations modeling, and implementation. For example, a project with four concurrent, interacting tactical teams will need 20 (4 × 5) days of quality assurance consulting per month. Six concurrent teams will require two consultants full-time (40 consulting days per month) because of even greater interaction in this project environment. The cost of this consulting support should be included in the project budget.

15.2.6 Schedule information engineering workshops

To be fully effective, all project participants (full-time and part-time) must be trained in information engineering, with emphasis on strategic modeling, tactical modeling or operations modeling, depending upon the project stage. This book can only provide the theory of information engineering; it cannot replace training. This is communicated in hands-on workshops (in conjunction with software) using case studies drawn from the project itself. Each workshop uses lecture sessions and immediate application of learned techniques to the project itself, over a period of five days. It enables the project team members to draw on their expert knowledge. They use that knowledge and apply the techniques for progressive solution of part of the project as a case study.

As part of the workshop, the participants learn how software is used to analyze the accuracy of their data model. Alternative strategies are automatically identified by software and they can consider the implications of those alternatives. Some may represent critical strategic gaps or opportunities that had been overlooked. Changes can be made to the model. Software examines the impact of changes on other parts of the model. It analyzes the evolving model for implementation plans, as discussed earlier in this chapter. Modeling sessions in the workshop then focus on priority areas.

The workshops expose the project team to potential problem areas. They learn to recognize problems that may emerge during a real-life project. They learn how to resolve those problems through strategic, tactical and operations modeling software, and techniques, as appropriate.

Project team members are trained in class sizes of up to 12 people. Two case study teams can thus be defined in a workshop, each with six students. Each case study team can be further broken down into two subgroups of three people. Each subgroup can focus on a specific project area of the case study. The subgroups develop data models relating to their project area and integrate those data models across subgroups.

If two case study teams both develop solutions for the same case study, those separate solutions can be reviewed during the workshop. Specific areas of difference can be used to evaluate alternative design solutions. The resulting case study solutions then provide initial input to the project. They are progressively expanded to focus first on priority areas identified by management.

Alternatively, the workshop attendees may participate as a group, with the instructor leading modeling sessions. This applies to the strategic modeling workshop, for example. A strategic model is progressively developed, then analyzed and processed by software. It is then refined based on the expertise of the attendees. This is discussed further in Chapter 16.

This chapter has covered the various tasks that must be undertaken in starting the project. These are summarized in Box 15.1.

Box 15.1
Starting the project

Identify project area

Define the project scope in terms of those business units to be included and those to be excluded from the project. These delineate the boundaries so the project does not later expand to cover areas that are not relevant at this time. Establish project priorities based on identified policies, goals, objectives, concerns and issues. Set project objectives, which define *what* is to be achieved, the deliverables and time for completion.

Select project software

Select software that can automatically derive implementation plans from a data model and automatically plot data maps in implementation sequence. Defined data should be capable of being directly linked to the strategic plan. Allocate clerical or data administration staff resources to use this software. Install all hardware and software prior to the start of the project.

Establish initial project plan

Develop an initial project plan based on estimates in Table 15.2. Each strategic, tactical or operations area contains around 30–40 entities and will take 1–2 months.

A *typical* project will have 50–90 strategic entities and 500–700 tactical entities. This covers 80% of organizations regardless of their size or turnover. It represents three strategic areas and four potentially concurrent tactical areas in each strategic area. If one strategic team and four tactical teams are allocated, the total project duration will be approximately six months. With only one tactical team, the project duration will expand to 22–28 months.

A *simple* project with only one business unit operating in a small industry niche may have 50–80 strategic entities and 300–800

Box 15.1 (cont.)
Starting the project

---

tactical entities. This represents two strategic areas and three concurrent tactical areas in each strategic area. If only one strategic team and two tactical teams are used, total project duration will be around 12 months. With one tactical team, the duration will be 24 months.

A *complex* project is one involving an organization with several diverse businesses. It may contain perhaps 200 strategic entities and more than 1200 tactical entities. This may be broken down into two concurrent, typical projects with durations indicated earlier.

Establish project teams

The project teams will be made up of approximately 80% managers and expert users; that is, those individuals with the greatest expert knowledge of the project area. Allocation of less experienced, but more available, users without this expertise must be resisted. The remaining team members will be drawn from the data administration or analyst staff of the DP department.

The project scope and total project duration define the project size. They determine the number of concurrent project teams required. Each project team will comprise up to six people. The criterion is quality, not quantity. For a more complex project of business units in different industry or market segments, several smaller, concurrent projects should be established. Total project duration is dependent on the number of concurrent project teams established.

Set project budget and funding

The project budget should include not only the time, and hence cost, of full-time and part-time project team members and administrative staff, but also required hardware and software support. The number and cost of training workshops and the cost of consulting support should also be budgeted. For an average project, each separate team will require an average of five days of quality assurance consulting support per month,

(cont'd)

Box 15.1 (cont.)
Starting the project

over a period of six months. A project with four concurrent, interacting project teams needs 20 days consulting support per month. Six concurrent project teams will require two consultants full-time because of project interaction.

Schedule information engineering workshops

All full-time and part-time project team members are trained in information engineering. This is presented in five-day strategic modeling, tactical modeling or operations modeling workshops, each with up to 12 people. Techniques learned are applied using the project as a case study. This begins the project. It expands immediately following the workshop to focus on priority areas.

CHAPTER 16

Preparing for the Project

In Chapters 10–13, we discussed the development of strategic statements used as input to the project. In Chapter 15, we established the project scope, defined an initial project plan, considered the allocation of project teams and project funding, and outlined the importance of information engineering workshops. This chapter covers preparation for the project.

16.1 | PROJECT STEPS

A number of steps are involved in an information engineering project, as illustrated in Figure 16.1. Each of these steps involves a number of tasks, which are discussed in this and subsequent chapters:

- Preparing for modeling.
- Conducting modeling sessions.
- Processing models.
- Conducting refinement sessions.
- Processing refined models.

The first two steps are discussed in both this chapter and Chapter 17. The remaining steps depend on the selected software; the approach used for processing; whether automatic strategic analysis is carried out; and refinement opportunities based on that strategic analysis. Many available software products are designed for use by DP analysts, rather than business experts. Their potential for automatic strategic analysis is

259

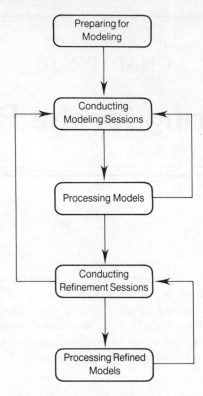

Figure 16.1 The steps of modeling and refinement.

therefore severely limited. The characteristics of software for automated information engineering are discussed in Part Four.

Figure 16.1 illustrates the iteration between modeling sessions and processing. Data defined in modeling sessions is automatically analyzed by software to identify alternative strategies. This helps identify potential data to be addressed. Similarly, data covered in refinement sessions is further analyzed to identify other data. This refinement may lead to further modeling.

We will now discuss the first step of modeling. This relates to preparation carried out after the project scope, but prior to starting any of the strategic, tactical or operations modeling stages of a project.

16.2 | PREPARING FOR MODELING

We saw in Chapter 15 that the project scope may involve one or several project areas. Each area should be addressed to determine the modeling

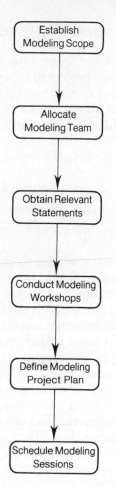

Figure 16.2 Modeling preparation tasks.

scope for that area. This is the first preparation task for modeling. The modeling preparation tasks are as follows (see Figure 16.2):

- Establish modeling scope.
- Allocate modeling team.
- Obtain relevant statements.
- Conduct modeling workshops.
- Define modeling project plan.
- Schedule modeling sessions.

16.2.1   Establish modeling scope

We will refer to the part of the organization covered by the modeling scope as the **project area**. Each project area represents a separate project. The project scope will involve one, or more, **strategic areas**. As we saw in Chapter 15, each strategic area includes a number of **tactical areas** and also **operations areas**. We will use this terminology to distinguish between them.

A strategic area may comprise:

- A division, branch or section of a government department.
- A company, business unit or division of a conglomerate.
- A division, department, branch or functional area of a company.

It is important initially to establish the scope of each strategic area (see Figure 16.2). This is defined in part by the strategic statements, but also from the organization chart, which identifies the management involved. For example, if the project scope involves the whole organization, then the strategic area scope includes senior management of the enterprise. On the other hand, if the project scope addresses only selected business units within the organization, then the scope involves senior managers only from those parts of the business.

There will be specific parts of a project area that are vital to its effective operation; there will be other parts that are ancillary. The strategic area scope identifies those areas that are essential and those that are less important. These latter areas may be excluded from the relevant modeling stage initially.

16.2.2   Allocate modeling team

During the project scope (Chapter 15), the project team is broadly defined according to the overall project plan. This plan defines the anticipated project duration and the likely number of concurrent strategic and tactical teams that could be supported. This step now allocates staff specifically to each modeling team (see Figure 16.2).

The selection of the strategic team is vital to the overall success of the project. Staff allocated to this team must either have direct management responsibility or extensive experience in the strategic area. This includes the senior managers responsible for the area, as well as managers who report to them and who are responsible for various business units or functional areas within it. It also includes staff who are considered experts in their area of the business. We will call these people the **senior experts**.

Selection of the right people is paramount. The project will decide what information will be provided to that manager in the future. The manager will likely assert that only he can participate, thereby eliminating his senior experts as well as DP staff. The correct approach is to include the manager and his senior experts – to a total of no more than five people. Managers and experts should be allocated to the project team so that together they have 80%–90% of the strategic management knowledge of their area of the business. One DP analyst or data administrator is also included in the team, for project management and for processing defined strategic data. This brings the total size of the strategic project team to no more than six people.

Each team member will apply strategic modeling techniques: the experts identify data fundamental to the strategic area; the manager evaluates the identified data, provides direction, sets priorities and decides the information needed for the future; the DP member uses the results of processing and derived implementation phase data maps for project planning.

Having allocated people to the project team, the next task (see Figure 16.2) is to obtain the relevant statements. These form the input to strategic modeling.

16.2.3   Obtain relevant statements

The relevant statements may come from informal strategic planning, as described in Chapters 11 and 12, or they may be generated by relevant managers and the project team completing the management questionnaire, as described in Chapter 13, or they may come from operations modeling documentation, such as existing systems or packages, source documents, report and screen formats, or file and record formats. These provide input to the stages of strategic, tactical and operations modeling.

Following definition of the modeling scope, appointment of people to the strategic team and documentation of the strategic statements, the team then attends the first workshop, the strategic modeling workshop.

16.2.4   Conduct modeling workshops

There are two alternative approaches that may be adopted by management during a strategic modeling project. These are:

- Active management participation.
- Passive management participation.

Active management participation is more effective, as managers identify the information they need to carry out their responsibilities. They directly participate in strategic modeling and attend a strategic modeling workshop (see Chapter 15). As management set directions for the future, it is therefore imperative that they participate actively.

If managers cannot attend the workshop, they can only participate passively. This, however, requires more of their time and the result is substantially less. Often, a subordinate acts as the manager's proxy. But this subordinate, while expert in the strategic area, may not be aware of the manager's information needs and may never ask the questions that clarify those needs. The result is the definition only of current information needs, based on presently identified issues or problems. It rarely extends to information needed for the future.

16.2.5   Define modeling project plan

Data defined in the workshop leads to a more detailed project plan for strategic, tactical and operations modeling. Using data maps, management identify priority areas. In modeling sessions, the project team focuses first on these areas and defines additional data needed to clarify issues and directions. In refinement sessions, the team addresses identified concerns, issues, policies, goals, objectives and strategies, and the strategic model grows. As it evolves, by considering further strategies, the software derives updated implementation phase data maps and the strategic project plan is further refined. Alternative strategic directions may be established and the strategic statements are changed to reflect these new directions. These statements are stored in a strategic planning dictionary (see Part Four) and are linked by software to strategic data in the model that supports achievement of those statements. The design dictionary and the strategic planning dictionary both grow during this period of strategic modeling and refinement, and both dictionaries are linked together to ensure that the data and statements support each other.

This period of strategic modeling and refinement is the most volatile period of the analysis phase. It is highly iterative, as shown in Figure 16.1. It requires expert software to analyze the identified data and derive updated implementation phase data maps. Strategic modeling and refinement take one to two months per strategic area (see Figure 15.6). At the end of this time, around 50–90 strategic entities will have been identified. The refined strategic statements present a clear, agreed strategic plan.

Strategic modeling and refinement is seen by management as computer-aided strategic planning (CASP). They gain many benefits from this interactive strategic planning: they obtain immediate feedback; they can test alternative strategies; they can identify new opportunities and discuss possibilities; and they see the strategic plan evolve under their direction along tight, clearly observed paths, and a clear return on investment is achieved.

Where software is not available for automatic strategic analysis, and for automatically deriving project plans, the project progresses in a disorganized way, and can take nine months or even longer. There is no direction or no clear purpose. After three months, management become concerned. After four months, there is no clear way through the mess. After five months, no end is in sight and management do not attend scheduled sessions, although their input is vital. After six months, the project starts to self-destruct. If fortunate, it dies quietly, or the team is ceremoniously dismissed! In such cases, an opportunity is lost which may never present itself again with the same management.

16.2.6   Schedule modeling sessions

The strategic modeling stage, as we have seen, extends over one to two months for each strategic area. During this period, modeling and refinement sessions involve a total of two to three weeks of a manager's time. This time can be reduced if spent away from the organization, such as on a residential basis at a hotel. This avoids interruptions for day-to-day problems which demand management action. Two residential intensive planning meetings (perhaps three), each of three days' duration with at least a week between for processing defined data, are most productive. If residential meetings cannot be used, regular modeling sessions must be scheduled. Each session is three hours and three sessions are typically scheduled per week.

Three sessions per week allows entry, processing and analysis of data defined at one session to be completed by the next session. This is essential to maintain continuity and impetus. But these sessions can be conducted more frequently, if required to reduce the duration of the strategic modeling stage. If conducted daily (perhaps each morning), processing can be completed each afternoon, but only if sufficient computer access is available. Several processing tasks must be carried out concurrently.

Strategic refinement sessions are similarly scheduled. Once the strategic data has been identified, entered and processed, it can be reviewed in refinement sessions. Strategic directions are refined iteratively. Management progresses rapidly through evolutions of strategic planning thought, with a clear definition emerging of information needed for decision making now and in the future.

Managers who did not attend the strategic modeling workshop participate passively in modeling and refinement sessions. The total time they must spend is greater and the quality of the data they define is less because of their lack of understanding. They will still participate in three sessions per week of at least three hours, but strategic modeling and refinement, instead of taking one to two months, may extend over an elapsed period of six months. This is too long. Consequently, the project will lose impetus and will have a high potential for failure.

With untrained managers, the project team normalizes data between sessions. It presents the results of business normalization to management for resolution at the next session. In such cases, strategic refinement rarely occurs, management receive little feedback and the result is less effective. Management contribute passively, led only by questions from the project team, rather than their own insight. This takes longer and is less precise than with active participation, but in some organizations it is the only alternative possible.

The steps to prepare for modeling are summarized in Box 16.1. The conduct of modeling sessions is discussed in the next chapter, in relation to an organizational example.

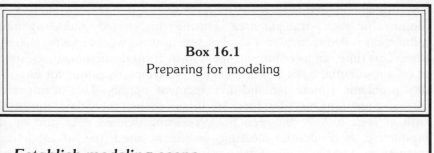

Box 16.1
Preparing for modeling

Establish modeling scope

The scope of each strategic area is defined in part by the strategic statements, but also from the organization chart. A strategic area may comprise: a division, branch or section of a government department; a division, department, branch or functional area of a company; a company, business unit or division of a conglomerate. Each strategic area represents a strategic modeling project.

Allocate modeling team

The strategic modeling project team comprises senior managers and senior experienced staff from the strategic area. These people are selected so that between them they have a detailed understanding of at least 80%–90% of management information needs, and associated data from which it is derived, in their area of responsibility.

Obtain relevant statements

The strategic team obtains, or documents itself, relevant strategic statements relating to the strategic area. These statements are gathered by distribution of the management questionnaire. Goal analysis may be carried out for refinement of the questionnaire responses.

Box 16.1 (cont.)
Preparing for modeling

Conduct modeling workshops

The strategic modeling workshop introduces strategic modeling and refinement, using the management questionnaire responses. Later workshops are conducted according to the project plan derived automatically from the data model at each stage of its development.

Define modeling project plan

Data defined during the strategic modeling workshop is analyzed by software to derive a project plan. Implementation phase data maps are automatically derived and plotted. These maps establish a firm project plan for modeling and refinement sessions. Using this software, strategic modeling and refinement take one to two months per strategic area. Without this software capability, strategic modeling may take nine months, or longer.

Schedule modeling sessions

Modeling sessions are scheduled in one of two alternative ways: intensive planning meetings on a residential basis at a hotel – two residential meetings (perhaps three), each of three days, are needed; or strategic modeling sessions of three hours each, with three to five sessions per week. Strategic refinement sessions are similarly scheduled.

CHAPTER 17

Conducting Modeling Sessions

This chapter discusses the preparation necessary for modeling sessions. It presents the steps that are used to discover, clarify and then represent strategic, tactical and operational data. It draws on the data modeling principles presented in Part Two, using an example to illustrate the application of these principles at each step. It shows the amount of definition necessary for subsequent processing and refinement. The processing of the data model defined in this chapter is then covered in Chapter 21.

17.1 MODELING SESSION PREPARATION

The structure and conduct of modeling sessions is important if the maximum input is to be obtained. Three catalysts are necessary for these sessions: the first catalyst is the relevant strategic, tactical or operational statements; the second is active management participation; the third is the leader of the modeling sessions.

17.1.1 The first catalyst – relevant statements

The mission statement is a catalyst for strategic modeling: it identifies data fundamental to the overall existence and operation of the strategic project area. Issues, which help identify problems, and policies, goals and objectives also provide input to strategic modeling (see Chapter 16). Markets, products and services, and channels statements give input for tactical modeling. Documentation of existing systems or packages is input to operations modeling. These statements are obtained during preparation for modeling (see Chapter 16). The use of some of these statements as catalysts is discussed in this chapter.

Modeling and refinement sessions are ideally carried out with the active participation of management and expert users from the project area. This is the second catalyst for modeling success.

17.1.2 The second catalyst – active management participation

Managers and expert users who participate in modeling and refinement sessions should have, between them, a detailed understanding of some 80%–90% of the data and activities of the relevant project area. They should be aware of planned future changes, as they will evaluate alternatives for the future which emerge through modeling. They should therefore attend the relevant information engineering workshops; this is active management participation.

For passive management participation, the criterion of 80%–90% understanding of the relevant project area is unlikely to be achieved. These managers do not participate directly; rather, less experienced subordinates attend the workshops in their place (see Section 16.2.4).

17.1.3 The third catalyst – the session leader

Modeling and refinement sessions bring together managers and their expert staff to plan for the future. These people may know each other very well, but they may rarely consider the future during day-to-day activity. The management hierarchy present at these sessions may inhibit lower-level individuals from expressing their opinion; from providing input to strategic, tactical and operations modeling. Similarly, internal politics and the desire to protect 'empires' may act as inhibitors to a free flow of ideas and discussions. These represent constraints to thought and, if not tackled directly, they inhibit identification of data and options that emerge during the sessions. In the worst case, they can totally destroy the chance of achieving a worthwhile result.

To avoid these problems, a session leader is nominated to provide formal control over the sessions. This leader must be objective and impartial. Ideally, he should come from outside the project area: his comments are then more likely to be accepted as objective. The individual should be of a management status and authority, so that his opinions are respected, but not of such a level that any suggestions are taken as law. He should be able to communicate well and to motivate people – a catalyst to a free flow of ideas and discussion. The most effective session leader is often an external consultant: one who has had extensive experience in leading strategic, tactical and operations modeling sessions for other organizations, and who will be impartial.

17.1.4   Tools and materials

Management questionnaire responses

The session commences with all individuals having copies of the strategic statements and summaries of the management questionnaire responses (see Chapter 13). These are generally the same people who prepared those statements.

White boards

At least two large white boards are needed, with color marking pens that can be wiped off with a rag. Modeling involves much discussion, represented in the form of data maps and entity lists on the white boards. These maps and entity lists change many times before all present agree on their content. If available, an electronic white board is invaluable. This is used to make paper copies of white board documentation, used for later processing of defined data by software.

Flip chart pads

If white boards are not available, agreed data is written on flip chart paper (typically 1 m^2). This allows reference by attendees to previously defined data when considering other data. Alternatively, electronic white board copies of relevant material are distributed to all session attendees.

Session secretary

A session secretary is needed: to record details of any data requiring further resolution; to record the emerging data models from the white boards or flip charts, if an electronic white board is not used; to prepare data input for entry to software; and to document actions to be carried out before the next session.

With these tools and materials, and active participation by management and senior experts from the project area, the modeling session can begin. As indicated in earlier chapters, each session is typically scheduled for three hours, ideally with three or more scheduled sessions per week.

17.2 | CONDUCTING A MODELING SESSION

The steps followed in a modeling session are illustrated in Figure 17.1. The session examines the relevant statements to identify the data needed for reference. This data is fundamental to the session focus. For example, a strategic modeling session concentrates on data needed to carry out the strategic area mission; a tactical modeling session concentrates on relevant markets, products and services, or channels of the tactical area;

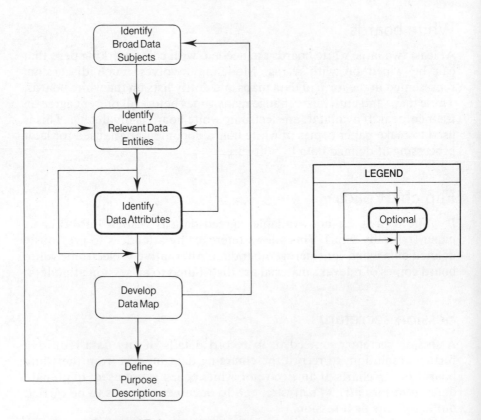

Figure 17.1 The steps followed in a modeling session.

operations modeling addresses relevant source documents, report and screen formats, and file and record formats for the operational area. The output from a modeling session is a data model. This comprises a data map and entity list of the relevant data (see Part Two).

17.2.1 Identify broad data subjects

Figure 17.1 indicates that the starting point is to identify data subjects. This is particularly applicable to strategic modeling. Data subjects are broad data terms: they may represent one or several data entities. They are also temporary; that is, they clarify initial thinking to identify specific entities. For tactical and operations modeling, data subjects represent strategic data that is subsequently normalized to tactical and operational levels of detail.

Strategic modeling identifies data at the highest level in the strategic area. Strategic data often represents summary data to assist management in decision making. Much of the data already exists as summary reports, which contain information derived from tactical and operational data at lower levels in the organization. Existing or desired management reports, as well as relevant strategic statements, provide useful input to identify data subjects during strategic modeling. This leads to the definition of strategic and tactical entities used to generate the information required in those reports.

In this chapter, we will use some of the strategic statements as a catalyst for strategic modeling based on a hypothetical company example. The principles that are introduced also apply to tactical and operations modeling, using the relevant statements for each of these stages.

An example of a strategic modeling session

The session leader examines, with all attendees, the strategic area mission statement to identify broad data subjects. These are suggested by nouns within the statement – either explicitly included or implied. Consider the following hypothetical mission statement for a large retail department store:

> '*We exist to serve our customers in a variety of markets, with high quality products offered at reasonable prices.*'

This organization is not a discount store, nor is it exclusive. It is a middle-of-the-road store that competes on quality. It charges for quality: not an excessive price, but 'reasonable'. Let us for the moment put aside any question of how we would define 'reasonable' and consider instead how to use the mission statement as a catalyst for identifying strategic data.

A reference in the mission statement to a particular market, or markets, is a data subject. It may later be decomposed into several data entities which represent those markets and the customers who belong to each market segment. Thus, the implied term 'market segment' would be identified as a strategic data subject: MARKET SEGMENT. This is written on the white board by the session leader.

Within the data subject MARKET SEGMENT, the session attendees first identify the existing and possible future market segments that support the mission These are listed under the data subject heading: MARKET SEGMENT. The retail store may address three market segments, such as CLOTHING, FURNITURE and APPLIANCE. At this point, the white board will appear as follows:

```
MARKET SEGMENT
   CLOTHING
   FURNITURE
   APPLIANCE
```

The word 'customers' appears in the mission statement. Next, the types of customers belonging to market segments are listed under the data subject heading: CUSTOMER. There may be several types of customers for the CLOTHING market segment. These are CHILDREN, WOMEN, MEN and FASHION (for high-fashion clothing). For the FURNITURE and APPLIANCE segments, there may be several common customer types: NEWLY-MARRIED (for newly married couples establishing their first home) or FAMILY (for established families buying additional furniture or appliances for the home). Each customer type is listed in relation to the appropriate market segment, as follows, to focus attention on various markets:

```
MARKET SEGMENT    CUSTOMER
   CLOTHING          CHILDREN
                     WOMEN
                     MEN
                     FASHION

   FURNITURE         FAMILY
                     NEWLY-MARRIED

   APPLIANCE         FAMILY
                     NEWLY-MARRIED
```

This can continue further to identify broad product or service types that address the needs of different customer types in the market segments, as shown in the following for the FURNITURE and APPLIANCE segments:

CUSTOMER	MARKET SEGMENT	PRODUCT
FAMILY	FURNITURE	BEDROOM
		KITCHEN
		LOUNGE ROOM
	APPLIANCE	LAUNDRY
		KITCHEN
		TELEVISION
		STEREO PLAYER
		HOME COMPUTER
NEWLY-MARRIED	FURNITURE	BEDROOM
		KITCHEN
		LOUNGE ROOM
	APPLIANCE	LAUNDRY
		KITCHEN
		TELEVISION

Only some examples of the different types of products or services are identified at this point, rather than an exhaustive list. There is a temptation to go into too much detail. However, the objective is to list examples only to act as a catalyst for thought prior to the next step. Note here that the products and services have been grouped with the relevant market segment, as some customers belong to more than one market segment.

For a strategic area within a larger organization, its markets may be other parts of the organization itself. Therefore, the data subject MARKET SEGMENT may include other parts of the organization which receive outputs (products, services or reports) produced by the strategic area. Once again, do not get carried away by listing too many instances of product or service types, or customer types, or market segments. This detail comes with the next step.

17.2.2   Identify relevant data entities

As indicated in Figure 17.1, each data subject is used to identify data entities. This step focuses on defining key attributes that uniquely identify the subject. If one or several key attributes can be readily identified, the data subject is potentially an entity. If other non-key data attributes suggest themselves, the entity is confirmed. However, these non-key attributes are not defined at this point – they are left until later. For example, in our hypothetical example, MARKET SEGMENT is a potential entity, with *market segement#* as a primary key.

As entities and their key attributes emerge, they are written on the white board in entity list format (see Part Two): entities are written in capitals; attributes are written in lower case. Both use unique, singular names. Key attributes are indicated with a # appended to the end of the name while primary keys are underlined. Those attributes that occur many times within an entity are surrounded by double left and right parentheses to indicate that they are repeating group attributes. Hence:

MARKET SEGMENT   (Market segment#,

The different types of market segments CLOTHING, FURNITURE and APPLIANCE are potential entities. Each entity is given a unique name, in the singular. Because each is a type of market segment, it is given the same primary key as used by MARKET SEGMENT – that is, *market segment#*. Additionally MARKET SEGMENT is given a foreign key of *market segment type#* because of the existence of different types of market segment. These new keys are shown in boldface with the new entity MARKET SEGMENT TYPE, also in boldface, as follows:

MARKET SEGMENT TYPE   **(Market segment type#,**

MARKET SEGMENT   (Market segment#, **market segment type#,**

CLOTHING MARKET   **(Market segment#,**

FURNITURE MARKET   **(Market segment#,**

APPLIANCE MARKET   **(Market segment#,**

It is now apparent that the entities CLOTHING MARKET, FURNITURE MARKET and APPLIANCE MARKET are fourth business normal form (4BNF) MARKET SEGMENT entities, while MARKET SEGMENT is third business normal form (3BNF). At this point you may wish to review 3BNF and 4BNF in Chapters 7–9.

We have not yet fully confirmed these entities. Strategic modeling focuses only on data of interest to management of the strategic area. More detailed data is left for later tactical and operations modeling. Only the managers can decide if we are moving to too much detail in identifying, at this early stage, these 4BNF entities. We can ask what they need to know about specific market segments. Their response may be:

'*We want total sales and profit this month for each segment, with comparisons against the same month last year, and comparisons against sales and profit quotas set for each segment.*'

We will consider the detailed information suggested from this statement in the next section. For the present, we will examine the implications behind their comment.

The managers want common information across segments, for sales and profitability comparisons of each segment with other segments. They do not appear to be interested in details unique to (say) the clothing market as distinct from the furniture market or appliance market. This detail may be of interest only at a lower management level. Their lack of interest in information unique to each segment suggests we have already moved to tactical detail with these managers by listing market segment types. We will therefore only note their existence here. We will address them in tactical modeling, but omit them from further definition at this stage. We will not include them in the strategic entity list unless we find strategic details unique to one market segment, and not to the others.

Foreign key attributes that identify related information are added to the entity list. The related entities are also added to the list. For example, in our customer type data subjects list given earlier, which lists customers for each market segment, some customers appear in more than one market segment. Each customer has a unique customer number. The foreign key *customer number#* is thus included in MARKET SEGMENT. This indicates the presence of additional entities: CUSTOMER and CUSTOMER TYPE. Because there are many customers in a market segment, *customer number#* is included in MARKET SEGMENT as a repeating foreign key, shown with double parentheses and in boldface in the following. Similarly, a customer may belong to more than one market segment: *market segment#* therefore is also a repeating foreign key in CUSTOMER.

MARKET SEGMENT TYPE	(Market segment type#,
MARKET SEGMENT	(Market segment#, market segment type#, **((customer number#))**,
CUSTOMER TYPE	(Customer type#,
CUSTOMER	(Customer number#, customer type#, **((market segment#))**,

Market segments and their customers are interested in different products. A repeating foreign key of *product number#* should thus be added to MARKET SEGMENT. This indicates that the entities PRODUCT TYPE and PRODUCT should also be added, as shown in boldface. Furthermore, *market segment#* is added as a repeating foreign key in PRODUCT, as illustrated in the following:

MARKET SEGMENT TYPE	(Market segment type#,
MARKET SEGMENT	(Market segment#, market segment type#, (customer number#)), **((product number#))**,
CUSTOMER TYPE	(Customer type#,
CUSTOMER	(Customer number#, customer type#, ((market segment#)),
PRODUCT TYPE	(Product type#,
PRODUCT	(Product number#, product type#, **((market segment#))**,

We have focused so far on the identification of primary and foreign key attributes to uncover potential data entities. We can now start to define some non-key data attributes for these entities. This is an optional step for strategic modeling, but is mandatory for tactical and operations modeling.

17.2.3 Identify data attributes

The definition of data entities continues, now by identifying non-key data attributes as shown in Figure 17.1. As already indicated, this step is optional for strategic modeling. The initial definition of strategic attributes is not essential for the identification of strategic entities. Attribute definition should be bypassed during strategic modeling. Instead, software used first should be to identify potential strategic, tactical and operational systems, as described in Chapter 21. This enables management to establish initial priorities for the development of important systems. Only then are detailed non-key attributes defined for those priority systems.

The identification of data attributes is always carried out for tactical and operations modeling. These stages identify relevant levels of non-key attribute detail based on defined management priorities after strategic modeling. It is at this point that non-key attributes which were ignored at the strategic modeling stage are eventually defined.

However, management priorities may dictate that certain strategic systems be delivered early. These priority strategic systems can initially be refined by the use of software that applies strategic analysis (see Chapter 21). Strategic analysis, carried out by software, examines defined strategies set by management in the context of an established strategic model. The software automatically identifies alternative strategies that may have been missed by management. Some strategic attributes may therefore need to be defined at this time. Normally, however, these strategic attributes would be left for definition during the tactical and operations modeling stages.

We will assume this situation exists: that management require priority strategic systems to be implemented early. We will therefore discuss the early definition of strategic attributes in this section. This will also serve to illustrate the principles used for definition of non-key attributes in tactical and operations modeling.

Early definition of strategic attributes

Strategic attributes are non-key attributes. Descriptive attributes may be noted, such as *market segment name* and *market segment type description*. Other attributes emerge that indicate summary information aggregated from more detailed tactical data. These are strategic attributes of particular interest to management, such as the earlier statement made by them in relation to market segment information. This indicates that the managers are particularly interested in the {*segment total sales revenue this month* } and {*segment nett profit this month* } for each market segment. These are derived non-key attributes that imply time dependency: they suggest the need for an additional primary key *period#*, where a period may be any duration of interest to management – a week, month or year.

Management want to compare this month's results against sales and profit quota targets for the month. This also implies comparison with quota achievement for the year to date (YTD) – perhaps expressed as a percentage of the target achievement. This suggests derived attributes of: {*segment sales quota this month%*}, {*segment sales quota YTD%*}, {*segment profit quota this month%*} and {*segment profit quota YTD%*}. It also indicates additional entities of QUOTA and QUOTA TYPE for different types of quotas, with repeating foreign keys of *quota number#* in MARKET SEGMENT and *market segment#* in QUOTA.

Management are also interested in performance for the same period last year. This suggests MARKET SEGMENT attributes of: {*segment sales last year*}, {*segment profit last year*}.

The entity list to this point for MARKET SEGMENT, QUOTA and QUOTA TYPE, showing any new changes in boldface, is as follows:

QUOTA TYPE	**(Quota type#**, quota type description,
QUOTA	**(Quota number#**, **period#**, quota type#, quota amount, ((market segment#)),
MARKET SEGMENT TYPE	(Market segment type#, **market segment type description.**
MARKET SEGMENT	(Market segment#, period#, market segment type#, ((customer number#)), ((product number#)), **((quota number#)), market segment name, {segment total revenue this month}, {segment net profit this month}, {segment sales quota this month%}, {segment sales quota YTD%}, {segment profit quota this month%}, {segment profit quota YTD%}, {segment sales last year}, {segment profit last year{,**

At this stage, it is not important to identify all attributes. Attributes of a more detailed nature are suggested by including only a group attribute, surrounded by single left and right parentheses. For the CUSTOMER entity, group attributes of (*account details*) and (*credit details*) are noted. This indicates the existence of more detailed tactical attributes that can be identified during tactical modeling.

The definition of strategic attributes up to this point has prompted further discussion of more detailed operational information that the managers cannot presently easily obtain, but would like:

'We need to evaluate customers in each market segment in terms of the revenue generated by their purchases, and their payment history. We would like to encourage those customers who pay promptly to buy more, so we want to see which products they prefer.'

This suggests detailed CUSTOMER attributes at the operational level. Normally, these would not be defined until the tactical or operations modeling stages. However, we will define them here, so that we can see some of the additional detail that does arise from tactical and operations modeling.

Management are interested in {*customer sales revenue this month*} for each customer. *Period#* is thus a primary key for the CUSTOMER entity. It indicates the need for customer history. Management want attributes of {*customer outstanding account balance*} and {*customer actual payment period*} (time taken to pay an outstanding account balance). Following this further for different products, they want {*product total sales this month*}, and {*product total sales this month last year*}, as well as the {*product average order value*} for each product. *Period#* is also a primary key for the PRODUCT entity. The strategic entity list to this point, with new changes again shown in boldface, is as follows:

QUOTA TYPE	(Quota type#, quota type description,
QUOTA	(Quota period#, quota amount, quota type#, ((market segment#)),
MARKET SEGMENT TYPE	(Market segment type#, market segment type description,
MARKET SEGMENT	(Market segment#, period#, market segment type#, ((customer number#)), ((product number#)), ((quota number#)), market segment name, {segment total revenue this month}, {segment nett profit this month}, {segment sales quota this month%}, {segment sales quota YTD%}, {segment profit quota this month%}, {segment profit quota YTD%}, {segment sales last year}, {segment profit last year}.
CUSTOMER TYPE	(Customer type#, **customer type description,**
CUSTOMER	(Customer number#, **period#,** customer type#, ((market segment#)), **(customer account details), (customer credit details), {customer sales revenue this month}, {customer outstanding account balance}, {customer actual payment period},**
PRODUCT TYPE	(Product type#, **product type description,**
PRODUCT	(Product number#, **period#,** product type#, ((market segment#)), **{product total sales this month}, {product total sales this month last year}, {product average order value},**

By including *period#* as part of a compound primary key for the entities above, an extra opportunity presents itself: the entity list allows a record to be kept of historical activity. Each occurrence of the entity for a different period indicates the values that were determined in that period. The strategic entity list thus represents:

- Market segment sales and profit history.
- Market segment quota performance history.
- Customer sales and payment history.
- Product sales history.

This historical data is of vital strategic interest. It indicates performance over time. Examples of a variety of reports can be used to illustrate the potential of these strategic attributes. For instance, consider the following strategic attributes:

MARKET SEGMENT   (market segment#, period#,

   ...

   {segment total revenue this month},...., {segment sales last year}, ...,

These lead to the presentation of sales information either in report or graphical form. Table 17.1 illustrates a typical sales report produced from this MARKET SEGMENT entity for the clothing market segment, comparing sales this period with sales for the same period last year. This report may also be presented to management in a graphical form, such as the sales performance graph in Figure 17.2. This figure plots sales revenue over a number of periods for the clothing market segment this year, compared to the same period last year. Each value for a time period is a representation of a single occurrence of that market segment for the period. Figure 17.2 clearly indicates that while sales increased steadily

Table 17.1 Typical sales report produced from the MARKET SEGMENT attributes, showing sales this period compared with that period last year, for the clothing segment.

Period	Sales This Period	Sales Last Year
January	185 000	165 000
February	198 000	167 000
March	194 000	170 000
April	212 000	173 000
May	208 000	174 000
June	202 000	173 000
July	199 000	176 000
August	193 000	178 000

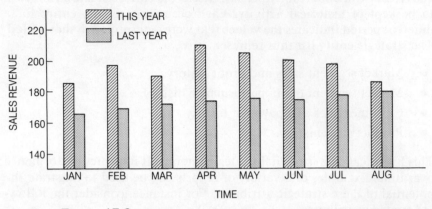

Figure 17.2 Graphical presentation of strategic attributes.

last year and for the first part of this year, clothing sales now seem to be in decline.

Continuing the example further, this graphical representation allows comparisons to be made of historical performance in other market segments, as shown in Figure 17.3. This shows that, while clothing increased, then declined this year, the furniture market has been in steady decline for all of the year. Contrast this with the appliance market, which has shown a steady increase in sales revenue over this same period.

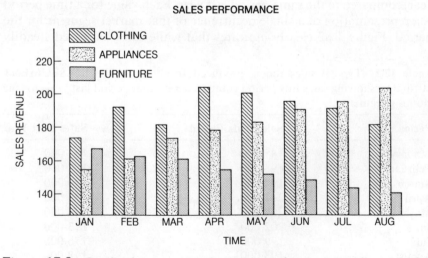

Figure 17.3 Graphical comparison of strategic attributes across different market segments.

Similar comparisons can be made of profit, sales quota performance, average customer sales revenue or average product order value. These strategic attributes address management's interest. They lead to other opportunities for further analysis and objectives setting. The definition of strategic attributes from objectives is normally carried out after strategic modeling, as part of strategic objectives modeling. However, we will illustrate some of the principles here.

Identification of strategic attributes from objectives

Each of the separate data entities defined for a data subject is expanded in turn, iterating through the definition of entities and then attributes. While strategic data subjects and entities are suggested from the mission statement, strategic attributes are identified from management goals and objectives, using strategic objectives modeling principles as introduced here. They may be nominated indirectly by session attendees, initially based on their need for specific reports, summaries or graphs, and their detailed knowledge of the strategic area, as we have seen here. However, these information needs should be expressed as specific goals and objectives, such as in the example of strategic objectives modeling which follows:

Goal 1

To increase revenue and profit from each market segment at an annual rate that exceeds the segment growth rate by at least 5% pa while maintaining our profit margin of at least 40% and profit growth of 10% pa.

Objectives

(1) *Each market segment will be managed to achieve an increase in revenue each year at least 5% greater than the annual growth of the market segment.*

(2) *Each market segment will be managed to achieve a minimum profit margin of 40% over revenue.*

(3) *Each market segment will be managed to achieve an annual profit growth rate of 10%.*

In Chapter 11, we saw that goals and objectives have three characteristics: a measure, a level and time. For example, the measure of objective 1 is '*increase in revenue*'; the level is '*at least 5% greater than the annual growth of the market segment*'; the time is '*each year*'. The measure of objective 2 is '*minimum profit margin over revenue*'; its level is '*40%*'; its time is implied as '*each year*'.

Chapter 11 also showed us that goals and objectives relate directly to attributes. They enable us to identify attributes directly. For example, to calculate '*increase in revenue*' for objective 1, we need attributes of {*segment total revenue this month*} and {*segment total revenue last year*}. Similarly, the measure of '*minimum profit margin over revenue*' for objective 2 needs attributes of {*segment total revenue this month*} and {*segment nett profit this month*}. Finally, the measure for objective 3 of '*annual profit growth rate*' needs attributes of {*segment nett profit this month*} and {*segment nett profit last year*}. All three objectives are time based and so need a primary key of <u>*period#*</u>.

These attributes have already been defined in MARKET SEGMENT, but with slightly different names: {*segment total revenue this month*}, {*segment nett profit this month*}, {*segment sales last year*}, {*segment profit last year*}. The latter two attributes in fact relate to {*segment total revenue last year*} and {*segment nett profit last year*} and should therefore be changed, as shown in the entity list at the end of this section. However, these attributes only allow us to determine whether *our* revenue and profit have increased: we cannot determine if this is faster than the annual growth of the market segment. We need to know how the market segment itself is growing. This suggests that we also need information relating to revenue performance of our competitors in each market segment. This brings us to an important principle:

> *The strategic model we have developed so far potentially applies to any retail organization. If each competitive retailer in a segment is also represented, we can find not only the total annual growth of each segment, but also our market share of that segment.*

Our share of each market segment is strategic information vital to senior management. It leads them to establish additional goals and objectives:

Goal 2
To increase market share in those segments that exceed the profit margin and profit growth targets (see goal 1), and reduce market share in any other segments that do not achieve those profit margin and profit growth targets.

Objectives
(1) Each market segment that achieves or exceeds the minimum profit and annual profit growth targets (see objectives 2 and 3 of goal 1) will be managed to increase our share of that segment at least 10% pa relative to our competitors.

(2) Following senior management approval, each market segment that does not achieve the minimum profit and annual profit growth targets (see objectives 2 and 3 of goal 1) will be vacated.

These goals and objectives indicate the need for strategic entities of ORGANIZATION and ORGANIZATION TYPE. They identify in ORGANIZATION a repeating group of attributes: {<u>*organization segment share*</u>}, with a repeating group key of <u>*market segment#*</u>, and a primary key of *organization#*. Further attributes are also identified for MARKET SEGMENT: {*segment total revenue*} and {*segment growth rate*}.

As we have seen in the foregoing, the definition of strategic entities and attributes is essential for a clear identification of information needed by management. The strategic entity list to this point is summarized below:

ORGANIZATION TYPE (<u>Organization type#</u>, organization type description,

ORGANIZATION (<u>**Organization#**</u>, <u>**period#**</u>, **organization name, organization type#, ((market segment#, organization segment share)),**

QUOTA TYPE (<u>Quota type#</u>, quota type description,

QUOTA (<u>Quota#</u>, <u>period#</u>, quota amount, quota type#, ((market segment#)),

MARKET SEGMENT TYPE (<u>Market segment type#</u>, market segment type description,

MARKET SEGMENT (<u>Market segment#</u>, <u>period#</u>, market segment type#, ((customer number#)), ((product number#)), ((quota number#)), market segment name, {segment total revenue this month}, {segment nett profit this month}, {segment sales quota this month%}, {segment sales quota YTD%}, {segment profit quota this month%}, {segment profit quota YTD%}, {**segment total revenue last year**}, {**segment nett profit last year**}, {**segment total revenue**}, {**segment growth rate**},

CUSTOMER TYPE (<u>Customer type#</u>, customer type description,

CUSTOMER (<u>Customer number#</u>, <u>period#</u>, customer type#, (market segment#)), (customer account details), (customer credit details), {customer sales revenue this month}, {customer outstanding account balance}, {customer actual payment period},

PRODUCT TYPE (<u>Product type#</u>, product type description,

PRODUCT (<u>Product number#</u>, <u>period#</u>, product type#, ((market segment#)), {product total sales this month}, {product total sales this month last year}, {product average order value},

Additional entities may be identified during strategic modeling (and also during strategic objectives modeling as we have just seen) and added to the list. The session delves deep into each data subject. A data subject may represent high-level management information, or it may suggest reports or summarized information derived from underlying tactical data entities. Management examine the entities and their attributes written on the white board. They focus on information that may be extracted or derived from entities to achieve the mission and purpose of their area of responsibility.

As each data subject is expanded, additional data subjects may emerge. The mission statement provides a catalyst for management thinking. Eventually, data subjects and data entities emerge more slowly. At this point, a change is necessary. Figure 17.1 indicates that the session moves from data identification mode to data mapping mode.

17.2.4   Develop data map

In Part Two, we discussed the development of a key map from an entity list. We saw that a key map can be developed for entities either in an unnormalized form or progressively normalized to third business normal form and, where appropriate, to fourth and fifth business normal form. At this point, data entities and attributes have been documented in the strategic entity list in an unnormalized form. The data is represented in an unnormalized strategic key map in Figure 17.4. This illustrates strategic data defined by senior management. It shows potential associations between the entity MARKET SEGMENT and each of ORGANIZATION, QUOTA, CUSTOMER and PRODUCT based on foreign keys in MARKET SEGMENT and ORGANIZATION.

The strategic key map in Figure 17.4 is next expanded into a strategic data map, by defining the association lines joining entities as

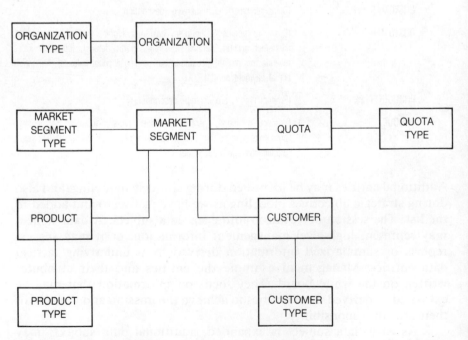

Figure 17.4   Strategic key map from strategic entity list in unnormalized form.

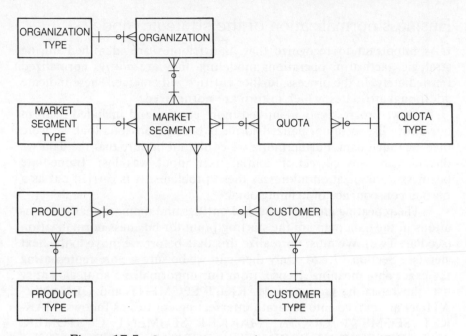

Figure 17.5 Strategic data map from key map in Figure 17.4.

one, many, mandatory or optional, as described in Part Two. This is illustrated in Figure 17.5. This figure shows associations from each of the TYPE entities to its relevant 3BNF principal entity as mandatory one-to-optional becoming mandatory many (see CUSTOMER TYPE to CUSTOMER). This data map also contains unnormalized entities with many-to-many associations. These reflect the repeating foreign keys defined within those entities. For example, the repeating groups of:

ORGANIZATION   (organization#, ..., ((market segment#, ...)), ...)

MARKET SEGMENT   (market segment#, ..., ((customer number#)), ((product number#)), ((quota number#)), ...)

are shown as many-to-many associations between MARKET SEGMENT and the entities ORGANIZATION, QUOTA, CUSTOMER and PRODUCT, based on foreign keys in those entities. Each of these associations is shown as mandatory many-to-optional becoming mandatory many: each has a mandatory reference to one or many market segments of interest to the organization; that market segment may not yet have any customers, but eventually will have at least one customer (product or quota) – the association at that end is optional becoming mandatory one or many.

Business normalization of the strategic model

It is important to recognize that as attributes are identified during strategic, tactical or operations modeling, they are *always* normalized immediately. In the process, further entities will emerge. These indicate additional attributes, which in turn are normalized.

As we progressively identified more entities and included them in our entity list in unnormalized form, it became obvious that we were missing much data. Furthermore, we could not be sure that the data we did identify was correct. Potential user input was lost. Immediate business normalization addresses these problems. It is carried out as a normal consequence of defining data.

The repeating groups in defined entities and many-to-many associations in the data map are the starting point for business normalization (see Part Two). We must normalize this data before we move to the next step (see Section 17.2.5). Only then can we be sure we are representing the exact data meaning. Hence, from our unnormalized strategic entity list, the repeating groups in MARKET SEGMENT and ORGANIZATION are moved into separate intersecting entities as follows: MARKET SEGMENT QUOTA, MARKET SEGMENT CUSTOMER, MARKET SEGMENT PRODUCT and ORGANIZATION MARKET SEGMENT. Relevant attributes are also moved out of MARKET SEGMENT into these entities, as shown in the following normalized entity list:

ORGANIZATION TYPE	(Organization type#, organization type description,
ORGANIZATION	(Organization#, period#, organization name, organization type#,
QUOTA TYPE	(Quota type#, quota type description,
QUOTA	(Quota number#, period#, quota amount, quota type#
MARKET SEGMENT TYPE	(Market sergment type#, market segment type description,
MARKET SEGMENT	(Market segment#, period#, market segment type#, {market segment name}, {segment total revenue this month}, {segment nett profit this month}, {segment total revenue last year}, {segment nett profit last year}, {segment total revenue}, {segment growth rate},
ORGANIZATION MARKET SEGMENT	(Organization#, market segment#, period#, {organization segment total revenue}, {organization segment share},
QUOTA MARKET SEGMENT	(Market segment#, period#, quota number#, {segment sales quota this month%}, {segment sales quota YTD%}, {segment profit quota this month%}, {segment profit quota YTD%},

PRODUCT MARKET SEGMENT

(<u>Market segment#</u>, <u>period#</u>, <u>product number#</u>, {segment product revenue this month}, {segment product profit this month}, {segment product sales last year}, {segment product profit last year},

CUSTOMER MARKET SEGMENT

(<u>Market segment#</u>, <u>period#</u>, <u>customer number#</u>, {segment customer revenue this month}, {segment customer profit this month}, {segment customer sales last year}, {segment customer profit last year},

CUSTOMER TYPE

(<u>Customer type#</u>, customer type description,

CUSTOMER

(<u>Customer number#</u>, <u>period#</u>, customer type#, (customer account details), (customer credit details), {customer sales revenue this month}, {customer outstanding account balance}, {customer actual payment period},

PRODUCT TYPE

(<u>Product type#</u>, product type description,

PRODUCT

(<u>Product number#</u>, <u>period#</u>, product type#, {product total sales this month}, {product total sales this month last year}, {product average order value},

As a review exercise, examine the unnormalized and normalized versions of each entity to ensure that you understand why the entities have been so normalized. Refer to the business normalization rules in Chapters 7–9.

The normalized data map developed from this entity list is illustrated in Figure 17.6. The associations in this figure have been defined based on the existence of at least one organization eventually interested in each market segment (optional becoming mandatory). Each organization must also have a market segment that it addresses (optional becoming mandatory), or it may not stay in business long. Each customer, product and quota are classified as belonging to at least one market segment. This is mandatory. However, a new market segment may not have any customers, products or quota allocated yet (optional becoming mandatory).

As discussed earlier in this section, strategic modeling focuses only on the definition of primary keys and repeating foreign keys to identify relevant related entities. This is achieved by business normalization, as shown here. Strategic objectives modeling then defines strategic attributes based on goals and objectives, while the definition of detailed non-key attributes is left until tactical and operations modeling. In this section, however, we combined elements of strategic objectives modeling with tactical modeling so we could identify a number of non-key attributes. This will help us to illustrate the application of the next step: defining purpose descriptions. This step determines whether we have captured the correct meaning for the entities and attributes defined so far.

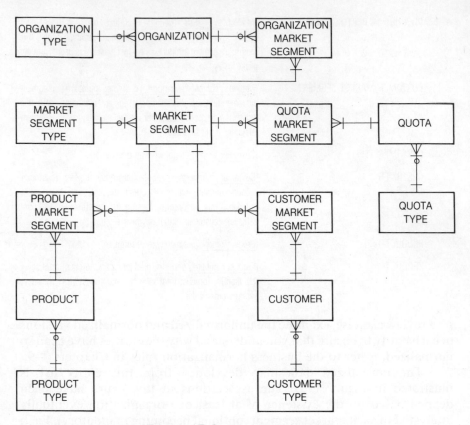

Figure 17.6 Normalized data map.

17.2.5 Define purpose descriptions

So far, we have identified some strategic entities and their attributes, and given them complete, meaningful names. We have developed a strategic data map in which we have represented strategic data unambiguously ... or have we? We chose names that indicated the purpose of each entity or attribute, but we cannot be sure that everyone views that data in exactly the same way. We must now ensure that there is agreement on the exact meaning of each entity and attribute by defining a purpose description for each.

The definition of purpose descriptions for entities and attributes uncovers misinterpretations. But be careful! People who interpret the data differently are not necessarily wrong. They may be thinking of different data. In resolving these inconsistencies, we may uncover additional data that had previously been overlooked, and subsequent to modifications of the data map. Hence, the iteration with earlier steps, as shown in Figure 17.1.

We generally leave purpose descriptions of associations until after strategic refinement, as associations represent processing and procedures. We have not defined associations sufficiently yet for the definition of their purpose descriptions to be productive here.

Entity purpose descriptions

The first task is to define the purpose of each entity; that is, its reason for existence. We do not define *how* it is used: that will come later when we examine strategies. Rather, we decide what purpose it serves.

We consider the name given to the entity, together with its component attributes defined to this point. Other related entities in the data map also provide an indication of the entity purpose. A narrative statement of purpose is then defined. This purpose description may be defined during the modeling session and immediately discussed, or it may be documented following the session by one or two people and discussed in the subsequent refinement session that addresses the model.

During discussion of the statement of entity purpose, homonyms (the same name used for different data) can emerge. Homonyms first become apparent when the entity purpose is expressed. *'That is not what I understand it to be! It should be this ...'* is usually the first indication that people are thinking of the same name in relation to completely different data. That name is a homonym. Each view of a homonym entity should be expressed. Different names must be defined to represent the additional entities that are apparent. They are added to the data map and entity list. Attributes are also identified for these entities. Purpose descriptions are immediately defined to resolve other homonyms that may exist for the entities.

Synonyms (different names used for the same data) also emerge at this stage. The first indication is often *'Is this entity intended to represent that? I thought (other entity name) was intended for that purpose!'* Two or more entities have been defined to represent the same data. They are synonyms. Those separate entities and their attributes are merged together to form one entity. The entity name is changed to one which all agree reflects the intent of the entity. The data map is changed. The entity purpose description is again defined.

Disagreement of entity purpose can arise because people consider only their perspective of the entity. Perhaps they are looking at a more detailed example of a particular entity type; that is, they are looking at a fourth business normal form of the entity. This detail may be left for tactical modeling, or it may represent important strategic data that should be addressed now.

It soon becomes obvious whether some people are thinking differently. If the entities are not homonyms or synonyms, they represent new entities. If they are relevant to the modeling scope, they should be defined now. Primary and foreign keys are agreed. Strategic non-key attributes are added if necessary at this point. The data map is changed. A purpose description for each entity and attribute is defined for discussion.

The entity purpose description is progressively changed until it expresses the view of all participants. When agreed, it is written down in narrative detail to express the full meaning of the entity. It may be a one-line statement, or a sentence, or one or several descriptive paragraphs. Purpose descriptions for entities in our hypothetical example are as follows:

ORGANIZATION
Records details of each organization, competitor or otherwise, of interest.

QUOTA
Records the total amount, and type, of the quota allocated for a specific period.

MARKET SEGMENT
This represents a part of the total market for a particular period. It records total revenue and profit earned in the period for the segment this year and also last year.

CUSTOMER
Records account and credit details for each customer in each period, including sales revenue, account balance and normal period for payment of accounts.

PRODUCT
Records total sales for each product in a period, and the average value of an order for the product.

ORGANIZATION MARKET SEGMENT
Records the total revenue and market share of each organization selling into a market segment for each period.

QUOTA MARKET SEGMENT
This records percentage achievement of sales and profit quota for each segment for the current month, and year to date.

CUSTOMER MARKET SEGMENT
This records sales revenue and profit from each customer in a segment for the current month, together with the total revenue and profit from that customer for last year on a moving 12-month basis.

PRODUCT MARKET SEGMENT
This records sales revenue and profit from each product in a segment for the current month, together with the total revenue and profit from that product for last year on a moving 12-month basis.

As can be seen, no homonyms or synonyms are apparent so far. In modeling, they usually do not begin to appear until business normalization is almost complete and attribute purpose descriptions are defined. Also, at that time, possible additional entities which have been omitted may become apparent. As you read each entity purpose description, review that entity and its component attributes as given in the normalized entity list. An examination of the attributes provides initial insight into a possible narrative entity purpose description. Each of the attributes in the entity is then examined in turn.

Key attribute purpose descriptions

A purpose description for each primary key attribute in an entity is similarly defined. That description also applies when the primary key exists in another entity as a foreign key. The purpose description of a key attribute is always defined once only, on its first use as a primary key. This description is used for every other occurrence of that key attribute as a primary key or a foreign key.

Homonyms and synonyms also emerge for key attributes as for entities. The name of an attribute is changed as appropriate. Additional key attributes are defined if necessary and if within the modeling scope. These may indicate other entities, which are added to the entity list and data map, and purpose descriptions are defined for all these new key attributes and entities. Or some homonyms may be defined as alias names, so that parts of the organization can refer to a key attribute using their own terminology.

Non-key attribute purpose descriptions

If non-key strategic attributes have been identified, their purpose descriptions must also be defined here. Homonym and synonym non-key attributes generally suggest incomplete business normalization. They indicate that a non-key attribute has been placed in the 'wrong' entity and so must be moved to another where it 'belongs'. The use of alias names is not appropriate here. Rather, the attribute should be fully normalized.

After correctly normalizing, the attribute purpose description is defined again. This may provoke considerable discussion! Even violent disagreement! Only when an attribute is normalized do homonyms and synonyms of that attribute become apparent. People think in the context of the entity in which an attribute resides. Complete business normalization resolves homonyms. For synonyms, all must agree on a standard name. Some representatives attribute purpose descriptions are as follows:

Market Segment Name
 Provides a unique name to identify each market segment of interest.

Period
 Uniquely identifies each time period as a period number. This number is sequential, and refers to a specific date and duration (week, month, year), as indicated in the specific occurrence of the PERIOD entity

Market Segment Type
> Uniquely identifies each type of market segment for customer and product planning, sales and profit management, market research and product promotion.

. . . .

Segment Total Revenue this Period
> Provides the total revenue earned for the specific period for all sales made to this market segment. This is also needed for comparison with last year's sales performance.

Segment Nett Profit this Period
> Provides the nett profit earned for the specific period for all sales made to this market segment. This is also needed for comparison with last year's profit performance.

. . . .

No homonyms or synonyms emerged during the definition of entity purpose descriptions. However, this is not the case for attribute purpose descriptions. These are listed, in part, in the foregoing descriptions.

Note that the purpose description of many of the attributes in MARKET SEGMENT have been defined. *Market segment*# presents no surprises, but this is not the case for *period*#. It is obvious from the attributes in MARKET SEGMENT that *period*# has been considered as if it was *month*# (a month of the year) so that comparisons can be made from month to month and against the same month last year. This is too restrictive. *Period*# is used as a key in this entity and also in other entities. We may wish to make comparisons in this and other entities on an annual or a weekly (or even daily) basis. Consequently, attribute names which are referred to as 'this month' (such as {*segment total revenue this month*} in MARKET SEGMENT) have been changed to refer to 'this period'. This and other attribute names are changed to refer to a period, rather than a month, as follows:

Old Attribute Name	**New Attribute Name**
Segment total revenue this month	Segment total revenue this period
Segment nett profit this month	Segment nett profit this period
Segment sales quota this month%	Segment sales quota this period%
Segment profit quota this month%	Segment profit quota this period%

Following further discussion, it seems a new entity PERIOD may be appropriate. This contains the following attributes:

PERIOD   (Period#, Starting date, period duration)

Period# is the primary key: a sequential number used to refer to an occurrence of the PERIOD entity. This occurrence indicates the specific starting date of the numbered period and its duration (day, week, month, quarter or year). The purpose description of *period*# is defined and included in the descriptions given earlier. The PERIOD entity is also added to the normalized entity list to this point, but now shown in the following final normalized entity list. This will be used subsequently in Chapter 21 for analysis of data to extract information reports.

PERIOD	(Period#, Starting date, period duration)
ORGANIZATION TYPE	(Organization type#, organization type description,
ORGANIZATION	(Organization#, period#, organization name, organization type#,
QUOTA TYPE	(Quota type#, quota type description,
QUOTA	(Quota number#, period#, quota amount, quota type#,
MARKET SEGMENT TYPE	(Market segment type#, market segment type description,
MARKET SEGMENT	(Market segment#, period#, market segment type#, [market segment name], {segment total revenue this period}, {segment nett profit this period}, {segment total revenue last year}, {segment nett profit last year}, {segment total revenue}, {segment growth rate},
ORGANIZATION MARKET SEGMENT	(Organization#, market segment#, period#, {organization segment total revenue}, {organization segment share},
QUOTA MARKET SEGMENT	(Market segment#, period#, quota number#, {segment sales quota this period%}, {segment sales quota YTD%}, {segment profit quota this period%}, {segment profit quota YTD%},
PRODUCT MARKET SEGMENT	(Market segment#, period#, product number#, {segment product revenue this period}, {segment product profit this period}, {segment product sales last year}, {segment product profit last year},
CUSTOMER MARKET SEGMENT	(Market segment#, period#, customer number#, {segment customer revenue this period}, {segment customer profit this period}, {segment customer sales last year}, {segment customer profit last year},
CUSTOMER TYPE	(Customer type#, customer type description,
CUSTOMER	(Customer number#, period#, customer type#, (customer account details), (customer credit details), {customer sales revenue this period}, {customer outstanding account balance}, {customer actual payment period},
PRODUCT TYPE	(Product type#, product type description,
PRODUCT	(Product number#, period#, product type#, {product total sales this period}, {product total sales this period last year}, {product average order value},

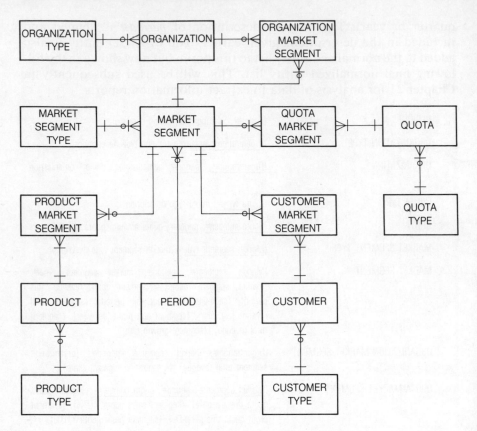

Figure 17.7 The final data map.

The final data map, to include the PERIOD entity, is shown in Figure 17.7.

The tools and materials, as well as the conduct of modeling sessions, are summarized in Box 17.1.

Box 17.1
Conducting modeling sessions

TOOLS AND MATERIALS

Management questionnaire responses

All individuals must have a copy of the relevant strategic statements for the strategic area, plus the consolidated responses of the management questionnaire.

Materials

At least two large white boards are needed, or two flip chart stands and pads. Alternatively an electronic white board is used, to make copies from the board of material for later reference by all attendees.

Session secretary

A session secretary is needed: to record details of various data subjects requiring further resolution; to record the emerging strategic model from the white boards and flip charts if an electronic white board is not used; to prepare data input for entry to software; to document actions to be carried out before the next session.

CONDUCTING A MODELING SESSION

Identify broad data subjects

The mission and purpose is used as a catalyst to identify broad data subjects. These are often suggested by nouns in the mission statement – either explicit or implied. They suggest possible entities which must be stored for later reference.

Identify relevant data entities

Listed examples within a data subject are used to identify data entities. Primary key attributes are defined to uniquely identify each entity. Foreign keys that indicate other related entities are added. If those other entities have not already been identified, they are added to the entity list.

(cont'd)

Box 17.1 (cont.)
Conducting modeling sessions

Identify data attributes

Within each data entity, non-key data attributes are defined at this point. This step is normally omitted for strategic modeling. It is included for strategic objectives modeling, and tactical and operations modeling, which focus on defining detailed data attributes in each entity.

Strategic attributes indicate information of interest to management of the strategic area. They may represent aggregated or summary attributes, derived from other attributes at the tactical or operational level. Non-key attributes are grouped in the entities where they belong. Group attributes (of details for later definition) are indicated with single left and right parentheses. Repeating groups are immediately normalized.

Develop data map

The normalized entity list is first used to develop a key map. The associations are then expanded to produce a normalized data map of the strategic model.

Define purpose descriptions

A narrative statement of the purpose of each entity is defined. This is often suggested by the attribute content of the entity. Homonyms and synonyms are identified and normalized further if necessary. The statement content is changed until all agree. The purpose description may be one line, a sentence, or one or several descriptive paragraphs.

A purpose description for each primary key attribute in an entity is defined when it is first encountered. This description applies for all other existences of that key, whether used as a primary key or foreign key in other related entities. Homonyms and synonyms also emerge. They indicate the possible existence of other homonym or synonym entities. These entities are defined and normalized. The key attribute name is changed or alias names are defined as appropriate, and purpose descriptions are defined. The purpose description may be one line, a sentence, or one or several descriptive paragraphs.

Box 17.1 (cont.)
Conducting modeling sessions

A purpose description for each non-key attribute in an entity is similarly defined. Homonyms and synonyms also emerge, as for entities. These attributes are further normalized. The attribute name and purpose description is changed as appropriate. The purpose description may be one line, a sentence, or one or several descriptive paragraphs.

PART FOUR

Automated Systems Development

CHAPTER 18

Software for Automated Development

Computer-aided software engineering (CASE) has emerged in the last few years as one of the most significant developments in the software industry. The term CASE relates generally to the automation of software development. Many products are now available. This chapter provides a method for evaluating CASE methodologies, tools and techniques. It discusses circumstances when CASE may be used and presents strategies for determining the most appropriate CASE product for each situation.

18.1 | DEFINITION OF CASE

Technological change has led to rapid improvements in the price and performance of hardware and communications. However, software development productivity has lagged behind. CASE promises to change that. Many products have emerged recently, all calling themselves CASE. Before we can distinguish between them, we must define the term. In the absence of an agreed definition of CASE, the following is proposed:

> *Computer-aided software engineering (CASE) is a generic term that refers to the automation of software development. It encompasses all stages of the software development life cycle. It is based on a rigorous methodology, with software tools to automate application of that methodology by DP staff and users.*

This is a general definition that encompasses most of the products on the market today, while also allowing us to distinguish between them. We will first discuss some principles, then present a CASE evaluation method.

18.2 | CASE FOUNDATIONS

According to the definition, the foundation of a CASE product is the methodology on which it is based. This depends on the analysis and design methods that are used, and the stage of DP growth in an organization. As we discussed in Chapter 1, it is not until the third of Nolan's DP growth stages – the control stage – that the need for data consolidation is recognized. The earlier stages concentrate on each separate redundant data version needed to support specific applications. The need to integrate these applications is recognized, but it is very difficult to achieve – it requires planning.

Rather than an overall plan for integrated development, organizations at stages 1 and 2 of Nolan's stages focus on building individual applications. How those separate applications fit together is not first determined. An overall plan (or lack of it) is the end result of the analysis and design methods employed.

18.2.1   Analysis and design methods

Stages 1 and 2 concentrate on *how* things are done rather than *what*; that is, they are procedure oriented. Applications are developed using the procedure-driven methods of systems analysis, structured analysis and structured design, and business systems planning (BSP). In contrast, stages 4–6 are data oriented. Data-driven methods such as information engineering are appropriate to these stages. The data resource is structured in a data model so that data shared throughout the organization can be readily brought together, or integrated. Data administration results and the organization moves smoothly to the stage of maturity.

If procedure-driven methods of analysis and design continue to be used for the latter data-oriented stages, the integration and data administration of stages 4 and 5 are difficult and costly to achieve, and expensive to maintain. This was illustrated in Figure 1.4(b) by the high proportion of maintenance for stages 4–6. With procedure-driven methods, the application backlog continues to grow.

Figure 1.4(a), in contrast, illustrated the effect of data-driven methods used in the later data-oriented stages. The data model provides the control needed in stage 3 and integration occurs naturally. Areas of high priority can be readily identified from the data model by management, and evolution through the later stages occurs easily. Fewer resources are needed for maintenance so that more resources are applied to new application development.

While procedure-driven methods are effective at stages 1 and 2, they are less productive for stage 3 and beyond. It is at stage 3 (or earlier) that the transition must be made to data-driven methods. Organizations at stages 1 and 2 can take either of two courses of action. They can accept the situation, use procedure-driven methods and then change later to data-driven methods in stage 3. Alternatively, they can apply a variation of the data-driven methods for stages 1 and 2, for these methods also work effectively at the early stages. The variation, however, is in the extent of user involvement.

In using data-driven methods at stages 1 and 2, DP staff act as catalysts or facilitators for the users, who carry out much of the design based on their business knowledge. As the organization then moves through stage 3 to stage 4, an interesting phenomenon occurs. Deeper business knowledge is needed to achieve the integration of the later stages. The users take the initiative. They do an increasing amount of the analysis and design themselves, based on their knowledge of the business rather than a knowledge of computers. The transition from the application orientation of stages 1 and 2 to the data orientation of stages 4–6 is smooth. Evolution to the later stages is orderly based on data-driven methods that are applied mainly by the users.

We can use Nolan's stages to determine the DP stage reached in an organization. We can use this to decide whether procedure-driven or data-driven methods are more appropriate to its needs. This will help us to select the most appropriate systems development methodology. The methodology on which a CASE product is based is one factor that must be considered. The other factor is the characteristics of the CASE software tools provided.

18.3 | CASE SOFTWARE CHARACTERISTICS

To provide effective support for automated development, a CASE product must provide support in three fundamental areas:

- Dictionary support.
- Modeling support.
- Documentation support.

18.3.1 Dictionary support

Two of the most effective tools for automated software development are data dictionaries and design dictionaries. These lead to the development of data models and procedure models, which are then implemented with the most appropriate software. This latter software includes third, fourth or fifth generation data base management systems (DBMSs). We will call these 3GD, 4GD or 5GD, respectively. It includes third, fourth or fifth generation languages (3GL, 4GL or 5GL, respectively).

Many dictionary products are available to capture definitions from data modeling and procedure modeling projects. These dictionaries may run on either mainframe computers, minicomputers or microcomputers. They include data dictionaries and design dictionaries and are categorized into four main classes:

- **Class 1**: Passive data dictionaries for 3GD, and for 3GL and 4GL.
- **Class 2**: Integrated active data dictionaries for 3GD and 4GD, and for 3GL and 4GL.
- **Class 3**: DP-driven design dictionaries for 3GD and 4GD, and for 3GL and 4GL.
- **Class 4**: User-driven expert design dictionaries for 3GD, 4GD and 5GD, and for 3GL, 4GL and 5GL.

Most of the data dictionary products on the market today fall into the first two classes.

Class 1 dictionaries provide no active support to the design process. They are data administrator (DA) and data base administrator (DBA) tools whose support is passively directed to the generation of various data base schemata for physical data base implementation once data definition and design have been completed. They are used primarily for third-generation DBMS products and languages, with some limited application for 4GLs.

Class 2 dictionaries provide more integrated support for 4GLs and for some 3GLs, integrating the languages they support with the third- or fourth-generation DBMS products on which those languages are implemented. They are often proprietary, developed specifically to support proprietary DBMS products and languages. They are referred to as 'active' dictionaries in their support for data base design and implementation. However, their support for analysis and design is *passive*; they are wholly dependent on the expertise of analysts. They are DP driven.

Class 1 and 2 dictionaries relate mainly to stages 1 and 2 of DP growth. This is illustrated in Figure 18.1.

Class 3 design dictionaries are DP driven. They are technical products developed for use by experienced analysts and information

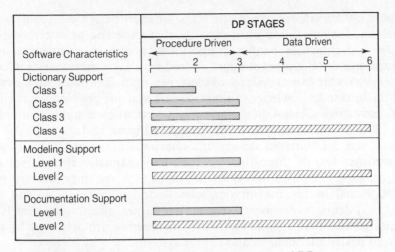

Figure 18.1   CASE software characteristics and DP stages.

center personnel, as well as DAs and DBAs. They provide assistance to the analysis and design process, supporting interactive graphical design by experienced DP staff. These design dictionaries record the resulting graphical design documentation (data flow diagrams, structure charts, data models, action diagrams, and so on) for later revision and refinement by DP staff. They are used to design both third- and fourth-generation data bases and systems which use 3GLs and 4GLs. DP staff provide the technical expertise, while users are involved only in reviewing the resulting diagrams and designs. Many of the CASE products on the market today are examples of class 3 dictionaries. They are CASE products that are DP driven (as for class 1 and 2 dictionaries). This may even be embodied in the names used for these products, with DP terms such as 'workbench' or 'facility' or some other DP acronym.

In contrast, Class 4 expert design dictionaries are user driven, not DP driven. It is this class of expert design dictionary that has greatest significance to a project. The expert design support of class 4 dictionaries enables that software to progressively 'learn' about the system being designed: it intelligently participates in the requirements specification, analysis, design, implementation and maintenance process. Because of the precision and cross-checking exhibited by the design methodology on which this software is based, this class of design dictionary is an expert system for automated analysis, design and development support. In its ultimate form, it can automatically generate fully executable systems directly from design specifications prepared by users.

Class 3 dictionaries relate to stages 1–3 of DP growth. Their complexity and dependence on DP experience is such that they hope only for 'user involvement' in the design process. They cannot provide the expert DP knowledge offered by class 4 expert design dictionaries. DP analysts, DAs or DBAs *must* provide that expertise as intermediaries. Class 3 dictionaries cannot support the active user-driven analysis, design and development support offered by class 4 dictionaries. Class 4 dictionaries are expert systems in their own right. They base their designs on the business knowledge of users: expert systems provide the required DP knowledge. Class 4 dictionaries, as a consequence, apply to all of the six DP growth stages. This is illustrated in Figure 18.1.

Class 3 DP-driven design dictionaries achieve productivity gains sometimes two or three times better than manually applied software engineering. However, they do not approach the productivity gains experienced by the user-driven class 4 design dictionaries and their expert systems. As discussed later in this chapter, effective gains of 10–20 times greater than manual software engineering are achieved by user-driven design dictionaries and expert systems.

> *The greatest productivity gains are achieved when the design is specified directly by the user from a business perspective rather than by a DP analyst or data administrator acting as intermediary.*

Class 4 design dictionaries also provide interfaces with the major data dictionaries in the first two classes. A class 4 dictionary actively supports the analysis, design and development of information systems, decision-support systems and expert business systems. Interfaces with class 1 and 2 data dictionaries may be required for compatibility with existing installation standards or to interface with the DBMS products and information systems that those passive dictionaries support. Passive class 1 and 2 dictionaries may therefore be loaded from an active class 4 expert design dictionary. The passive dictionaries only exist to provide an interface with the past: all new design and development is carried out by the class 4 dictionary.

18.3.2 Modeling support

The modeling support provided by a CASE product should address both data models and procedure models. If structured analysis and structured design are supported, data flow diagrams (DFDs) and structure charts are also modeled.

A data model comprises a data map and data definitions documented in an entity list. As discussed in Chapters 3 and 4, a data map provides a graphical representation of data entities and the associations between them, for detailed management and user review. It provides feedback to users for identification of information requirements based on the strategic plan. It ensures precise implementation of data needed to support those information needs. A data map and its data definitions directly support each other in a data model.

A procedure model can be derived from a data model. It comprises a procedure map and processing definitions in a procedure list. It documents the logic required to process the data represented by the data model. A procedure map provides a graphical representation of procedural logic and business conditions to be satisfied. It provides feedback to users for identification of their processing needs. A procedure map and its process definitions directly support each other in a procedure model.

A data model and its procedure models are directly integrated. Data and procedure definitions are stored in a data dictionary or a design dictionary, as described earlier. Data maps graphically represent defined data while procedure maps represent defined logic. Modeling combines the two in an iterative process: changes in definitions must be reflected as appropriate in the supporting data and procedure maps, and vice versa.

Software based on computer-aided design (CAD) principles provides automated modeling support. There are two levels of support, which relate to the degree of integration of the modeling process with the selected dictionary, as follows:

- **Level 1**: Passive modeling.
- **Level 2**: Expert modeling.

Level 1 modeling software provides a passive drafting capability for production and maintenance of graphical data and procedure maps, or DFDs and structure charts. These maps must be manually entered, the design and layout must be manually specified, and subsequent maintenance must be separately specified and re-entered each time. Support is provided for the physical process of preparing and maintaining graphical maps, but little support is offered for consistency checking of defined data or logic. Such passive modeling systems are unable to capture sufficient design detail from the user to automate the subsequent generation of systems. While they may provide spectacular graphics support, their benefit is superficial. They are totally dependent on an experienced analyst or data administrator to provide modeling expertise. They are DP driven, not user driven. The productivity gains achieved are thus severely limited by the passive user involvement that results.

Most of the automated modeling systems and CASE products on the market today are level 1. There is generally no integration with a class 4 expert design dictionary; they may at best support a class 3 dictionary. Consistency checking between graphical maps and relevant definitions in the dictionary must therefore be carried out manually, with a consequent opportunity for error. If carried out by the software, the strong DP emphasis restricts users to passive interaction. The result is DP interpretation of the feedback, rather than business knowledge applied by the users directly. These products relate mainly to stages 1 and 2 of DP growth, as illustrated in Figure 18.1.

Level 2 modeling software, by contrast, provides an expert modeling capability fully integrated with a class 4 expert design dictionary. Data definitions are entered by users and accepted directly by the design dictionary. These definitions are then automatically plotted as graphical data maps – no manual specification is necessary. The software analyzes the data and automatically groups it into subject data bases. A subject data base contains a related group of entities that are able to be implemented separately from other entities. It automatically groups subject data bases into implementation clusters. Implementation clusters represent potential application systems and business functions. They highlight management responsibility and control implications, and suggest alternative organization structures and reporting paths. Clusters automatically derived from a data model by level 2 modeling software help management identify priority systems for rapid implementation and delivery. They result in automatic derivation of project plans from a data model for high concurrent development activity. This leads to the productive development of application systems, information systems and decision-support systems, as will be discussed shortly.

Level 2 modeling software provides automated quality assurance. It plots data maps that are fully consistent with data definitions, derived subject data bases and implementation clusters. These data maps are plotted in implementation sequence and can be read directly both as data maps and as project plans.

Procedure maps are then automatically derived from the data maps. These provide the fundamental logic necessary to process the defined data. Users can readily review the derived business logic and provide additional refinement where necessary. This refinement is reflected in the procedure maps as further conditional logic. The procedure models, the data model and their supporting definitions are then automatically updated by the software where necessary.

The special manual drafting step of level 1 systems (required for entry, design, layout, plotting and subsequent maintenance of graphical maps in conjunction with class 3 dictionaries) with its consequent opportunity for error and dependence on DP expertise is eliminated with level 2 data modeling software as the production of data and procedure maps is fully automated from the design dictionary. These products apply to all of the stages of DP growth, as illustrated in Figure 18.1.

18.3.3   Documentation support

Much documentation is produced throughout the systems development life cycle. This undergoes constant change through requirements specification, analysis, design, implementation and subsequent software maintenance. This documentation must be maintained so that it is complete, consistent and up to date. The production of documentation, and its maintenance to ensure that all changes are recorded so it represents the current status of the project, is a major task. In the pressure of meeting deadlines, the quality of documentation is often the first area to suffer.

Most CASE products provide automated documentation support. There are two levels of support, which relate to the generation of documentation based on the underlying methodology, as follows:

- **Level 1**: Manual documentation.
- **Level 2**: Active documentation.

Level 1 documentation provides an electronic storage medium for production and maintenance of graphical and textual documentation. This documentation must be manually entered and documentation changes needed to record a design change must be separately specified and re-entered each time. Support is provided for the physical process of preparing and maintaining documentation, but little support is offered for consistency checking. Such manual documentation systems are unable to capture sufficient detail from the underlying methodology to automate the generation of documentation changes. They are totally dependent on an experienced analyst, data administrator or programmer to provide documentation maintenance expertise.

Most of the CASE products on the market today are level 1. There is no generation of documentation as an automatic byproduct of the underlying methodology. Consistency checking of documentation must therefore be carried out manually, with a consequent opportunity for error. They relate to stages 1–3 of DP growth, as illustrated in Figure 18.1.

Level 2 documentation software, by contrast, provides an active documentation capability fully integrated with a class 4 expert design dictionary. Design changes entered by users are automatically checked for consistency and then accepted by the design dictionary. All required documentation is automatically updated as a byproduct of the underlying methodology, so no manual documentation is necessary.

The software automatically produces updated documentation fully consistent with the applied changes. Subject data bases, implementation clusters and project plans are automatically derived, highlighting the impact of the change. Data maps are automatically regenerated and plotted in implementation sequence. Supporting detailed data and strategic plan documentation is automatically produced. Changes in priority areas can be readily identified for early development and delivery of systems.

Procedure maps are then developed from the derived clusters and updated data maps. Users can review the business impact of the change and refinements can be made where necessary, leading to further active and automatic maintenance of documentation. The procedure models, the data model and their supporting definitions are automatically updated by the software where necessary. The associated documentation is automatically maintained so that it is complete, up to date and consistent with the latest status of the project.

The manual documentation and maintenance of level 1 systems, with its consequent opportunity for error and dependence on DP expertise, is eliminated with level 2 software, as the production of documentation is fully automated. This software applies to all stages of DP growth, as illustrated in Figure 18.1.

18.4 | CASE METHODOLOGIES AND TOOLS

We are now ready to discuss the evaluation of CASE methodologies and tools. In this section, we will categorize the various approaches used by CASE products on the market today. Representative examples of products in each category will be provided, but the market is changing too rapidly for such products to remain current for long.

Three main CASE categories have emerged, which are categorized according to the extent of the systems development life cycle supported, as follows:

- CASA/CAP products.
- DP CASE products.
- USER CASP/CASE products.

18.4.1   CASA/CAP products

The term CASA/CAP refers to computer-aided structured analysis/computer-aided programming. Products in this category provide automated support for analysis, design and implementation based on structured analysis and structured design. Many variations of the procedure-driven structured techniques are supported, such as Yourdon, De Marco and Gane and Sarson. Some of the data-driven techniques may also be supported, such as Warnier-Orr and Jackson.

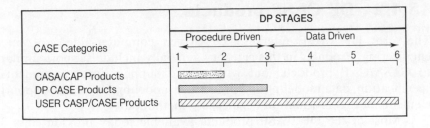

Figure 18.2 CASE categories related to DP stages.

Most of the CASA/CAP products available today provide class 3 dictionary support, but only level 1 modeling support and level 1 documentation support. They are technical DP tools that assume intimate knowledge of the methodologies supported. They provide passive support for electronic storage and maintenance of structured diagrams and documentation. Completeness, consistency, currency and accuracy of the evolving design is the responsibility of the analysts, data administrators and programmers to whom these tools are directed.

Because of their DP emphasis, together with a strong procedural emphasis, these products apply to stages 1 and 2 of DP growth, as illustrated in Figure 18.2. Examples of products in this category are listed in Figure 18.3, together with their suppliers. Some of these products are discussed in Chapter 19.

CASE PRODUCTS	SUPPLIERS
CASA/CAP Products Recoder, Inspector	 Language Technology, Inc
DP CASE Products Excelerator Analyst/Designer Toolkit Corvision Promod DSEE III Information Engineering Workbench Information Engineering Facility FOUNDATION	 Index Technology, Inc Yourdon, Inc Cortex Corporation Promod, Inc Apollo Computer, Inc Arthur Young International and Knowledgeware, Inc Texas Instruments, Inc Arthur Andersen & Co
USER CASP/CASE Products IE: CASE (USER: Expert Systems)	 Information Engineering Systems Corporation

Figure 18.3 Typical CASE products and suppliers.

18.4.2 DP CASE products

The term DP CASE refers to DP-driven computer-aided software engineering. Products in this category generally include support similar to CASA/CAP products, but with added support for requirements specification, data modeling and procedure modeling. Some also support elements of the information engineering methodology.

Most of the DP CASE products available today provide class 3 dictionary support, but only level 1 modeling support. They are dependent on initial manual entry of data models, procedure models and data flow diagrams. They are unable to generate data maps and procedure maps automatically from users' specifications. Subsequent maintenance of these maps is carried out manually, with a consequent opportunity for error. No automatic analysis of the business implications of the manually entered models is possible: these products accept the manual definition as the only business representation. Any changes from a business perspective must be manually reentered, so no automatic analysis of the business impact of the changes, or of strategic gaps or opportunities arising from the changes, is possible.

Some DP CASE products provide level 2 documentation support. This is based on active maintenance of the documentation produced. This documentation, however, reflects the DP emphasis of the methodologies on which these products are based. Support may be provided to document business functions and organization structure, but no opportunity is provided for automatic analysis and identification of alternative business strategies or organization structures. In addition, no automatic identification of strategic gaps and opportunities, based on the strategic plans set by management, is possible.

These products are technical DP tools that assume an intimate DP knowledge of the methodologies supported. They are intended for use mainly by analysts and data administrators. They emphasize 'user involvement', but this is passive. They are not tools that allow users to actively carry out requirements specification, analysis and design completely by themselves. A high level of DP expertise is required before active access to class 3 knowledge bases is possible. The very design of a class 3 knowledge base prevents it from providing this DP expertise. Experienced DP staff must act as intermediaries between the user and his business experience, which contradicts the objective of increased user involvement.

Completeness, consistency and currency of the evolving design is automatically provided by many of these products. However, this is carried out by the software from a DP perspective, not from a business perspective. Because of the passive user involvement, these products depend on the DP interpretation of analysts and data administrators to whom these tools are directed, not the business interpretation of users and managers.

Because of their DP emphasis, together with a procedural and a data emphasis, these products apply mainly to stages 1–3 of DP growth. This is illustrated in Figure 18.2. Examples of products in this category are listed in Figure 18.3, together with their suppliers. Some of these products are discussed in Chapter 19.

18.4.3   USER CASP/CASE products

The term USER CASP/CASE refers to computer-aided strategic planning / computer-aided software engineering. This includes the support of the CASA/CAP and the DP CASE products, but with a much greater user emphasis. Products in this category fully support the information engineering methodology, with complete support for strategic planning at all levels of management. These products allow systems to be developed that directly support the plans set by management. They also provide rapid feedback for management refinement of those plans in days, rather than the months and years for feedback using traditional strategic planning methods.

Systems are designed by users at the business level, with expert systems evaluating the impact of the design and subsequent changes, from a business perspective. They identify strategic gaps and opportunities arising from the changes. This rapid feedback permits further business refinement. Data maps and procedure maps are automatically generated, so organizational restructuring opportunities become apparent. Once all implications have been considered and accepted by management, the supporting documentation and maps are automatically produced and maintained up to date.

The USER CASP/CASE products available today provide class 4 dictionary support, with level 2 modeling support. They generate data maps and procedure maps automatically from users' specifications. Subsequent maintenance and regeneration of these maps is carried out automatically, with no opportunity for analyst error. Automatic analyses of the business implications of changes are made from a business perspective by the expert systems embodied in this software.

Subject data bases, implementation clusters and project plans are automatically derived from the data model. Application systems, information systems, decision-support systems and expert business systems can be developed. Based on business requirements, priority systems can be selected for early development and delivery.

USER CASP/CASE products provide level 2 documentation support. This is based on active and automatic maintenance of the documentation produced. This documentation reflects the user emphasis of the information engineering methodology on which these products are based. Support is provided to document business functions and organization structure. Automatic analysis and documentation of alternative business strategies or organization structures is carried out. Strategic plan documentation is maintained up to date to relate those plans directly to the data that supports their achievement. Automatic identification of strategic gaps and opportunities is achieved.

These products comprise both USER and DP tools. They provide expert DP knowledge, together with expert knowledge of the information engineering methodologies on which these products are based. They are intended for use by managers and users with no knowledge of DP, as well as by analysts, data administrators and programmers.

They support active, direct participation of users in requirements specification, analysis, design, implementation and maintenance. DP and information engineering expertise is built into the knowledge base on which the class 4 dictionary is based, to permit this active user participation. Business knowledge is captured and used to automatically create a business knowledge base. These products are able to learn more and more about the organization as development progresses. They thus become active partners with managers, users and DP in the development process. Completeness, consistency, currency and accuracy of the evolving design is automatically provided by these products. This is carried out by the software both from a DP perspective and a business perspective.

Because of both their USER and DP emphasis, together with a procedural and a data emphasis, these products apply to all stages of DP growth. This is illustrated in Figure 18.2. Examples of products in this category are listed in Figure 18.3, together with their suppliers. Some of these products are discussed in Chapter 19.

In their ultimate form, the USER CASP/CASE products will eventually enable the supporting computer systems to be automatically regenerated, based on the strategic and business plans set by management. Data bases can be automatically generated and installed today. In the future, programs will be automatically generated in target languages. Systems will be automatically installed on mainframes, minis or micros. Translation, migration and installation for different physical environments will be totally automatic. The designed systems can be maintained logically, at the business level, in a machine-independent, DBMS-independent and language-independent form. Systems development and maintenance will then be fully automatic, based on strategic and business plans set by management.

USER CASP/CASE products have proved the rigor of the user-driven information engineering methodology on which they are based, with the use of this methodology since 1976 at DP and management levels in thousands of organizations worldwide. The expert systems software that they use has been on the market since 1984. Projects that previously may have taken two to three years using software engineering are now being implemented in two to three months, with automatic generation of SQL/DS, DB2, ORACLE and other relational data bases directly from a data model defined wholly by managers and users. Productivity gains of 10–20 times greater than software engineering are being regularly achieved today, as discussed later in Chapter 22. But the upper limit of productivity gain has not yet been reached: the potential exists for even greater software development productivity. We can see the day, soon, when all analysis and design will be carried out by managers and users at the business level, with automatic generation of the supporting application systems, decision-support systems and data bases in hours. This will change the DP industry as we know it today.

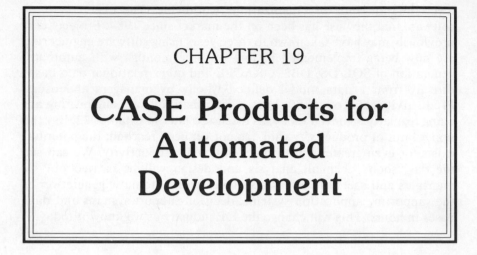

CHAPTER 19

CASE Products for Automated Development

This chapter introduces a number of CASE products that support automated systems development. Many products are available, with more being released every week. Only a selection of products have been included, because of this variety. Some offer support for software engineering, while others support information engineering. As our emphasis is on information engineering, products in this category are discussed in more detail. These products capture business expertise directly from managers and users, for the development of systems based on the strategic plans set by management.

19.1 SELECTED CASE PRODUCTS

During the project scope stage (see Chapter 15), software tools for analysis, design and generation are selected and installed. Products addressed in this chapter are listed in Table 19.1. As all of these products are undergoing continual enhancement, the best source of information is the software developer or its suppliers. Reference details are provided for the developer, and the suppliers in some countries, where further information can be obtained. Each will be discussed in terms of the CASE criteria discussed in Chapter 18 and their support for information engineering, as follows:

318

Table 19.1 CASE products discussed in this chapter.

Product	Supplier
Excelerator	Index Technology Corporation
Analyst/Designer Toolkit	Yourdon Incorporated
Corvision	Cortex Corporation
FOUNDATION	Arthur Andersen & Co
Information Engineering Workbench	Arthur Young/Knowledgeware Incorporated
Information Engineering Facility	Texas Instruments Incorporated
USER: Expert Systems/IE:CASE	Information Engineering Systems Corporation

- **Step 1**: The first step is to assess the present position of your organization in terms of Nolan's DP growth stages and the target stage to which you want to progress. You are then ready to evaluate the products in this chapter.

- **Step 2**: An overview is given of each product, except for pricing. As part of this overview, each product is discussed in terms of the support offered in the CASE software areas introduced in Chapter 18 – namely, dictionary support, modeling support and documentation support. The support offered in these areas provides the second part of the CASE evaluation. Figure 18.1 is used to relate this support to your target Nolan stage from step 1.

- **Step 3**: As we saw in Chapter 18, CASE products are classified into three categories. The CASE category provides the third part of the evaluation. Given your target Nolan stage from step 1, Figure 18.2 identifies the most appropriate CASE category.

- **Step 4**: The classification of products into each of the CASE categories in step 3 is the final step in the evaluation.

19.1.1 Excelerator

Excelerator was developed by Index Technology Corporation (101 Main Street, Cambridge, MA 02142, USA). It is also referred to as InTech. It is the most widely used CASE product, with 7500 copies installed as of September 1987.

Excelerator is a very effective workbench for systems analysts. It runs on IBM microcomputers, and supports facilities for creating and modifying data flow diagrams (DFDs), structure charts, data models, screens and report designs. It provides analysis of designs for consistency and completeness. A project dictionary stores details of objects, such as DFDs, processes, data stores, data models and structure charts, and tracks relationships between them.

An additional product, Customizer, is also available. This customizes the output of Excelerator for systems analysis and design. It allows users to modify the dictionary structures, menus and graphical shapes, and to add custom procedures to support an organization's specific methodology or techniques. It includes a system dictionary, shape editor, screen and report design, and uses high-resolution graphics and a mouse.

Excelerator supports a class 3 design dictionary, through the support offered by its project dictionary. It is dependent on the existing knowledge of its analyst users for effective use. Given that knowledge, it supports structured analysis, structured design and data modeling. It provides consistency and completeness checking of diagrams.

DFDs can be drawn based on Gane and Sarson notation, or Yourdon, or others as defined using the Customizer. It allows data models to be drawn and linked to the data stores of DFDs. It generates record structure definitions in a variety of languages, including COBOL, PL/1 and C. However, it does not generate program code. Interfaces are provided to other CASE products and tools covering areas not directly supported by Excelerator. This includes an interface to Telon, a mainframe code generator from Pansophic Systems.

Excelerator is dependent on manually drawn diagrams. It supports level 1 modeling, providing an electronic repository for these diagrams. These are manually modified as required and then saved in their modified form. Once designed, however, it produces relevant design documentation automatically, with level 2 documentation support.

Because of its support for data modeling, in addition to structured analysis and structured design, it does not belong in the CASA/CAP category. With its DP emphasis as an analyst tool, it is classified as a DP CASE product.

Its support for a class 3 design dictionary and level 1 modeling, together with its dependence on analyst use, indicate that it is most effective when used for analysis and design of application systems. It applies particularly well to Nolan's stages 1–3. However, its procedural emphasis on structured analysis and design limits its effectiveness when used within the data-oriented environment of corporate-wide systems in Nolan's stages 4–6.

19.1.2 Analyst/Designer Toolkit

The Analyst/Designer Toolkit was developed by Yourdon Incorporated (1501 Broadway, New York, NY 10036, USA). It is based on the widely used software engineering methodology (as defined by Ed Yourdon and Tom De Marco) for structured analysis and structured design.

The Analyst/Designer Toolkit is extremely useful for organizations who standardize on the Yourdon structured techniques. It runs on IBM microcomputers, with facilities for creating and modifying context diagrams, entity relationship diagrams, state-transition diagrams, DFDs and structure charts. It provides analysis of designs for consistency and completeness.

A project dictionary stores details of objects such as data groups, data elements, entities, modules, processes, prompts, relationships, textual requirements, states and terminators, and the relationships between them. The project dictionary is compatible with dBASE III, for easy generation of customized reports.

Two other options are available: Rule Tool and COMPOSE. The Rule Tool adapts the Toolkit to other methodologies, allowing the creation of unique sets of symbols and rules for connectivity. The COMPOSE option supports the merging of diagrams with textual documentation.

The Analyst/Designer Toolkit supports a class 3 design dictionary through the support offered by its project dictionary. It is dependent on the existing knowledge of its analyst users for effective use. Given that knowledge, it supports structured analysis, structured design and entity–relationship modeling. It provides consistency and completeness checking of diagrams.

DFDs, state-transition diagrams and structure charts can be drawn based on Yourdon notation, or others as defined using the Rule Tool. Data models are drawn based on the Chen entity–relationship notation (see Chapter 4). This allows entity relationship models to be drawn and linked to the data stores of DFDs.

The Analyst/Designer Toolkit is dependent on manually drawn diagrams. It supports level 1 modeling, providing an electronic repository for these diagrams. These are manually modified as required and then saved in their modified form. Once designed, it produces relevant design documentation automatically with level 2 documentation support.

Because of its support for entity–relationship modeling, as well as structured analysis and structured design, it does not belong in the CASA/CAP category. Its emphasis as an analyst tool classifies it as a DP CASE product.

Its support for a class 3 design dictionary and level 1 modeling, together with its dependence on analyst use, indicate that it is most effective when used for analysis and design of application systems. It applies particularly well to Nolan's stages 1–3. However, its procedural emphasis on structured analysis and design limits its effectiveness when used within the data-oriented environment of corporate-wide systems in Nolan's stages 4–6.

19.1.3   Corvision

Corvision was developed by Cortex Corporation (138 Technology Drive, Waltham, MA 02154, USA). It supports the design and generation of systems to be executed on DEC VAX computers.

Corvision is a design workbench for systems analysts. It uses either DEC VT terminals or IBM microcomputers with a VAX minicomputer. It supports an entity diagrammer, for development of data models and definition of data-sets (files) and attributes (fields). A data view diagrammer shows access paths through the data model, for development of transactions comprising screens and reports. A menu diagrammer supports progression from function to function within an application. A screen painter and a report painter allow screens to be painted based on data defined in data sets and fields [1]. These are used by the Corvision action diagrammer to generate program logic for file accessing, and screen and report preparation and processing. This is generic logic to access files and process the specified screens to produce defined reports. These are skeleton action diagrams. The analyst then defines additional logic unique to the application, using Builder, a 4GL developed by Cortex. This 4GL was earlier supplied as part of The Application Factory, the predecessor of Corvision.

The VAX provides a central design repository. This provides guidance and control of concurrent development carried out on several terminals or micros communicating with the VAX. It provides analysis of the diagrams for consistency and completeness. When complete, the application is then automatically generated as executable machine code. It does not translate to an intermediate language, such as COBOL, but its performance is claimed by Cortex to be comparable to compiled COBOL or FORTRAN programs on the VAX.

Corvision supports a class 3 design dictionary, through the support offered by its VAX repository. It is dependent on the existing knowledge of its analyst users for effective use. Given that knowledge, it supports data modeling and action diagramming. It provides consistency and completeness checking of diagrams. It does not support development of DFDs, because of its data-driven emphasis. It generates application systems only for execution in a VAX environment. However, it supports access against both DEC VMS files as well as DEC RDB data bases.

Corvision is dependent on manually drawn diagrams and supports level 1 modeling, providing an electronic repository for these diagrams. These can be manually modified as required and then saved in their modified form. Once defined, however, it produces relevant design documentation automatically, with level 2 documentation support.

Because of its support for data modeling and action diagramming, it does not belong in the CASA/CAP category. With its DP emphasis as an analyst tool, it is classified as a DP CASE product.

Its support for a class 3 design dictionary and level 1 modeling, together with its dependence on analyst use, indicate that it is most effective when used for analysis and design of application systems. It applies particularly well to Nolan's stages 1–3. It is data driven, but its application system emphasis limits its effectiveness for stages 4–6 where integrated, corporate-wide systems are required.

19.1.4 FOUNDATION

FOUNDATION was developed by Arthur Andersen & Co (69 West Washington Street, Chicago, IL 60603, USA). It supports planning, analysis and design on IBM micros, with a central design encyclopedia, and generation of systems on an IBM mainframe.

FOUNDATION is designed for use by both users and systems analysts. It uses IBM micros operating in a stand-alone mode, or communicating with an IBM mainframe. It supports two micro-computer-based CASE products, DESIGN/1 and METHOD/1, and a mainframe-based CASE product, INSTALL/1.

DESIGN/1 supports development of flowcharts, DFDs and structure charts using the graphics facilities of the micro, together with the painting of screens and reports. It transfers design definitions to METHOD/1 for use in project management.

METHOD/1 provides a project management capability. As discussed in Part Three, project management is a critical area that is often overlooked. The best designed system is useless if the project fails due to poor project management. METHOD/1 supports tailoring of project plans to the unique requirements of each organization, with precise project estimating. It accepts design definitions from DESIGN/1, with interactive access to project plans, reporting on progress of tasks in the project against the plan.

INSTALL/1 accepts output from DESIGN/I and METHOD/1, but it can also be used independently. It operates on an IBM mainframe with the IBM DB2 relational DBMS, which is used as a central DB2 data dictionary. Common and reusable system tasks are precoded and are automatically included in generated programs. INSTALL/1 automatically generates data structures, screens, records, file maintenance applications, SQL statements, conversation flows, validation logic, copybooks and I/O modules. It generates both COBOL II and 0S/VS COBOL for execution in a DB2 envinonment.

FOUNDATION supports a class 3 design dictionary and is dependent on the existing knowledge of its analyst users for effective use. It uses manually drawn diagrams. It supports level 1 modeling and provides an electronic repository for these diagrams. These can be manually modified and saved in their modified form. Design documentation is produced automatically, with level 2 documentation support.

Its emphasis is on the existing functions of an organization as a starting point and it provides support primarily for analysts. It is therefore classified as a DP CASE product.

Its support for a class 3 design dictionary and level 1 modeling, with an analyst emphasis, indicate that it focuses on the analysis and design of application systems. It applies particularly well to Nolan's stages 1–3. Although it provides support for data modeling, its function and procedural emphasis limits its effectiveness for stages 4–6 where integrated. corporate-wide, data-oriented systems are required.

19.1.5 Information Engineering Workbench

The Information Engineering Workbench (IEW) was developed by KnowledgeWare Incorporated (3340 Peachtree Road, NE, Atlanta, GA 30026, USA) and is marketed by Arthur Young International. It supports the planning, analysis and design of systems on IBM microcomputers, with a central design encyclopedia on an IBM mainframe. It starts from a definition of the functions of an organization, which are used as a basis for planning new systems.

IEW is designed for use by systems analysts. It uses IBM microcomputers operating in a stand-alone mode, or communicating with an IBM mainframe. It supports a number of analyst tools. A Decomposition Diagrammer is available for hierarchical definition of activities or organizational structures to lower detail levels. An Entity Diagrammer is supported for definition of data models both at the planning level and at the detailed operational level. A Data Flow Diagrammer shows the flow of information throughout an application. This can be tailored to Yourdon, Martin or Gane and Sarson notation.

An Action Diagrammer is used by the analyst to define minispecs which specify the program logic for file accessing, and screen and report preparation and processing. The analyst also defines logic unique to the application. This logic can then be transferred to Gamma, a mainframe-based code generator also provided by KnowledgeWare. This translates the defined programs to COBOL.

The IBM mainframe provides a central design repository, called the encyclopedia. This controls concurrent development carried out on several micros communicating with the mainframe. It provides consistency checking of the defined diagrams. Each micro may alternatively use its own stand-alone encyclopedia.

IEW supports a class 3 design dictionary through the mainframe-based encyclopedia. It is dependent on the existing knowledge of its analyst users for effective use. Given that knowledge, it supports data modeling, data flow diagramming and action diagramming with consistency and completeness checking. With its support for DFDs, its focus is more procedure driven than data driven.

IEW depends on manually drawn diagrams. It supports level 1 modeling, providing an electronic repository for these diagrams. These can be manually modified as required and then saved in their modified form. It produces the relevant design documentation automatically, with level 2 documentation support.

Its emphasis on the functions of an organization as a starting point assumes the present organization structure is also acceptable for the future, perhaps with some refinements. It does not provide support for the automatic derivation of potential new functions and application systems directly from a data model. With its DP emphasis as an analyst tool, it is therefore classified as a DP CASE product.

Its support for a class 3 design dictionary and level 1 modeling, with an analyst emphasis, indicate that it focuses on the analysis and design of application systems. It applies particularly well to Nolan's stages 1–3. Although it provides support for data modeling, its function and procedural emphasis limits its effectiveness for stages 4–6 where integrated, corporate-wide, data-oriented systems are required.

19.1.6   Information Engineering Facility

The Information Engineering Facility (IEF) was developed by Texas Instruments, Incorporated (PO Box 655621 MS 8474, Dallas, TX 75265, USA). IEF offers analysis and design on IBM or TI micros, with a central design encyclopedia and code generation on an IBM mainframe. As with IEW, it starts from the existing functions of an organization, which are used for planning new systems.

IEF is designed for use by systems analysts. It uses IBM or TI micros operating in a stand-alone mode, or communicating with an IBM mainframe. It supports two micro-based toolsets, the Analysis Toolset and the Design Toolset, and two mainframe-based toolsets, the Construction Toolset and the Database Generation Toolset.

The Analysis Toolset supports five diagrams using the graphics facilities of the micro: entity relationship, entity hierarchy, process decomposition, process dependency (similar to a DFD) and process action diagrams. These are transferred automatically to the Design Toolset, which supports three additional diagrams: dialog flow, screen design and procedure action diagrams. The action diagrammer capabilities of these toolsets are used by the analyst to define minispecs for file accessing, and screen and report preparation and processing. The analyst also defines logic unique to the application. This logic is then used by a mainframe-based code generator also provided by Texas Instruments. This translates the defined programs to COBOL.

The mainframe toolsets, together with a central design repository (the encyclopedia), require IBM's DB2 relational DBMS to operate. The encyclopedia manages multiple projects, with concurrent development using micros based on data downloaded from the mainframe.

IEF supports a class 3 design dictionary through the mainframe-based encyclopedia. It is dependent on the existing knowledge of its analyst users for effective use. Given that knowledge, it supports data modeling, data flow diagramming and action diagramming with consistency and completeness checking. With its support for DFDs (the process dependency diagram) and action diagrams, its focus is more procedure driven than data driven.

IEF depends on manually drawn diagrams. It supports level 1 modeling, providing an electronic repository for these diagrams. These can be manually modified as required and then saved in their modified form. It produces the relevant design documentation automatically, with level 2 documentation support.

As with IEW, its emphasis on the existing functions of an organization as a starting point assumes the present organization structure is also acceptable for the future, perhaps with some refinements. It does not provide support for the automatic derivation of potential new functions and application systems directly from a data model. With its DP emphasis as an analyst tool, it is therefore classified as a DP CASE product.

Its support for a class 3 design dictionary and level 1 modeling, with an analyst emphasis, indicate that it focuses on the analysis and design of application systems. It applies particularly well to Nolan's stages 1–3. Although it provides support for data modeling, its function and procedural emphasis limit its effectiveness for stages 4–6 where integrated, corporate-wide, data-oriented systems are required.

19.1.7   IE: CASE Information Engineering Development System

IE: CASE was initially developed in Australia by Information Engineering Systems Limited of Sydney. Later development was carried out in the USA by its subsidiary, Information Engineering Systems Corporation (1235 Jefferson Davis Highway, Arlington, VA 22202, USA). IE: CASE is part of the USER: Expert Systems software family, first released in October 1984. It supports planning, analysis, design and data base generation on IBM micros, for migration to micros, minis or mainframes. As distinct from IEW and IEF, it provides two alternative starting points. It can start from the existing functions of an organization or it can automatically derive potential new functions and application systems directly from a data model.

IE: CASE is designed for use by both users and systems analysts. It uses IBM micros operating independently, with automatic merging, identifying and resolving of conflicts across multiple projects. IE: CASE fully automates information engineering, as described in this book. It supports three micro-based CASE products. These are IE: Analysis, IE: Design and IE: Generation.

IE: Analysis supports strategic, tactical and operations modeling using the analysis and data modeling conventions described in this book. It accepts strategic plans defined by management. It analyzes these plans based on strategic analysis, to identify alternative strategies. Some of these alternative strategies may represent critical strategic gaps or opportunities overlooked by management. It supports computer-aided strategic planning (CASP).

The data models developed by IE: Analysis are automatically analyzed to determine separately implementable subject data bases and implementation clusters. These are plotted in implementation sequence (as implementation phase data maps) completely automatically, for project planning purposes. This offers a level 2 expert modeling capability.

IE: Analysis supports an expert design dictionary and a strategic planning dictionary, for use by users and analysts alike. It provides expert information engineering support, progressively capturing business expertise directly from managers and users. Data definitions from this dictionary can be transferred to other environments (such as other CASE products or data dictionaries on mainframes or minis) by using the Universal Export Facility (USER: UEF), supplied as part of IE: Analysis.

IE: Design accepts data models and strategic planning directions from IE: Analysis. It automatically generates a PROLOG knowledge base from the data transferred from IE: Analysis. It produces relevant design documentation, including data file or data base formats, screen form and report definitions, and cross-reference reports.

IE: Generation generates data base creation statements for a number of relational DBMS products, including SQL/DS and DB2 (from IBM), ORACLE (Oracle Corporation) and INGRES (Relational Technology). It also generates data bases for Powerhouse (Cognos). Data base queries can be prototyped for review by the users. SQL queries may be tested with IE: SQL, which is supplied as part of IE: Generation. This is a microcomputer-based, major subset of IBM DB2. It is used for prototyping SQL systems that will be implemented with SQL/DS, DB2, ORACLE or INGRES.

IE: CASE supports a class 4 expert design dictionary with IE: Analysis, which provides information engineering expertise and captures business knowledge directly from the users. It supports level 2 expert modeling through IE: Analysis. This generates graphical data models automatically. Design documentation is produced automatically by IE: Design, with level 2 documentation support.

IE: CASE can be based on either the existing functions of an organization as a starting point or on the automatic derivation of potential new functions and application systems directly from a data model. With IE: Analysis, it provides expert support for both users and analysts. It is therefore classified as a USER CASP/CASE product.

Its support for class 4 dictionaries and level 2 modeling makes it extremely versatile. It can focus on either analysis and design of individual application systems or on the development of corporate-wide systems. It therefore applies across all of Nolan's stages 1–6, for separate application systems or for integrated, corporate-wide, data-oriented systems, as required.

19.2 FIRST RULE OF CASE

In this chapter, we have covered a number of CASE products. Most of these belong to the DP CASE category, as described in Chapter 18. At the time of writing, at least one product is available in the USER CASP/CASE category – IE: CASE. The automated support provided by USER CASP/CASE products, which are designed for both users and analysts and which capture business knowledge directly from the users, leads us to define an important rule of CASE. This rule is overlooked by most of the products on the market today, except perhaps for the last product discussed above:

> The potential for a CASE product to provide **automatic code generation directly from user specifications** is inversely proportional to the number of **graphical diagramming input methods** employed.

The variety of graphical diagrams, manually input with level 1 modeling for most of the CASE products described in this chapter, reflects the need for analysts to express their knowledge of the user's requirements as clearly as possible. The users and other analysts review these diagrams for correctness. However, this is a poor substitute for the active definition by managers and users of data models which precisely reflect the unique business requirements, constraints, audit and management controls, and data and information needs of an organization.

The logic that is implicit in data models developed by the experts of the business can be used directly for code generation. This is based on only one graphical diagramming input method: the data model. This logic is defined using the information engineering principles introduced in this book, together with detailed training in strategic, tactical and operations modeling. The potential for automatic code generation directly from a data model developed by users is covered in Chapter 22. This also discusses derivation of other diagrams from a data model.

Because of the opportunities offered by active analysis and design carried out by the experts of a business, the concluding chapters of the book will describe the IE: CASE Information Engineering Development System, together with its component products.

Reference

[1] Jones, R. (1988). The case for automating the automation business. *DEC User* (March).

CHAPTER 20

Automated Information Engineering

This chapter introduces one example of a USER CASP/CASE product – the IE: CASE Information Engineering Development System, part of the USER: Expert Systems family. IE: CASE provides expert, automated support for planning, analyzing, designing and generating data bases. This software comprises a group of expert systems that facilitate the rapid development of information systems, decision-support systems and expert business systems, developed for users and by users. Such systems capture expert business knowledge of strategic and functional managers, to position their organization for the effective exploitation of both its information resource and its knowledge resource.

The information engineering methodology described in this book is fully automated by IE: CASE. It allows management and DP staff to reduce the application backlog, and to develop systems that require significantly less maintenance than systems developed using traditional means.

20.1 INTRODUCTION

IE: CASE provides expert design support to information engineering projects for strategic, tactical and operations modeling. IE: CASE supports all of the development phases. The IE: CASE components are shown in Figure 20.1. We will discuss the support for analysis, design and generation first, leaving discussion of the support for operations until last.

330

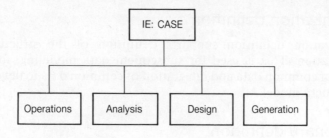

IE: CASE Information Engineering Development System

IE: Analysis   Planning and Analysis System
IE: Design   Design System
IE: Generation   Data Base Generation System

Figure 20.1   Information engineering development phases.

20.2   ANALYSIS PHASE

IE: Analysis (planning and analysis system) comprises a class 4 expert design dictionary and a strategic planning dictionary. It provides expert design support to both users and analysts. It completely automates strategic planning and analysis using information engineering. A clear definition of the strategic data resource of an organization is established. Figure 20.2 illustrates IE: Analysis, used for the analysis phase.

20.2.1   Data modeling

Data modeling uses both an expert design dictionary and a strategic planning dictionary. It provides expert support to both users and analysts. It fully automates the strategic, tactical and operations modeling stages of information engineering. It allows clear definition of the strategic data resource of an organization to be established, to integrate common data automatically. It provides the following capabilities.

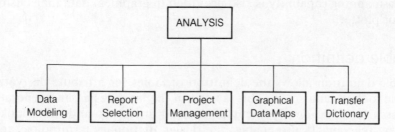

Figure 20.2   Components of the analysis phase.

Organization definition

Organization definition supports definition of the structure of an organization. This is used for subsequent data modeling, for identification of common data and integration of common data to develop a corporate data model.

Dictionary definition

Dictionary definition supports the interactive definition of entities, attributes and associations within and across the functional areas making up the organization structure. This supports the main design dictionary activity for data model definition, processing and analysis. It represents a design repository that accumulates increasing knowledge of the project and related business expertise. It provides a design knowledge base on which later processing and analysis is carried out.

Strategic plan definition

Strategic plan definition accepts the definition of strategic statements of policies, issues, goals, objectives, strategies and tactics as text in a strategic planning dictionary. These strategic statements are linked to the relevant defined data in the design dictionary.

Business strategy definition

Business strategy definition analyzes the definition of data in the design dictionary. It identifies current strategies, which are represented as associations between related entities. Possible alternative strategies are identified by strategic analysis, some of which represent strategic gaps or opportunities that may have been overlooked.

Model select and view

Model select and view allows graphical data maps to be displayed on a graphics screen, for limited analysis review. A more extensive automatic data-mapping capability is also provided in graphical data maps using a color plotter.

Table definition

Table definition allows the definition of tables for attribute derivation, table lookup, and so on. This is used in the later design and generation phases for code development of derived attributes and table lookup, where relevant. It also enables the design dictionary terminology to be tailored uniquely to an organization's needs.

20.2.2   Report selection

Report selection allows a variety of analysis reports to be printed for review, evaluation and refinement during data modeling and strategic planning. The representative reports listed here can be selected for printing either immediately, or in a batch mode for unattended printing.

Data entities report

This is an alphabetical report of entities, purpose descriptions and attributes in each functional area, or across functional areas.

Attribute report

This is an alphabetical report of attributes (and purpose descriptions) in each functional area, and across all functional areas, as a 'where-used' report.

Association report

This is an alphabetical report of associations (and purpose descriptions) in each functional area, and across all functional areas. Associations are printed schematically, and also as narrative text.

Policy/issues report

This is a textual report of policies/issues and supporting data entities, within or across functional areas.

Objectives report

This is a textual report of goals/objectives and supporting attributes, within or across functional areas.

Strategies report

This is a textual report of strategies/tactics and related associations, within or across functional areas.

Extended purposes report

This is a textual report of extended purpose descriptions of entities, attributes and associations.

Report batching

This is a batch definition of the foregoing reports for unattended, non-stop printing.

20.2.3 Project management

Project management provides expert support for the identification and progressive generation of subject data bases. It automatically derives an implementation plan from defined data in the expert design dictionary. This indicates the sequence in which subject data bases should be implemented, based on defined business strategies. These subject data bases can be progressively delivered as information systems. This provides input to the design and generation phases.

Project management comprises two steps: association edit and implementation strategies. Association edit checks all associations for implementation validity, and produces a report of cautionable or unimplementable associations. Implementation strategies further analyzes the design dictionary to develop implementation plans for project planning, data mapping and implementation purposes. It produces a report of entities grouped within subject data bases for progressive implementation, together with a report identifying subject data bases in implementation priority sequence, representing potential application systems. This provides input for plotting graphical data maps in implementation sequence and provides input to the design and generation phases for designing and generating data bases. It also carries out quality assurance of the definition of data models.

20.2.4 Graphical data maps

These provide automatic plotting of schematic data maps on a color plotter. The data maps can be plotted in either a compressed form or in expanded form for improved layout and readability. They can be plotted in implementation sequence for all defined data or for selected implementation clusters as identified by project management. These data maps can be used to identify alternative strategies. They provide immediate feedback to users during the analysis process to ensure that essential management and audit controls are addressed, and business conditions are satisfied.

20.2.5 Transfer dictionaries

These are used to transfer the design and strategic planning dictionaries from the analysis phase to the design and generation phases. They install subject data bases for designing and generating application systems and information systems. They provide an open architecture export facility. Data defined in the expert design dictionary and strategic planning dictionary can be transferred to the data dictionary or other software products on microcomputers, minicomputers or mainframes.

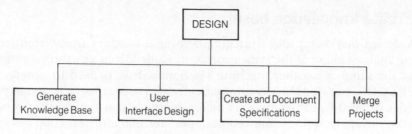

Figure 20.3   The design phase.

20.3 DESIGN PHASE

The design phase uses IE: Design (design system). Four design options are provided, as shown in Figure 20.3. These are used: to load the analysis model from the analysis phase and generate a knowledge base; to design the user interface, comprising screen forms and reports; to produce design documentation of data files, screen forms and reports; and to merge two projects to produce a third consolidated (merged) project. Together with the documentation from IE: Analysis of policies, objectives and strategies in the strategic planning dictionary, and of entities, attributes, associations and purpose descriptions in the design dictionary, complete design documentation is produced. This documentation is an automatic byproduct of the analysis and design process. IE: Design then provides input to IE: Generation for automatic generation of data bases for target data base management systems.

20.3.1 Generate knowledge base

This uses the design dictionary and strategic planning dictionary defined in the analysis phase. It creates a design knowledge base in PROLOG, which contains all entity, attribute and association definitions, all organizational definitions, all strategic planning statements and links to relevant design dictionary definitions. Application groups are defined and physical attribute definitions are established.

Load external project

A design dictionary and strategic planning dictionary can be transferred from the analysis phase of the same project, or from an external project on the same or another machine. In the latter case, the transfer is via a floppy disk and is loaded into the design phase of the current project.

Create knowledge base

A design dictionary and strategic planning dictionary transferred from the analysis phase of the same project, or loaded from an external project on the same or another machine via floppy disk, is used to generate a PROLOG knowledge base automatically. This contains facts and expert rules derived from the analysis phase definitions. A typical data model from the analysis phase may contain perhaps 800 entities, 1000 associations and 2000 attributes, progressively developed over several months. This results in a PROLOG knowledge base of approximately 5000 facts and expert rules, automatically generated on a micro in a matter of only hours. Manual development of this knowledge base, using knowledge engineering techniques, may have taken years.

Define applications

Implementation clusters derived during project management processing in the analysis phase are used to define application groups. An application group represents one or more application systems. One or several clusters can be combined and given a unique application group name for use in the design and generation phases.

Physical attribute assignment

An application group is selected for definition of physical attribute characteristics. Each attribute is defined in terms of data type (currency, integer, text, date, time, Boolean), size and output format for physical implementation.

12.3.2   User interface design

This is used to design screen forms and reports from defined data entities and attributes in the analysis phase. Each implementation cluster of related entities in an application group is used for the painting of screen forms and for the design of reports.

Screen design

Screen forms are painted based on installation-defined standards. Each related entity in a module is included (with appropriate attributes) on the form. The attribute name can be used to label the data field on the screen, or a different label can be entered in conjunction with the data field. The data field and its label can be positioned anywhere on the form, independently of each other. Additional text, such as instructions, or a displayed heading or footing for the form, can be entered and moved around the screen. In this way, the generated screen is dynamically modified until acceptable in utility and appearance, and then saved. It can be further modified later, if required, and saved again.

Logical inferencing techniques are used during forms design, for inclusion of related data from entities in installed implementation clusters. This achieves automatic joining of related entities in a screen form.

Report design

A defined application group of related entities and attributes provides input to report design. Each selected attribute is positioned as a report column. The attribute name can be used as a column heading, or different text can be entered by the user. Text can be entered for a report header or footer, or as other text in the report, and then saved. It can be further modified later, if required, and saved again.

Logical inferencing techniques are used during report design, for inclusion of related data from entities in installed implementation clusters. This achieves automatic joining of related entities in a report.

20.3.3 Create and document specifications

Data file specifications, screen forms and reports, and related documentation are produced. The record format for each entity in an application group is printed in a data file specification report. Screen forms and reports are printed in screen or report image, with relevant specifications of attribute name, row and column positioning. Documentation can be directed to a screen, printer or data file.

Data file specification

The record format represented by each entity and all of its attributes is documented as a data file specification report. This indicates the name of each entity and each attribute, together with its logical data type and the corresponding physical data type, size and format of each defined data field. This is used for data file or data base implementation in environments not supported for automatic data base generation by IE: Generation.

Screen specifications

Each designed screen form is printed both as an exact image of the screen and with printed forms design specifications, indicating for each data field, label or text field the attribute name (for data fields) or displayed text (for label or text fields), the starting row and column position on the screen, the length (number of columns) and the display format. This documentation is used for subsequent program coding.

Report specifications

Each designed report is printed both as an exact layout of the report and also with printed report layout specifications, indicating for each data column, column heading or report text field the attribute name (for data columns) or displayed text (for column headings or report text fields), the starting line and column position on the report, the column width (number of print positions) and the data presentation format. This documentation is used for subsequent program coding.

Cross-reference reports

A number of 'where-used' cross-reference reports allow the impact of a design change in one part of an application to be evaluated in terms of its effect on other possible areas.

20.3.4   Merge projects

This provides support for automatic merging of multiple projects established in either or both of the analysis and design phases. It merges a primary project and secondary project into a merged project, with automatic detection and resolution of conflicts. This allows a large project to be distributed across many project teams, each with its own hardware. These teams may be centralized or distributed, operating concurrently and independently on different parts of the project.

This facility supports the automatic merging of projects in a number of environments. Three examples will illustrate. Firstly, it merges multiple concurrent subprojects from a larger project, which were developed independently for high development productivity. Secondly, two independent projects carried out in different areas of an enterprise can be automatically combined into a single, larger consolidated project. Thirdly, later versions of a project can be merged with earlier versions, so automatically updating the earlier project versions.

A range of merge reports is provided which can be directed to screen, printer or disk file. These reports contain details of all conflicts detected while merging projects and the action taken to resolve them.

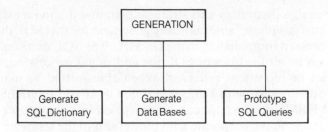

Figure 20.4   Components of the generation phase.

20.4 | GENERATION PHASE

The generation phase uses IE: Generation (data base generation system). This accepts definitions from the design phase of files, screens and reports. It automatically generates data base creation statements to install data bases on mainframes, minis and micros for target data base management systems (DBMS). The dictionaries from IE: Analysis can also be generated automatically for the target DBMS. Data base or dictionary queries are prototyped with SQL, the Structured Query Language adopted as a standard fourth-generation language by the American National Standards Institute in October 1986. This is illustrated in Figure 20.4.

An SQL version of the design dictionary and strategic planning dictionary is automatically generated for IE: SQL, a major implementation of DB2, SQL/DS, and a major subset of ORACLE and INGRES. It is supplied with IE: Generation. The SQL dictionary and application data bases can be transferred to other computers, such as mainframes, minis or micros, for processing independently of IE: CASE. They can be installed on those systems using DB2, SQL/DS, ORACLE, INGRES or other relational DBMS products as appropriate. Data bases can also be generated for Powerhouse.

20.4.1 Generate SQL dictionary

SQL commands to create an SQL design dictionary and strategic planning dictionary are automatically generated. This is referred to as the SQL dictionary. It is installed on the micro for processing with IE: SQL. It can be later transferred to mainframes, minis or micros for installation using DB2, SQL/DS, ORACLE, INGRES or other relational DBMS products. CREATE TABLE commands are generated for SQL, together with the relevant SQL INSERT commands for loading data defined in the analysis phase.

The design dictionary and strategic planning dictionary definitions from the analysis phase, automatically generated for this SQL dictionary, can be processed immediately using IE: SQL. The SQL dictionary can be operated on by all facilities of SQL for additional processing, or for *ad hoc* queries or reports as required. When transmitted to mainframes, minis or other micros with DB2, SQL/DS, ORACLE, INGRES or other relational DBMS products, it can be processed in a multi-user environment for access to the corporate data model and to the strategic planning dictionary defined in the analysis phase.

20.4.2   Generate data bases

Data bases are generated automatically for specified application groups. These can be installed for prototype processing with IE: SQL on the micro, or they can be transferred to mainframes, minis or other micros for processing with Powerhouse, or for relational data bases such as DB2, SQL/DS, ORACLE, INGRES or other relational products.

Each entity definition from the analysis phase is used to generate a CREATE TABLE command, to create an SQL table for that entity. Primary keys and foreign keys are generated as NOT NULL columns to eliminate duplicate keys and for subsequent referential integrity control between SQL tables. Common primary and foreign keys used for automatic joining of related tables for screen forms and reports establish referential integrity control between SQL tables.

Third, fourth and fifth business normal form (3BNF, 4BNF, 5BNF) entities are automatically generated as SQL tables. All generated SQL commands can be later modified by the data base administrator, if required for different data base design strategies.

20.4.3   Prototype SQL queries

IE: SQL, supplied with IE: Generation, is used on the micro for prototype processing of the SQL dictionary or SQL data bases generated as just described. Two versions of SQL are provided: an interactive version, with full syntax checking and access to all SQL facilities, and a menu-driven SQL version for training programmers and users in SQL, and for easy access via menus to all created SQL tables and columns for rapid construction of SQL commands.

IE: SQL is a major implementation of DB2 SQL and SQL/DS, and a major subset of ORACLE SQL. It operates in a single-user mode for prototyping DB2, SQL/DS and ORACLE applications on the microcomputer. SQL applications, defined as application groups of one or several clusters in the design phase, can be concurrently developed across multiple microcomputers with IE: SQL.

Menu-driven SQL

The menu-driven version of IE: SQL provides rapid menu access to all created SQL tables. This allows selected table names to be automatically inserted in SQL commands. It provides rapid menu access to all columns (attributes) in each selected SQL table, for column names to be automatically inserted in SQL commands. Free-form entry of some SQL command clauses is also provided. Syntax checking of SQL commands is carried out, with immediate execution if no syntax errors are found. The results are displayed on the screen.

Interactive SQL

The interactive version of IE: SQL provides full syntax checking of SQL commands, with immediate execution if no syntax errors are found. Results are displayed on the screen. Full access is provided to all SQL commands, entered free form. Syntax checking of SQL commands is carried out, with immediate execution if no errors are found. Detected syntax errors are clearly indicated with appropriate error messages, for correction.

Utilities

Utilities are provided for access to all SQL tables, whether for the SQL dictionary or for application data bases. This offers a capability analogous to the SQL catalog of DB2, SQL/DS or ORACLE. Access is provided to details of all created SQL tables, including all table definitions, columns, names, sizes, data types, and so on.

20.5 OPERATIONS

Operations is not a separate development phase, but is used to define the operating environment and to carry out administrative services for the other phases. Additionally, it provides menu-driven access to many common DOS commands, and access to all DOS commands in a DOS shell from any development phase. The facilities available are illustrated in Figure 20.5.

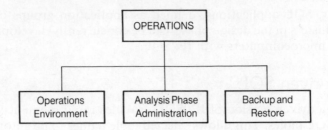

Figure 20.5 The IE CASE operations environment.

20.5.1 Operations environment

This supports the definition of a specific operating environment for use by IE: CASE, and provides access to a DOS shell, with menu selection of common DOS commands.

The analysis phase dictionaries (design dictionary and strategic planning dictionary), the design knowledge base, the SQL dictionary and the generated application data bases reside in a DOS directory allocated for each named project. This allows multiple projects to be resident on the same machine. A project is associated with a specific project name, which is made the current project at sign-on time. Menu access is provided to common DOS commands, allowing access to files associated with the current project, if required. A DOS shell is provided to enter relevant DOS commands.

20.5.2 Analysis phase administration

This option provides an administration facility during the analysis phase. It creates, sizes and initializes dictionaries for multiple projects. It verifies dictionary integrity and automatically carries out repairs in the event of corruption of data due to power failure or other processing interruption. It supports multiple projects, each with a separate design dictionary and strategic planning dictionary, and allows the creation, expansion or compression of different size design dictionaries and strategic planning dictionaries. It initializes these dictionaries for a new project, or for use in training, and allows the report headings to be changed as required.

20.5.3 Backup and restore

This provides convenient access to DOS backup and restore facilities. It calculates the number of disks needed to backup all of the data relating to the current project. It formats disks, carries out the backup and restores a previous backup version of the current project.

20.6 | AUTOMATED MAINTENANCE

With IE: CASE, much of the time-consuming, error-prone manual coding task of traditional development methods is reduced. The high cost of conversion, in moving from one hardware and software environment to another, is also reduced. Maintenance changes, needed because of changes in the business, no longer result in redevelopment of large parts of existing systems, as often occurs with the traditional development methods. Instead, those design changes are applied to the data model with IE: Analysis. Affected subject data bases and implementation clusters are derived again. The design knowledge base is automatically rebuilt by IE: Design and affected screens and reports are modified where necessary. Changed data bases are regenerated for target DBMS environments with IE: Generation for migration to micros, minis and mainframes.

CHAPTER 21

Automated Development Example

In this chapter, we will use the example presented in Chapter 17 of a large retail department store to illustrate some of the processing principles involved in the analysis phase, together with the reports produced by IE: Analysis.

21.1 INTRODUCTION

The final normalized entity list (see p. 295) and final data map (see Figure 17.7, p. 296) were defined to IE: Analysis. This provided a number of reports for review by the project team, as described in this chapter. It analyzed the data model and identified subject data bases and potential application systems. It carried out strategic analysis to determine whether any alternative strategies exist, which had been overlooked. This enables management to identify potential strategic gaps or opportunities. These are addressed in this chapter.

In discussing the processing and relevant reports in the following, the emphasis is only to illustrate the principles involved: not to provide a full solution for this data model. Consequently, only part of the reports are included, to focus on salient points, rather than to provide unnecessary detail. And, of course, this example involves only 15 entities. A typical strategic model will include 50–90 entities, while a data model expanded to operational detail will comprise perhaps 800 entities.

21.2 | ANALYSIS PHASE

21.2.1 Data list report

We will only examine one entity here: MARKET SEGMENT, defined as follows:

MARKET SEGMENT   (Market segment#, period#, market segment type#, market segment name, segment total revenue this period, segment nett profit this period, segment total revenue last year, segment nett profit last year, segment total revenue, segment growth rate)

This entity is of most interest to senior management. It includes market performance attributes which will enable a sales analysis system, developed using this entity, to produce sales reports for specific market segments. An example of part of an annual sales report based on this entity is shown in Table 17.1. A sales analysis system may present this report in graphical form, as illustrated in Figure 17.2.

This entity also enables management to evaluate the performance of different market segments over several time periods to identify trends, as illustrated in Figure 17.3. It is most significant in addressing the goals and objectives, as defined in Chapter 17.

Once entities and attributes have been defined to IE: Analysis, they can be printed in a data list report for review by other interested areas of the business. A typical strategic model of 50–90 entities will occupy several pages of this report. That part of the report that includes MARKET SEGMENT is illustrated in Figure 21.1. This figure documents each attribute defined in the MARKET SEGMENT entity. It indicates that *market segment number* and *period number* are primary keys, to identity each market segment in each period. The primary key may comprise one or more key attributes to achieve uniqueness, as we saw in Chapter 3. *Market segment type* is a foreign key.

Figure 21.1 further indicates that a secondary key (a selection attribute) has been defined based on *market segment name*, to provide access by name rather than *market segment number*. The remaining (non-key) attributes are documented alphabetically in terms of the authority of the strategic area to change those attributes.

At this stage all attributes are shown to have SHARED ADD/ DEL/CHG AUTHORITY. Other departments may add (ADD), delete (DEL) or change (CHG) values contained in each attribute. Most of these are derived attributes: they represent aggregate values derived from operational data. The operational areas of the business will update these

IE: CASE Retail Department Store Example
Data List: All
FUNCTIONAL AREA: **STRATEGIC MODEL** Page 1 Date: 1-Aug-1989

ENTITY: MARKET SEGMENT Entity Type : PRINCIPAL ENTITY
Functional Area role : SHARED DDD/DEL/CHG AUTHORITY

Entity Purpose : TOTAL REVENUE AND PROFIT IN THE PERIOD FOR THE SEGMENT THIS YEAR AND LAST YEAR

PRIMARY KEYS : **MARKET SEGMENT NUMBER**
PERIOD NUMBER

SECONDARY KEYS : **MARKET SEGMENT NAME** NON DERIVED

ATTRIBUTES : **SEGMENT GROWTH RATE**
Attribute Role : SHARED ADD/DEL/CHG AUTHORITY
DERIVED TO BE ALLOCATED LATER

SEGMENT NETT PROFIT LAST YEAR
Attribute Role : SHARED ADD/DEL/CHG AUTHORITY
DERIVED TO BE ALLOCATED LATER

SEGMENT NETT PROFIT THIS PERIOD
Attribute Role : SHARED ADD/DEL/CHG AUTHORITY
DERIVED TO BE ALLOCATED LATER

SEGMENT TOTAL REVENUE
Attribute Role : SHARED ADD/DEL/CHG AUTHORITY
DERIVED TO BE ALLOCATED LATER

SEGMENT TOTAL REVENUE LAST YEAR
Attribute Role : SHARED ADD/DEL/CHG AUTHORITY
DERIVED TO BE ALLOCATED LATER

SEGMENT TOTAL REVENUE THIS PERIOD
Attribute Role : SHARED ADD/DEL/CHG AUTHORITY
DERIVED TO BE ALLOCATED LATER

FOREIGN KEYS : **MARKET SEGMENT TYPE** MANDATORY

Figure 21.1 Partial data list report.

attributes with appropriate values for each period, so they also have shared authority. Derivation details have not yet been defined at this point: the derivation formula is indicated TO BE ALLOCATED LATER.

21.2.2   Association list report

The association lines joining entities in a data map are expressed automatically in English by IE: Analysis in an association list report, as illustrated in Figure 21.2. The associations defined by management are given a brief purpose description, illustrated by the MARKET SEG-MENT ANALYSIS IN A PERIOD association in Figure 21.2. Other associations relating to products of interest to a market segment have also been included. You may wish to refer back to the data map in Figure 17.7 in relation to this report.

You will notice in Figure 21.2 that mandatory associations are indicated with *must*, as with the TYPE OF PRODUCTS association where a PRODUCT must (mandatory) have one PRODUCT TYPE. This expresses the strategy (say) that '*products are only stocked that belong to product types of interest to our market segments*'. An optional tending-to-mandatory association is indicated by *will*. It indicates time dependency. A product type may be introduced to a market segment to assess market interest. No products are stocked initially, but if sufficient interest is expressed in specific products, they will be stocked. This is shown with PRODUCT TYPE which will (eventually) have one or more PRODUCT. Similarly, an optional association is indicated by *may*. There are no optional associations shown in the partial association list report in Figure 21.2. An alternative version of this report may also be printed, listing each entity alphabetically with all associations between that entity and other, related, entities shown using the schematic association notation.

21.2.3   Attribute list report

All attributes defined to IE: Analysis and documented in the data list report are also printed in an attribute list report, as illustrated in Figure 21.3. All attributes in each entity across all functional areas are printed, in alphabetical sequence by attribute name. A purpose description is defined for each attribute, which later leads to the definition of appropriate objectives.

The edit rule (for data entry) and the security level (the attribute role) of each attribute is printed. Derived attributes are identified, together with their relevant derivation formula names. Repeating and

IE: CASE Retail Department Store Example
Association List : All

Page 1   Date: 1-Aug-1989

MARKET SEGMENT ANALYSIS IN A PERIOD
Purpose : ANALYZES MARKET GROWTH AND MARKET SHARE PERFORMANCE BY PERIOD
    MARKET SEGMENT   must have one PERIOD
    PERIOD   will have zero, one or many MARKET SEGMENT

MARKET SEGMENTS FOR A PRODUCT
Purpose : USED FOR ANALYSIS OF A PRODUCT ACROSS MARKET SEGMENTS
    PRODUCT   must have one or more PRODUCT MARKET SEGMENT
    PRODUCT MARKET SEGMENT   must have one PRODUCT

PRODUCTS IN A MARKET SEGMENT
Purpose : PRODUCTS WHICH RELATE TO A MARKET SEGMENT, FOR ANALYSIS PURPOSES
    MARKET SEGMENT   will have one or more PRODUCT MARKET SEGMENT
    PRODUCT MARKET SEGMENT   must have one MARKET SEGMENT

TYPE OF MARKET SEGMENTS
Purpose : TYPE OF SEGMENTS USED FOR MARKET PERFORMANCE ANALYSIS
    MARKET SEGMENT TYPE   will have one or more MARKET SEGMENT
    MARKET SEGMENT   must have one MARKET SEGMENT TYPE

TYPE OF PRODUCTS
Purpose : TYPE OF PRODUCTS OF INTEREST TO MARKET SEGMENTS
    PRODUCT TYPE   will have one or more PRODUCT
    PRODUCT   must have one PRODUCT TYPE

Figure 21.2   Partial association list report.

(cont'd)

IE: CASE Retail Department Store Example
Attribute List: All

Page 1   Date: 1-Aug-1989

MARKET SEGMENT NAME

		Attribute type	SECONDARY KEY
Purpose	DEFINES THE NAME OF A MARKET SEGMENT, FOR ALTERNATIVE REFERENCE AND ACCESS		
Edit Rule	ADD NOW & MODIFY LATER		
Entity	MARKET SEGMENT		
Attribute type	NON DERIVED		

MARKET SEGMENT NUMBER

		Attribute type	KEY ATTRIBUTE
Purpose	UNIQUELY IDENTIFIES EACH MARKET SEGMENT FOR SALES ANALYSIS PURPOSES		
Edit Rule	ADD NOW, CANNOT MODIFY LATER		
Key use	USER CONTROLLED		
Entity	MARKET SEGMENT	Key role	PRIMARY KEY
Entity	ORGANIZATION MARKET SEGMENT	Key role	PRIMARY KEY
Entity	PRODUCT MARKET SEGMENT	Key role	PRIMARY KEY
Entity	CUSTOMER MARKET SEGMENT	Key role	PRIMARY KEY
Entity	QUOTA MARKET SEGMENT	Key role	PRIMARY KEY

MARKET SEGMENT TYPE

		Attribute type	KEY ATTRIBUTE
Purpose	UNIQUELY IDENTIFIES EACH TYPE OF MARKET SEGMENT FOR SALES ANALYSIS PURPOSES		
Edit Rule	ADD NOW, CANNOT MODIFY LATER		
Key use	USER CONTROLLED		
Entity	MARKET SEGMENT TYPE	Key role	PRIMARY KEY
Entity	MARKET SEGMENT	Key role	FOREIGN KEY
		Foreign key use	MANDATORY FOREIGN KEY

Figure 21.3   Partial attribute list report.

IE: CASE Retail Department Store Example
Attribute List: All

PERIOD NUMBER

	Attribute type	KEY ATTRIBUTE
Purpose	UNIQUELY IDENTIFIES EACH PERIOD FOR SALES ANALYSIS PURPOSES	
Edit Rule	ADD NOW, CANNOT MODIFY LATER	
Key use	USER CONTROLLED	
Entity	MARKET SEGMENT	Key role	PRIMARY KEY
Entity	PRODUCT MARKET SEGMENT	Key role	PRIMARY KEY
Entity	CUSTOMER MARKET SEGMENT	Key role	PRIMARY KEY
Entity	QUOTA MARKET SEGMENT	Key role	PRIMARY KEY
Entity	PRODUCT	Key role	PRIMARY KEY

SEGMENT GROWTH RATE

	Attribute type	NON KEY ATTRIBUTE
Purpose	RECORDS THE GROWTH RATE OF A MARKET SEGMENT IN A PERIOD	
Edit Rule	ADD NOW AND MODIFY LATER	
Entity	MARKET SEGMENT	
Attribute role	SHARED ADD/DEL/CHG AUTHORITY	
Attribute type	DERIVED	Derivation formula TO BE ALLOCATED LATER
Repeating	NON REPEATING	
Group	UNGROUPED	

SEGMENT NETT PROFIT THIS PERIOD

	Attribute type	NON KEY ATTRIBUTE
Purpose	RECORDS THE NETT PROFIT FOR A MARKET SEGMENT IN A PERIOD	
Edit Rute	ADD NOW AND MODIFY LATER	
Entity	MARKET SEGMENT	
Attribute role	SHARED ADD/DEL/CHG AUTHORITY	
Attribute type	DERIVED	Derivation formula TO BE ALLOCATED LATER
Repeating	NON REPEATING	
Group	UNGROUPED	

SEGMENT NETT PROFIT LAST YEAR

		Attribute type	NON KEY ATTRIBUTE
Purpose	RECORDS THE NETT PROFIT FOR A MARKET SEGMENT IN THE SAME PERIOD LAST YEAR		
Edit Rule	ADD NOW AND MODIFY LATER		
Entity	MARKET SEGMENT		
Attribute role	SHARED ADD/DEL/CHG AUTHORITY		
Attribute type	DERIVED	Derivation formula	TO BE ALLOCATED LATER
Repeating	NON REPEATING		
Group	UNGROUPED		

SEGMENT TOTAL REVENUE

		Attribute type	NON KEY ATTRIBUTE
Purpose	RECORDS THE TOTAL REVENUE, YEAR TO DATE, FOR A MARKET SEGMENT		
Edit Rule	ADD NOW AND MODIFY LATER		
Entity	MARKET SEGMENT		
Attribute role	SHARED ADD/DEL/CHG AUTHORITY		
Attribute type	DERIVED	Derivation formula	TO BE ALLOCATED LATER
Repeating	NON REPEATING		
Group	UNGROUPED		

SEGMENT TOTAL REVENUE LAST YEAR

		Attribute type	NON KEY ATTRIBUTE
Purpose	RECORDS THE TOTAL REVENUE FOR A MARKET SEGMENT IN THE SAME PERIOD LAST YEAR		
Edit Rule	ADD NOW AND MODIFY LATER		
Entity	MARKET SEGMENT		
Attribute role	SHARED ADD/DEL/CHG AUTHORITY		
Attribute type	DERIVED	Derivation formula	TO BE ALLOCATED LATER
Repeating	NON REPEATING		
Group	UNGROUPED		

SEGMENT TOTAL REVENUE THIS PERIOD

		Attribute type	NON KEY ATTRIBUTE
Purpose	RECORDS THE TOTAL REVENUE FOR A MARKET SEGMENT IN A PERIOD		
Edit Rule	ADD NOW AND MODIFY LATER		
Entity	MARKET SEGMENT		
Attribute role	SHARED ADD/DEL/CHG AUTHORITY		
Attribute type	DERIVED	Derivation formula	TO BE ALLOCATED LATER
Repeating	NON REPEATING		
Group	UNGROUPED		

Figure 21.3 (cont.) Partial attribute list report.

grouped attributes are indicated, and the entity (or entities) in which an attribute resides is identified. A non-key or secondary key attribute resides in only one entity after business normalization: a primary key or foreign key attribute may reside in one or several entities.

Entities, attributes and associations are linked directly to their relevant strategic statements in the strategic planning reports.

21.2.4   Strategic planning reports

Strategic planning reports are printed by IE: Analysis. These include text defined for each policy, objective or strategy statement, together with data supporting achievement of those statements. Thus, policy or issue statements are printed together with the entities to which they are linked; goals or objectives are printed with the attributes that measure their achievement; strategies or tactics are printed together with the associations to which they are linked.

The statement defined for goal 1 – market growth – has been linked to related attributes by IE: Analysis. This is printed in an objective report in Figure 21.4. This shows one screen page of text. Up to six screen pages are printed on each report page. A goal (or an objective) can include up to 32 767 screen pages – or approximately 3000 single spaced A4 (letter size) pages. It can be linked to any number of entities (and to the relevant attributes within them) that measure achievement of that goal, within or across functional areas.

Similarly, policy and strategy reports can be printed, each containing up to 32 767 screen pages. A policy (or an issue) is linked to the entities implementing that policy or affecting that issue; a strategy (or a tactic) is linked to the associations implementing procedures needed to carry out the strategy. Any number of entities and/or associations can be linked to a policy or strategy, within or across functional areas.

21.2.5   Project management reports

The processing carried out by IE: Analysis as a result of an analysis of the data model is indicated in Figures 21.5 and 21.6. This shows the subject data bases report (Figure 21.5) and the application systems report (Figure 21.6). (Refer to the discussion in Chapter 15 relating to these reports.)

No fourth (4BNF) or fifth business normal form (5BNF) entities have been defined in this simple data model: only third business normal form principal, type or intersecting entities such as MARKET SEGMENT, MARKET SEGMENT TYPE and PRODUCT MARKET SEGMENT. Figure 21.5 shows that each entity has consequently been grouped into a separate subject data base. If 4BNF and 5BNF entities are

IE: CASE Retail Department Store Example
Objective Listing All:
Functional Area:

STRATEGIC MODEL

Page 1   Date: 1-Aug-1989

GOAL: MARKET GROWTH   Page 1
To increase revenue and profit from each market
segment at an annual rate which exceeds the
segment growth rate by at least 5% pa while
maintaining our profit margin of at least 40%,
and profit growth of 10% pa.
.... linked to the following attributes (cancelled links in parentheses) ....

MARKET SEGMENT
SEGMENT TOTAL REVENUE THIS PERIOD, SEGMENT TOTAL REVENUE LAST YEAR,
SEGMENT NETT PROFIT THIS PERIOD, SEGMENT NETT PROFIT LAST YEAR,
SEGMENT GROWTH RATE

Figure 21.4   An objective report, linked to attributes.

SUBJECT DATA BASE	*ENTITIES*
MARKET SEGMENT	MARKET SEGMENT
MARKET SEGMENT TYPE	MARKET SEGMENT TYPE
PERIOD	PERIOD
PRODUCT	PRODUCT
PRODUCT TYPE	PRODUCT TYPE
PRODUCT MARKET SEGMENT	PRODUCT MARKET SEGMENT

Figure 21.5 Partial subject data bases report.

later defined, they will be automatically incorporated into these subject data bases by IE: Analysis. Each subject data base has taken the name of the principal, intersecting or type entity within it (listed to the right of the subject data base name).

Figure 21.6 shows part of the application systems report automatically derived from the data model. We will discuss cluster 1, which represents a potential product analysis system. It is of interest to three functional areas: the corporate, market research and sales departments.

As discussed in Chapter 15, each separate subject data base is listed according to the phase number (in brackets) in which it will be developed. A subject data base with no preceding phase number indicates phase 0. Cluster 1 thus shows that PERIOD, MARKET SEGMENT TYPE and PRODUCT TYPE are all able to be developed in phase 0 if sufficient development resources are available; that is, they are not dependent on

IE: CASE Retail Department Store Example
APPLICATION SYSTEMS REPORT   Page 1   Date: 1-Aug-1989

	Application System	Functional Area
1. PERIOD	Product Analysis System	• Corporate
MARKET SEGMENT TYPE		• Market Research
(1) MARKET SEGMENT		• Sales Department
PRODUCT TYPE		
(1) PRODUCT		
(2) PRODUCT MARKET SEGMENT		

Figure 21.6 Partial application systems report.

any other entities. Similarly, the remaining type entities in the other clusters are all able to be developed in phase 0. As a rule, all type entities are normally implemented as tables; further, they may be developed together and consolidated as a single table.

MARKET SEGMENT is then implemented in phase 1, as it is dependent on both PERIOD and on MARKET SEGMENT TYPE. Similarly, PRODUCT is implemented in phase 1, as it is dependent on PRODUCT TYPE.

Finally the intersecting entity PRODUCT MARKET SEGMENT is implemented in phase 2, as it is dependent on each of the previous entities. It represents operational processing activity which will be subsequently aggregated into the PRODUCT and MARKET SEGMENT entities.

Four implementation clusters were derived from the data model by IE: Analysis. Each represents a different potential application system, as shown in Figure 21.7. Notice that a number of subject data bases in

---

IE: CASE Retail Department Store Example
APPLICATION SYSTEMS REPORT   Page 1   Date: 1-Aug-1989

	Application System	Functional Area
1. PERIOD	Product Analysis System	• Corporate
MARKET SEGMENT TYPE		• Market Research
(1) MARKET SEGMENT		• Sales Department
PRODUCT TYPE		
(1) PRODUCT		
(2) PRODUCT MARKET SEGMENT		
2. PERIOD	Customer Analysis System	
		• Corporate
MARKET SEGMENT TYPE		• Market Research
(1) MARKET SEGMENT		• Sales Department
CUSTOMER TYPE		
(1) CUSTOMER		
(2) CUSTOMER MARKET SEGMENT		
3. PERIOD	Quota Performance System	• Corporate
MARKET SEGMENT TYPE		• Sales Department
(1) MARKET SEGMENT		
QUOTA TYPE		
(1) QUOTA		
(2) QUOTA MARKET SEGMENT		
4. PERIOD	Competitive Analysis System	• Corporate
MARKET SEGMENT TYPE		• Market Research
(1) MARKET SEGMENT		
ORGANIZATION TYPE		
(1) ORGANIZATION		
(2) ORGANIZATION MARKET SEGMENT		

Figure 21.7   Application systems report from data model.

Figure 21.7 are common to each cluster: PERIOD, MARKET SEG-MENT TYPE and MARKET SEGMENT. From its knowledge, IE: Analysis has determined that these three subject data bases are shared by each of the strategic systems identified so far. Once the first application system that uses these subject data bases has been developed, they are immediately available for use by subsequent systems without the need for redevelopment. The remaining subject data bases listed in each cluster are then specific to the relevant application system.

This is of course a simple example: the commonality of the three subject data bases is intuitively obvious. Not so with a typical strategic model of 50–90 entities. And common, shared subject data bases are certainly not obvious in an operational model of perhaps 800 entities. However, processing carried out by IE: Analysis allows common development opportunities to be readily identified. Other concurrent development opportunities also emerge, based on defined management priorities, as discussed next.

Notice that each application system in Figure 21.7 is of interest to at least two functional areas. Systems for each functional area are summarized in Figure 21.8.

Management have manually prioritized these functional areas alphabetically: from A, the highest priority, to Z which is lowest. We see that the sales department systems have been given the highest priority by management: its systems provide aggregate values required by corporate and market research.

Each application system has also been prioritized numerically by management: from 1, which is highest priority. The product analysis system and the customer analysis system have each been given the same high priority. Next, is the quota performance system, with the competitive analysis system having lowest priority.

IE: CASE Retail Department Store Example
APPLICATION SYSTEMS BY FUNCTIONAL AREA   Page 1   Date: 1-Aug-1989
Priority Functional Area   **Priority Application System**

Priority	Functional Area	Priority	Application System
B	CORPORATE	1	Product Analysis System
		1	Customer Analysis System
		2	Quota Performance System
		3	Competitive Analysis System
C	MARKET RESEARCH	1	Product Analysis System
		1	Customer Analysis System
		3	Competitive Analysis System
A	SALES DEPARTMENT	1	Product Analysis System
		1	Customer Analysis System
		2	Quota Performance System

Figure 21.8   Application systems by functional area.

Notice that the high-priority systems (clusters 1 and 2 in Figure 21.7) are of interest to each functional area. While the operational detail of these systems will be defined by sales department personnel, corporate and market research personnel will also need to participate. The information they require will be derived from the operational data in the product analysis system and customer analysis system. Other information opportunities may also emerge which need their input.

The significance of this derivation of application systems and functional areas from the data model, as carried out by USER CASP/CASE products such as IE: CASE, cannot be over-emphasized. Strategic directions set by management may need new or changed functions and application systems. This may lead to reorganization into new functional areas. DP CASE products that do not carry out strategic analysis as outlined here may not be able to derive new functions and organization structures from a data model. They depend on DP expertise, rather than on business expertise, as for USER CASP/CASE products. They start from the existing functions of an organization, which may be inappropriate to new strategic directions, and this may inhibit identification of new functions and organization structures.

21.2.6   Implementation plan

Finally, the implementation phase data map is shown in Figure 21.9. This was plotted by IE: Analysis based on the project management processing just discussed. It indicates the implementation sequence for the subject data bases in Figure 21.5, according to implementation clusters in Figure 21.7.

Each entity is positioned vertically according to its implementation phase number. Phase 0 is at the left-hand side of the plot, with phase numbers increasing from left to right. PERIOD, and each of the type entities, are plotted at the left: they are all able to be implemented in phase 0 if sufficient development resources are available (see Figure 21.9). MARKET SEGMENT, PRODUCT, CUSTOMER and QUOTA are plotted to their right – as these are implemented in phase 1. Finally, the intersecting entities at the end of each cluster are plotted in phase 2.

Intersecting entities are indicated by interspersed dashes in the entity box. As we discussed in Chapter 15, these entities represent areas of highest potential processing activity. Secondary (4BNF) entities are plotted with interspersed dots in the entity box, plotted underneath the principal (3BNF) entities to which they are related. (There are no secondary entities in Figure 21.9.) They can be plotted in a hierarchically structured format, as illustrated in Figure 15.2, or they can surround the 3BNF entity in an unstructured format, if specified.

Figure 21.9 provides a clear layout for a data map: the implementation sequence of the subject data bases is immediately apparent. All of

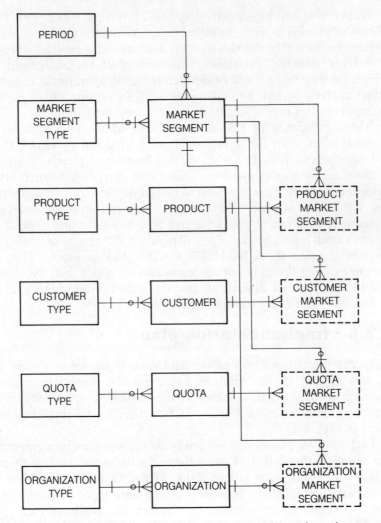

Figure 21.9 Implementation phase data map, plotted based on the processing carried out in Figures 21.5 and 21.7.

the phase 0 entities (PERIOD and the type entities) can be implemented concurrently if there are sufficient development resources available.

It is now obvious from Figure 21.9 that PERIOD, MARKET SEGMENT TYPE and MARKET SEGMENT are common to each cluster. These, together with PRODUCT TYPE and PRODUCT, must be completed before PRODUCT MARKET SEGMENT can be completed in the product analysis system. Similarly, CUSTOMER TYPE and CUSTOMER must also be completed before the CUSTOMER MARKET SEGMENT can complete the customer analysis system.

By viewing the right-most entities (the highest phase number), the potential application systems are immediately apparent. These are represented by each intersecting entity. The implementation phase data map is used visually to evaluate different development opportunities, before establishing the priorities indicated in Figure 21.8.

21.2.7   Alternative strategies

The data map in Figure 21.9 represents explicit strategies for associations defined between entities. We defined 14 associations explicitly. IE: Analysis then analyzed the data model to identify any alternative strategies we may have overlooked, of which there were many, even in this simple example! Figure 21.10 includes some of the more interesting of these. IE: Analysis identified 64 alternative strategies at this stage of development of the strategic model.

You will remember in Chapter 17, during the definition of purpose descriptions, that we determined the need for 'period', rather than the more limiting reference to 'this month'. We made a number of changes to the names of attributes to clarify their meaning. Our focus had been too specific. IE: Analysis has accepted this change and evaluated the impact of PERIOD on the data model that we explicitly defined (see the association between PERIOD and MARKET SEGMENT in Figure 21.9).

Figure 21.10 indicates that there is also a potential strategy between PERIOD and each of the subject data bases listed against it on the right-hand side. It is asking if we are interested in time dependency; that is, are we interested in historical data for each of these subject data bases? Now that is something we certainly did overlook! MARKET SEGMENT is

---

IE: CASE Retail Department Store Example
INCREMENTAL ALTERNATIVE STRATEGIES REPORT   Page 1   Date: 1-Aug-1989

Between Entity: PERIOD   and Entity: ORGANIZATION
                                               QUOTA
                                               ORGANIZATION MARKET SEGMENT
                                               QUOTA MARKET SEGMENT
                                               PRODUCT MARKET SEGMENT
                                               CUSTOMER MARKET SEGMENT
                                               CUSTOMER
                                               PRODUCT

Figure 21.10   Alternative strategies, identified by IE: Analysis.

related to each of the intersecting entities in Figure 21.9, and we have said we are interested in its time dependency. We can thus extract historical data for each intersecting entity indirectly. This may be appropriate for performance monitoring in a number of areas of the business. But Figure 21.10 also implies the following: Do we wish to establish a stronger, more explicit strategy for some, or all, of these intersecting entities? Do we want to obtain historical data also on CUSTOMER and on PRODUCT? In fact, while these represent alternative strategies for keeping historical details on each subject data base listed, they indicate critical strategic gaps that we missed. Period includes not only the past, but also the present . . . and the future. *Remember*, the future is also history . . . but it is history that has not yet happened!

IE: Analysis has asked us a number of important questions: Are we interested in using historical demand, to establish future:

(1) Forecasts of market segment demand by organization, customer and product?
(2) Forecasts of total demand by organization, customer and product?
(3) Forecasts of market segment demand by quota, to set future quotas?

These are important planning questions, and ones we are certainly interested in! For example:

- *Question 1* forecasts sales demand by organizations and customers, for products in each market segment.
- *Question 2* forecasts total sales demand for products across all market segments.
- *Question 3* sets future sales quotas by market segment based on this demand.

Perhaps we would have covered these as we progressed into tactical and operations modeling. Perhaps not. But we are now certain to address them. IE: Analysis inferred from our definition of PERIOD that we are also interested in the future. We are interested not only in monitoring the performance of the past, but also in planning for the future. This raises the possibility not only of reactive performance monitoring, but also of proactive trend analysis. We can now see, from the the strategic analysis of Figure 21.11, a possible decision early warning system, such as was discussed in Figure 11.4, p. 185.

As a rule of thumb, for each explicit strategy defined in a strategic model, IE: Analysis will often identify between 5 and 10 alternative strategies that are possible. For example, with the 14 explicit strategies identified in this strategic model, a further 64 alternative strategies were identified. For a tactical or operational model, there may be even more.

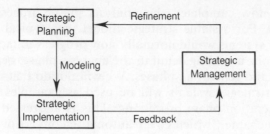

Computer-Aided Strategic Planning using Information Engineering

Strategic Planning	Automatically identifies strategic alternatives
Strategic Implementation	Precise communication to all management levels Misinterpretation is obvious, and corrected easily
Strategic Management	Rapid feedback cycle (days and weeks) Performance monitoring clearly identified

Figure 21.11   Computer-aided strategic planning feedback.

Typically, 10%–20% of these indicate critical strategic gaps or opportunities that have been overlooked. That is, for each explicit strategy we define . . . there is at least one critical area we miss!

Computer-aided strategic planning, such as used by IE: Analysis, at least draws them to our attention. We can then plan accordingly. In Chapter 10, when we discussed traditional strategic planning, we were concerned with the long strategic feedback cycle of three to five years (see Figure 10.1). No wonder many organizations do not survive, if they depend only on the feedback from traditional strategic planning! We have seen that computer-aided strategic planning, used with information engineering, leads to rapid strategic feedback. This is summarized in Figure 21.11.

We would normally evaluate alternative strategies identified by IE: Analysis, determine if any strategic gaps or opportunities have been identified and then refine the strategic model accordingly. This feedback may lead to the definition of additional strategic data, which is processed and analyzed once more. IE: Analysis evaluates the impact of this later data on the strategic model as earlier defined, to determine whether still additional alternative strategies exist. Thus, iterative strategic refinement occurs. Management evaluate each strategic alternative and carry out still further refinement as appropriate. Or some of these alternatives can be left until a later time when they are more appropriate to initiate, perhaps based on the action of competitors, or on customer demand, or on some other factor. Only when iteration results in no further change is the strategic model stable.

We have now completed the analysis phase processing of this strategic model. For a stable strategic model in a typical project, the highest priority systems would normally now progress to tactical modeling and operations modeling detail in the analysis phase, before moving into the design and generation phases. We will not do that in this book. Instead, these strategic systems will be used as examples to illustrate design and generation phase processing. This is addressed in the final sections of this chapter, which cover automatic conversion of the data model into a PROLOG knowledge base, and the definition of application groups based on processing carried out in the analysis phase. The physical characteristics of attributes in the data model are defined. Screen forms and reports are designed and data bases are generated.

21.3 | DESIGN PHASE

There are three stages of interest to us in the design phase:

- Stage 1: Create a design knowledge base from data defined in the analysis phase.
- Stage 2: Paint screen forms and reports from the knowledge base.
- Stage 3: Print design specification reports.

21.3.1 Stage 1: Create knowledge base

This reads the design dictionary and the strategic planning dictionary defined in the analysis phase. It creates a PROLOG knowledge base, available for use by expert systems in the design and generation phases, and by external expert systems shells.

The knowledge base contains all the functional area definitions, all the entity, attribute and association definitions, all the policy, objective, strategy and purpose description text and links to relevant data definitions, all the tables (system and user) and all the implementation clusters defined in the analysis phase. This knowledge base represents fifth-generation computer technology. It provides an inference engine to extract the analysis decisions, together with the relevant facts and expert rules. These are used in the design phase to paint screen forms and reports, and generate data bases based on the results of expert systems used in the analysis phase. The knowledge base is used internally by IE: CASE, without the users requiring any understanding of fifth-generation technology or expert systems to utilize it. Knowledge of the business and of its information and processing, as embodied in the data model, is needed instead.

Define application groups

Implementation clusters, derived during project management processing in the analysis phase (see Chapter 15), are selected to define application groups. An application group is potentially an application system. One or several clusters can be combined and given a unique application group name for use in the design and generation phases.

We will use the example introduced earlier in this chapter. Each application system in the application systems report in Figure 21.7 is represented now in the implementation phase data map of Figure 21.12.

We will use the first two clusters only, to design and generate the high-priority systems identified by management in Figure 21.8. These are a product analysis system and a customer analysis system. These two systems are of interest to the corporate, market research and sales department functional areas.

The implementation clusters in Figure 21.7 are illustrated as application systems in the data map of Figure 21.12. These applications represent application groups. A definition is now appropriate:

> *An application group is defined as a grouping of related subject data bases (and hence entities) from one or several implementation clusters, to represent a potential business function.*

An application group may be defined as one application system, or perhaps several application systems in a later development phase. The two application groups relate directly to the sales analysis system shown in Figure 21.12.

Notice that each application group in Figure 21.12 has been named based on the *intersecting* entity in each of the clusters in Figure 21.7. This is generally the last subject data base listed in a derived cluster. By examining the detailed definition of each of the entities in the cluster, together with its attributes, one or several potential application systems are suggested. Only one potential application system is shown for each cluster in Figure 21.12. The identification of potential application systems at this point is a useful starting point for the subsequent design of screen forms and reports based on those application groups.

Define physical data fields

Next, we will define the physical characteristics of attributes in entities, but first we must review the terminology we established in Chapter 3 to distinguish between logical and physical representations of data.

Cluster 1: Product Analysis System

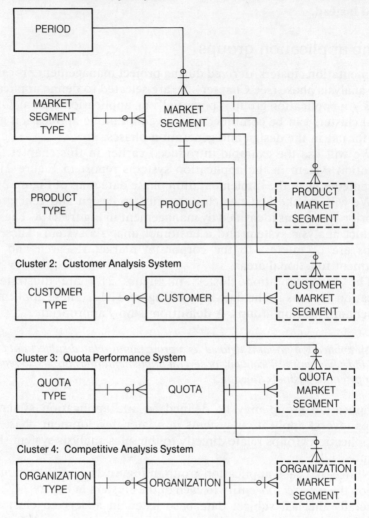

Cluster 2: Customer Analysis System

Cluster 3: Quota Performance System

Cluster 4: Competitive Analysis System

Figure 21.12   Implementation phase data map (from Figure 21.9).

The terms *attribute* and *entity* are logical terms. We will now use their physical counterparts. To differentiate between logical and physical representations of data, we will use different terminology: *data field* is the physical term used to represent a logical attribute; *record* is the physical term used to represent a logical entity. A physical data field (sometimes also called a data element or data item) resides with other data fields in a physical record, in an analogous way to attributes residing in entities. Thus, a primary key attribute resides in a physical record as a primary key field; a foreign key attribute as a foreign key field; a secondary key attribute as a secondary key field; a non-key attribute as a non-key field.

A record occurrence is analogous to an entity occurrence. Many record occurrences reside in a physical *file* or a physical *data base*. A physical record may reside as a *record type* in a physical file, using file access methods; or as a data base *record type* or *segment* in a physical data base, using network, hierarchical or inverted list DBMS; or as a *table* in a relational DBMS.

In a relational data base environment (such as with IBM's DB2 or SQL/DS, Oracle Corporation's ORACLE or IE: SQL in IE: CASE, an entity is referred to as a *table*, an entity occurrence is referred to as a *row* and an attribute is referred to as a *column*. A table is made up of many rows (analogous to records in files) and many columns (analogous to fields in records). As for fields, a primary key attribute resides in a table as a primary key column; a foreign key attribute as a foreign key column; a secondary key attribute as a secondary key column; a non-key attribute as a non-key column.

Keys, whether primary keys, foreign keys, or secondary keys, are physically implemented as indices using hierarchical, CODASYL, network, inverted list or relational DBMS products or file access methods. Because a primary or foreign key represents unique values, it is normally defined as a UNIQUE INDEX for SQL. A secondary key is not unique, and so is *not* defined as a unique index.

In this book, whenever we refer to *entities* and *attributes*, we refer to *logical* representations of data only. When we refer to *records* and *fields*, we refer to *physical* representations of data in general, unless we use the terms *tables*, *rows* and *columns*, when we refer specifically to physical representations of data only in a *relational data base* environment.

An application group is selected for the definition of physical attribute characteristics. Each of the entities in that group is presented for selection. For each entity, each attribute is then defined in terms of a logical data type (currency, integer, text, date, time, boolean, and so on). Based on standards defined for an installation, each logical data type definition is converted into the relevant physical data type, size and output format for physical implementation as a data field or column. For example, in one installation an attribute that represents *date* may be specified as a data field physical date format 'mm-dd-yy', such as 08-01-89 for 1st August, 1989. The standards set by another installation for *date* may instead be 'day, dd mon yyyy', which is converted to Monday, Aug 1989.

An installation's standards may change. For example, in the USA, the expansion of zipcodes from five digits to nine digits represented a horrendous problem: all programs where zipcode fields were physically defined as a five-digit numeric field had to be changed. With IE: CASE, however, an installation defines the logical data type for the attribute *zipcode* to be changed from a five-digit numeric physical field to a nine-digit field. All affected programs using *zipcode* are then documented in the cross-reference reports produced by IE: CASE (see later).

With the knowledge base installed and logical attributes now physically defined as data fields, we are now ready to paint screen forms and reports.

21.3.2   Stage 2: Paint screen forms and reports

Screen forms are painted from the data model, based on installation standards. Each related entity in an application system is included (with appropriate attributes) on the form. The defined attribute name is used to label the data field on the screen, or a different label can be entered in conjunction with the data field. The data field and its label can be moved to any area of the form. Text such as instructions, or headings or footings, can be entered and moved around the screen. The generated screen is thus dynamically modified until acceptable in utility and appearance, and then saved. It can be further modified if required and saved again.

Logical inferencing techniques are used during forms design, for inclusion of related data from entities in installed implementation clusters. This achieves automatic joining of related entities in a screen form to ensure referential integrity is maintained in all systems developed from the designed form.

Similarly, reports are designed and painted, based on the unique reporting format required.

We have completed the physical definition of entities and attributes as records and data fields; we have painted screen forms and reports; we are now ready to print design specifications.

21.3.3   Stage 3: Print specifications

Each entity that has been physically installed in a field definition is printed in a data file specification report as a record format for physical implementation. Designed screen forms and reports are printed in screen or report image, with relevant specification of attribute name, row and column positioning for physical implementation. Design phase cross-reference reports are also produced.

Data file specification

The record format represented by each entity and all of its attributes is printed as an application group contents report, as illustrated in Figure 21.13. This indicates the name of each entity and attribute, and the physical data type, size and format of each defined data field (attribute).

APPLICATION GROUP CONTENTS REPORT   1-Aug-1989   Page 1

Application Group   **PRODANAL**

PERIOD

K	period_number	numeric	integer short	5
N	starting_date	date	dd-mm-yy	8
N	period_duration	time	hh:ddd	6

MARKET_SEGMENT_TYPE

K	market_segment_type	numeric	integer short	5
N	market_segment_type_description	char		20

MARKET SEGMENT

K	market_segment_number	numeric	integer short	5
K	period_number	numeric	Integer short	5
K	market_segment_type	numeric	integer short	5
S	market_segment_name	char		20
N	segment_total_revenue_this_period	currency	$	8.2
N	segment_nett_profit_this_period	currency	$	8.2
N	segment_total_revenue_last_year	currency	$	8.2
N	segment_nett_profit_last_year	currency	$	8.2
N	segment_total_revenue	currency	$	8.2
N	segment_growth_rate	percent		4.1

PRODUCT_TYPE

K	product_type	numeric	integer short	5
N	product_type_description	char		20

PRODUCT

K	product_number	numeric	integer long	7
K	period_number	numeric	integer short	5
S	product_name	char		20
K	product_type	numeric	integer short	5
N	product_total_sales_this_period	currency	$	8.2
N	product_total_sales_this_period_last_year	currency	$	8.2
N	product_average_order_value	currency	$	8.2

PRODUCT MARKET SEGMENT

K	market_segment_number	numeric	integer short	5
K	period_number	numeric	integer short	5
K	product_number	numeric	integer long	7
N	segment_product_revenue_this_period	currency	$	8.2
N	segment_product_profit_this_period	currency	$	8.2
N	segment_product_sales_last_year	currency	$	8.2
N	segment_product_profit_last_year	currency	$	8.2

K – Key Attribute,   S – Secondary Key,   N – Non Key Attribute

Figure 21.13   Application group contents report from Fig 21.12.

The application group contents report in Figure 21.13 is used for implementation and program development in environments (file access methods, DBMS products or operating systems) not supported for automated data base generation by IE: CASE. It provides the record format for all physical records in an application group. It can be used to determine the total record length of the physical record (entity) for different physical implementation approaches.

Form layout specification

Each designed screen form is printed as an exact image of the screen, with each data field, label and text field identified. Following this, a report is printed of the form design specifications, indicating the attribute name (for data fields) or displayed text (for label or text fields), the starting row and column position on the screen, the length (number of display positions) and, if appropriate, the display format.

Report layout specification

Each designed report is printed both as an exact layout of the report and also with printed report layout specifications, indicating, for each data column, column heading or report text field, the attribute name (for data columns) or displayed text (for column headings or report text fields), the starting line and column position on the report, the column width (number of print positions) and, if appropriate, the data presentation format. A typical report designed this way, based on MARKET SEGMENT, is as follows:

```
MARKET SEGMENT              (market segment#, period#, . . .
                           {segment total revenue this month}, . . .
                           {segment sales last year}, . . .
```

The MARKET SEGMENT attributes outlined here are used to paint the sales analysis report format in Table 17.1. This can be processed with a spreadsheet graphics package to produce the sales analysis graph in Figure 17.2. Chapter 17 provides a more detailed discussion of these reports and graphs.

Cross-reference reports

A number of 'where-used' cross-reference reports are provided, indicating:

- For each entity, the application groups that use that entity.
- For each attribute, the application groups that use that attribute.
- For each attribute, the screen forms that use that attribute.
- For each attribute, the reports that use that attribute.
- For each application group, the screen forms used by that group.
- For each application group, the reports used by that group.

These reports allow the impact of a design change in an application to be evaluated in terms of its effect on other possible areas of the application.

21.4 GENERATION PHASE

There are two stages in the generation phase which are of interest to us:

- Stage 1: Generate SQL dictionary.
- Stage 2: Generate application data bases.

21.4.1 Stage 1: Generate SQL dictionary

An SQL design dictionary and strategic planning dictionary are automatically generated based on data defined in the analysis phase. This SQL dictionary can be installed on the micro for processing with IE: SQL, or can be transferred to mainframes, minis or other micros for installation using DB2, SQL/DS, ORACLE, INGRES or other relational DBMS products. SQL CREATE TABLE and CREATE INDEX commands are generated, together with the relevant SQL INSERT commands, for loading data defined in the analysis phase. The design dictionary and strategic planning dictionary definitions from the analysis phase can thus be processed immediately using IE: SQL. This SQL dictionary can be operated on by all facilities of SQL for additional processing, or for *ad hoc* queries or reports as required. When transmitted to mainframes, minis or other micros, to be processed with DB2, SQL/DS, ORACLE, INGRES or other relational DBMS products as appropriate, multi-user access can be provided to the data model – both to the design dictionary and to the strategic planning dictionary.

21.4.2 Stage 2: Generate application data bases

Generation of the data base creation statements to install designed application group data bases in target DBMS environments is discussed here for a representative group of the supported DBMS products.

DB2 and SQL/DS generation

SQL CREATE TABLE commands are generated for each selected entity, for migration to, and installation on, the mainframe. Each entity definition from the analysis phase is used to generate an SQL CREATE TABLE command. Primary keys and foreign keys are generated as NOT NULL columns, to eliminate duplicate keys and for referential integrity between DB2 or SQL/DS tables. All generated SQL commands are ready for immediate transmission to DB2 or SQL/DS, or can be modified by the data base administrator for different data base design strategies.

ORACLE and INGRES generation

SQL commands for CREATE TABLE are generated for each selected entity, for migration to a mainframe, minicomputer or micro supporting ORACLE or INGRES. Each entity definition is used to generate a CREATE TABLE command, to create an SQL table for that entity. Primary keys and foreign keys are generated as NOT NULL columns, to eliminate duplicates and for subsequent referential integrity control between SQL tables. All commands are ready for immediate transmission to ORACLE or INGRES, or can be modified later by the data base administrator for different data base design strategies.

CHAPTER 22

Future Directions in Information Engineering

This chapter details productivity gains achieved by using information engineering and IE: CASE as described in this book. It indicates potential cost savings that are achieved when compared with traditional techniques. It then discusses likely directions in information engineering. These include automatic derivation of design diagrams and automatic generation of code directly from data models developed by users.

22.1 SYSTEMS DEVELOPMENT PRODUCTIVITY

We will discuss the productivity of systems development, using for comparison the application development approaches first discussed in Chapter 1.

22.1.1 Traditional techniques

Application development using traditional analysis, design and implementation techniques (such as software engineering) breaks down the development process into the traditional stages of:

- Requirements specification.
- Analysis and design.

- Implementation.
- Maintenance and refinement.

Figure 22.1 illustrates the proportion of time spent in each of these stages, where traditional techniques (TRADITIONAL in this figure) represent 100 time units.

Requirements specification and analysis and design typically comprise some 40% of the development time. This will of course vary based on the complexity of different application systems and organizations.

Implementation in Figure 22.1 relates to programming, data base installation and testing of the designed application systems. Its relative proportion of total development time is dependent on the programming language and DBMS products utilized, whether third or fourth generation.

Maintenance relates to changes that may need to be made during systems development, *prior* to cutover of the final system into production. Its proportion of the total time is often inversely proportional to the amount of time spent in requirements specification, analysis and design. The less time spent in these stages, the greater the potential number of changes necessary before the system is ready for use.

We will now discuss two approaches to information engineering development, based on these development stages:

- Information engineering applied manually (MANUAL IE).
- Information engineering applied automatically (AUTO IE).

Manual information engineering (MANUAL IE) relies on passive data dictionaries, word processing or manual documentation. DP CASE

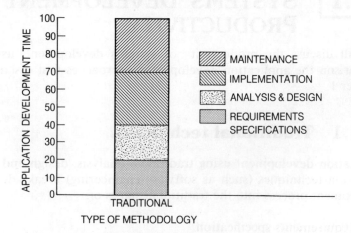

Figure 22.1 Traditional application development stages.

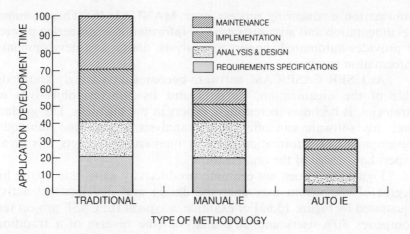

Figure 22.2 Application development time savings using the information engineering methodology.

information engineering products that do not carry out both level 2 modeling (see Chapter 18) and strategic analysis also fit into this category. Once documented, the design must be continually (and manually) cross–checked for consistency as design progresses.

Automated information engineering (AUTO IE) uses level 2 modeling and strategic analysis to continually (and automatically) cross-check the design for consistency, and produce relevant documentation as an automatic byproduct of the analysis and design process. USER CASP/CASE products such as IE: CASE fall into this category.

Figure 22.2 now compares TRADITIONAL with MANUAL IE and AUTO IE. These comparisons assume that the programming language and DBMS products used remain constant across all approaches.

22.1.2   Manual information engineering

The reduction in application development time in Figure 22.2 for MANUAL IE, when compared with traditional techniques, is based on the experience of hundreds of organizations worldwide who have used information engineering manually. It reflects the increased experience gained by those organizations in multiple projects, as their staff move up the learning curve in their use of information engineering.

22.1.3   Automated information engineering

The further reduction in time for AUTO IE in Figure 22.2 reflects the expert design support that USER CASP/CASE software provides to the information engineering process over MANUAL IE. This automates documentation and administration of information engineering projects. It provides automated support to analysis, design and development of information systems.

As USER CASP/CASE software becomes increasingly knowledgeable of the organization, its data and its policies, objectives and strategies, it becomes increasingly expert in the business. The guidance that this software can offer to the analysis, design and subsequent development of information systems increasingly reflects this greater expert knowledge of the organization.

Figure 22.2 does *not* estimate productivity gains due to the high degree of concurrent user analysis, design and development activity illustrated by Figure 15.6. For example, a typical IE: CASE project team comprises 80% users and 20% analysts (the reverse of a traditional project team). The same number of analysts can potentially support four times the number of AUTO IE projects as can support TRADITIONAL projects. Also, IE: CASE implementation phase data maps are used to identify concurrent development opportunities. The extent of project concurrency and productivity achieved is, however, dependent on personnel, equipment and funding resource availability.

Figure 22.2 illustrates the *minimum* productivity gains achieved during the analysis phase of a project, through strategic, tactical and operations modeling. This ranges from four times the improvement for AUTO IE, to 10–20 times the improvement – experienced by organizations where management is actively involved in analysis, and where the project team is made up of 80% users. These productivity gains are *directly* dependent on the extent of management and user participation. With this input, projects that previously needed two to three years to carry out requirements specification and analysis are now completed in two to three months.

In addition, Figure 22.2 only illustrates the *minimum* productivity gains experienced during analysis. It does *not* include the additional productivity gains resulting from automated design of screen forms and reports. It does *not* include any productivity gains from automatic generation of data base designs and data base creation statements, and automatic installation of data bases on mainframes, minis or micros. These productivity gains are dependent on the DBMS products used by the existing systems and those automatically generated with appropriate USER CASP/CASE software, such as IE: CASE.

Finally, Figure 22.2 makes no attempt to evaluate savings subsequent to development. These may result from exhaustive cross-checking by USER CASP/CASE software of data definitions, or from the automatic integration of common data, the identification of strategic gaps and opportunities for management evaluation (which may otherwise be overlooked), the earlier delivery of priority systems, or the eventual benefits provided by the earlier delivered systems.

Depending on management participation and the existing environment of an organization, regardless of whether it is government or commercial, AUTO IE can lead to productivity gains that significantly exceed the 10–20 times improvement over the traditional development techniques.

22.1.4 Maintenance after cutover

Figure 22.2 makes no judgment of the savings to an organization in maintenance and refinement of the developed systems *after* they have been cutover into production. With traditional development techniques, maintenance may absorb some 60%–80% of analyst–programmer resources, leaving only 20%–40% for new applications. The maintenance of manually developed systems (as organizations change) is very high. The cost of this maintenance over a typical five-year life time of a system using traditional techniques can sometimes be more than four times the original development cost!

With IE: CASE, maintenance after cutover with AUTO IE is typically reduced from 60%–80% to 10%–20%. Much of the remaining maintenance is further automated: changes are made in the data model and the affected data bases are regenerated.

22.1.5 Potential cost savings

Table 22.1 illustrates the potential cost saving for a project, based on an average salary (including overheads) of approximately $175 per day (approx $35 000 pa). The traditional development time for a 5-person year project has been estimated in Table 22.1 to be approximately $220 000. This must be adjusted based on the experience of each organization in its use of the traditional techniques, and based on its specific salary ranges. Regardless of the actual development cost using

Table 22.1 Potential cost savings for a five-person year project.

Method	Total Cost	Savings
TRADITIONAL	$220 000	
MANUAL IE	$110 000	$110 000
AUTO IE	$66 000	$154 000

traditional techniques in each organization, the relative costs illustrated in Figure 22.2 for each approach still apply. Table 22.1 shows the total development cost across all stages.

These cost savings directly reflect the reduced development time that MANUAL IE and AUTO IE have over the traditional development approach. Other projects can also be evaluated from Figure 22.2 and Table 22.1. For example, a 50-person year project results in 10 times the total cost for each approach, and 10 times the saving. Even greater productivity gains and cost savings may eventually be achieved based on some of the future directions discussed in the concluding section.

22.2 FUTURE INFORMATION ENGINEERING DIRECTIONS

The emphasis to this point has been on the development of the data model, rather than on definition of procedures. In Chapter 19, the first rule of CASE postulated that only one diagramming method was needed – the data model – and that code can be generated automatically from a data model. We will discuss automatic code generation in this section and will also see that a variety of diagrams can be generated from a data model.

In Chapter 21, we saw how the data model can be analyzed by software to identify subject data bases and implementation clusters. We saw that these clusters represent functions or systems. They may refer to existing functions or systems, or may indicate potential new functions or systems. They may suggest new organizational structures for improved operation; or for better use of, or access to, the information resource represented by the data model.

Data models, developed by users and managers through business normalization, can incorporate far more business expertise than data models developed by analysts based on computer expertise. Data models developed using information engineering incorporate logic, and this inherent logic can be used to automatically generate many of the programs needed to process the relevant data. For example, each entity occurrence in a data base must be created (added to the data base). It can then be read and displayed on a terminal for enquiry purposes. It may need to be modified, to reflect changes in the data content. Eventually, the entity occurrence will be deleted from the data base. The actions ADD, READ, MODIFY and DELETE represent the logic that is required to ensure that the data is maintained up to date. This is referred to as **maintenance logic**.

Maintenance logic represents much of the programming carried out against data. Edit rules and other validation tests are applied to ensure accuracy when data is first added, or when modifications are required, or when data needs to be deleted. Maintenance programs are responsible for adding, reading, modifying and deleting data according to edit rules and validation tests. We will see that much of the logic associated with maintenance programs can be automatically generated from a data model. Other programs – for specific reports, analysis or for aggregation of data – can also be generated from a data model. Or these programs can be written explicitly using appropriate third-, fourth- or fifth- generation languages.

The automatic generation of programs from a data model is based on expert rules that carry out **procedure modeling**. This can be used for **automatic systems design** and for **automatic systems generation**. The details of procedure modeling are not important to us at this point: what can be achieved through automated procedure modeling is, however, extremely important. We will therefore discuss automatic systems design and automatic systems generation. This concluding section is based on experience gained from unreleased, prototype USER CASP/CASE software. It indicates potential future directions in information engineering.

22.2.1 Automatic systems design

Program modules and structures can be automatically derived from a data model. Menus, screen forms and reports can also be automatically designed. They can be used with derived program modules to automatically generate program logic for maintenance processing of data in the resulting information systems. This logic can be generated as **pseudocode**. Pseudocode is an English-like expression of logic which is program-language independent. It can be used automatically to generate graphical system design documentation such as: menu structures, data flow diagrams, program flowcharts, structure charts and organization charts. This graphical documentation provides a clear representation of generated logic. This can be produced from pseudocode as automatically generated program specifications. Together with data model documentation of relevant policies, objectives and strategies, and also of entities, attributes, associations and purpose descriptions, complete design documentation can be automatically produced from only one form of input: the data model. This documentation is an automatic byproduct of the analysis and design process. It can provide input for automatic generation of programs and complete systems in target third- or fourth-generation languages, for target data base management systems and data communication facilities. Access to generated systems also requires the provision of security control logic. These automatic systems design characteristics are discussed next.

While the following design and generation tasks were also discussed in Chapter 20, they were carried out manually in that chapter, with automated support. The following section discusses the automatic execution of these tasks by future information engineering software.

Access security

User classes can be defined for relevant organizational areas. A number of access levels can be defined in each user class. Functional areas, or defined groups or individual users, can then be allocated to an appropriate user class and access level. These establish security constraints for access to, and operation of, generated systems.

The structure of an organization, together with its user classes and access levels, can be defined. This can be later used to restrict menu access for generated systems to authorized personnel, and also to enforce data access and actions via screen forms to those authorized personnel only.

User interface design

This is used to design menus, screen forms and reports based on defined data entities and attributes from the analysis phase. Each implementation cluster of related entities in an application group can be used for the automatic design of menu structures and screen forms, and for interactive design of reports.

Menu design   Menus can be automatically generated from defined entities and associations in the data model, and according to an organization's defined installation standards. These automatically generated menus can be modified if required, or all or selected menus can be defined completely manually. A variety of menu design options can be supported, such as horizontal or vertical menus, pop–up or full–screen multiple choice menus. Menus can be positioned anywhere on the screen, either in absolute position or relative to other defined menus.

Unique menu entries can also be defined to invoke existing application programs transparently from the generated systems. A consistent interface can thus be maintained not only for new systems generated from the data model, but also for invocation of existing systems from the same menu structure. A prototyping capability can also be provided, so that the effectiveness of the designed menus can be tested.

Program module definitions can later be automatically generated according to defined menu structures, based on related entities according to associations in the data model.

Screen design This can automatically generate screen forms for data input, display, modification and output from installed implementation clusters. It can generate screen forms with inclusion or exclusion of attributes as fields in the forms, according to edit rules defined for each relevant attribute. Logical inferencing techniques can be used during forms design, for inclusion of related data from entities in implementation clusters. These can achieve automatic joining of related entities in a screen form so that referential integrity can be maintained in all systems generated from the designed form. Modifications to a screen can be recorded and automatically reapplied later, when the screen form is regenerated.

Report design Reports can be interactively designed from installed implementation clusters, for inclusion or exclusion of attributes as columns in the reports, according to edit rules defined for each relevant attribute. Logical inferencing techniques can be used for inclusion of related data from entities in installed implementation clusters. These can achieve automatic joining of related entities in a report to ensure referential integrity can be maintained in all systems generated from the designed report. All modifications to a report can be recorded and automatically reapplied, when the report is regenerated.

Create design specifications

Design specifications for menus, modules, screen forms and reports can be created, together with the relevant pseudocode for processing them. This pseudocode can be used to produce graphical design documentation automatically, such as data flow diagrams, program logic flowcharts, program module structure charts and organization charts. The pseudocode can be later translated to target languages and DBMS products during systems generation.

Menu design specifications The menu structure (established in menu design) can be used to generate pseudocode for menus. This specifies each designed menu structure and establishes control logic to enforce access security. It can also establish the logic required to implement designed menus. This pseudocode can be later translated to target data communication, language and operating environments.

Logic module specifications Program module definitions can be automatically created according to the defined menu structure, based on related entities according to associations in the data model. Individual modules can be defined or all modules can be automatically defined for the entire data model. Entities can be automatically included in each defined module so that generated logic can ensure referential integrity of data files and data bases in later, automatically generated pseudocode.

Screen design specifications   The designed screens (established in screen design) can be used to generate pseudocode automatically. This specifies the logic required to create the forms, to be used by programs generated later. This pseudocode can be later translated to screen-mapping languages used by target data communication, language and operating environments. Control logic can be automatically established to enforce access security for screen forms, based on menu design and module specifications.

Report design specifications   The designed reports (established in report design) can be used to generate pseudocode automatically. This can specify the logic required to produce the reports. This pseudocode can be later translated to report writers used by target language and operating environments. This can establish control logic to enforce access security for reports, based on menu design and module specifications.

Pseudocode   The menus, program logic modules, screen forms and reports can all be used to generate logic automatically, as pseudocode. This defines logic for programs that are invoked by the menus. Logic can be automatically generated to accept data from the defined screens, process the defined data files or data bases, and produce reports or screen output as required. This is object-oriented logic, automatically derived from a data model.

   Pseudocode can be automatically generated for house keeping, screen accesses, data file or data base accesses, application processing, report production and screen output. All program logic required against each included entity in a program module can be generated. Pseudocode can also be generated to enforce access security for screen forms, data files, data bases and reports based on earlier defined user classes, access levels and menus, and to enforce referential integrity of data files and data bases. Pseudocode can also be generated to implement single-user or multi-user access to data files or data bases, with locking at the record level, and for transaction rollback against data files or data bases, either operator requested or system invoked.

Data flow diagrams   Many organizations have standards that specify that every application system must be completely documented using data flow diagrams (DFDs). Logic represented by pseudocode, and generated as discussed, can be used to create DFDs automatically. These illustrate the flow of data. They can be later used for automatic documentation of the generated systems.

DFDs can be automatically generated from installation-defined standards. DFD processes can be indicated by generated program modules. Generated transactions can indicate the flow of data using screen forms and reports. Data files or data bases can represent data stores. DFD levels can be automatically created based on generated module structures.

Flowcharts The logic represented by pseudocode can be used to create program flowcharts automatically. These illustrate the decision logic of generated program modules. They can be later used for automatic documentation of generated programs. Program flowcharts can be automatically created for each generated program module, based on installation-defined standards. Generated transactions can be flow-charted to indicate the access logic used for screen forms, data files or data bases, and reports.

Structure charts As well as DFD documentation standards, many organizations require every program module to be completely documented using structure charts. The module structure, generated as just discussed, can be used to create structure charts automatically. They can be used for the automatic documentation of generated systems. Structure charts can be generated based on installation-defined standards. Generated modules can indicate the structure of programs, with structure chart levels automatically created based on these module structures.

Organization charts The definition of organization structure, user classes and levels establishes the control hierarchy of an organization. This can be used to generate an organization chart automatically, and can later be used as part of the automatic documentation of the generated systems.

Organization charts can be automatically generated according to installation standards. These charts indicate the overall structure of an organization. They can be created to indicate functions available to each part of an organization. The menus defined for user classes and levels can establish the functions of a system authorized for use by those classes and levels.

Document design specifications

Designed screen forms and reports, data file specifications, generated pseudocode and related program documentation can be produced. The record format for each entity in an application group can be printed in a data file specification report. Screen forms and reports can be printed in screen or report image, with specifications of attribute name, row and column positioning. Defined menu structures and program module structures can be printed. Pseudocode for each program module can also be printed. Graphical design documentation comprising data flow diagrams, program flowcharts, structure charts and organization charts can be plotted on printers, plotters or laser printers.

Prototype-designed systems

The designed user interface, as represented by menus, screens, reports and access security, can be prototyped before moving to systems generation. This is called **user interface prototyping**. It enables human factors and the effectiveness of the designed systems to be evaluated.

An SQL version of the design dictionary, strategic planning dictionary and application data bases can also be automatically created for data base prototyping, similarly to that described in Chapter 21 for IE: CASE. In systems generation, the SQL dictionary and application data bases can be transferred to other computers, such as mainframes, minis or micros. They can be generated for those systems and installed using target relational or other DBMS products as appropriate.

User interface prototyping The user interface comprises menus, screen forms and reports. No data is used during user interface prototyping: only the appearance and effectiveness of the designed man–machine interface is evaluated. This can confirm security controls for menu usage based on defined user classes and access levels. The positioning, style and linking of related menus, and the style and utility of designed screen forms and reports, can be evaluated. Based on the effectiveness of the designed user interface, changes can be immediately made and prototyped again, as required.

SQL prototyping SQL commands can be automatically generated from data defined in the analysis phase. These commands can create an SQL dictionary, together with application data bases to be prototyped using SQL. The dictionary and data bases can be installed for prototype processing on a micro. *Ad hoc* queries and reports can then be produced using SQL, or additional processing can be carried out.

Each entity defined in the analysis phase can be used to generate an SQL table. Primary keys and foreign keys can be generated as NOT NULL columns, to eliminate duplicate keys and for later referential integrity control between SQL tables. Common primary and foreign keys can be used for automatic joining of related tables for screen forms and reports, and to establish referential integrity control between SQL tables.

A number of facilities can be provided to assist in prototyping. These can allow SQL commands to be defined, tested and modified, or saved to be loaded at a later time for execution. Menu-driven and interactive versions of SQL can be supported. Utilities can be provided for access to SQL tables.

22.2.2 Automatic systems generation

This accepts specifications from automatic systems design of menus, screens, reports and program module definitions, in pseudocode. Data base creation statements can be automatically generated to install application data bases and information systems on mainframes, minis and micros using target data base management systems (DBMS) products. The dictionaries from the analysis phase can also be generated automatically for installation using the target DBMS products.

Pseudocode can be translated to target third- or fourth-generation languages automatically. These programs can use target data communication facilities. They can access generated application data bases installed for the target DBMS products. The generated applications thus become directly executable, independent of the development software.

Target environment

The target environment can be defined for the systems to be generated. This can specify the operating system, the programming language, the data base management system and the data communications software of the target machine on which generated systems will be installed. This definition can be used to estimate performance of designed systems in the target environment and to generate systems for that environment.

Performance analysis

The logical performance of designed transactions and data bases in a target environment can be estimated and evaluated. This allows response-critical transactions, as well as heavily used data base access paths, to be identified. The performance of these transactions and data bases can be optimized by making data model and systems design changes. The performance can then be re-evaluated, or changed further, until satisfactory.

System generation

This can translate application systems, built from menus, program modules, screen forms, reports and associated logic in pseudocode and prototyped earlier, into source programs for the specified target language, operating system and data communication environment, with the relevant DDL and DML statements for the target DBMS.

Code generation Pseudocode can be translated to target languages. Pseudocode can be translated automatically to relevant screen-mapping commands required to communicate with screens using target data communication facilities. Pseudocode can be automatically translated to appropriate DML statements to access the target DBMS for processing generated data bases. All application logic defined in pseudocode can be translated to target languages.

Code for referential integrity of generated data bases can also be translated automatically from pseudocode. This can ensure that referential integrity is enforced for target DBMS products or file access methods which currently provide no support for referential integrity.

Menu generation Menu pseudocode can be automatically translated to screen-mapping commands needed to implement the menu structure using target communication facilities. Screen-mapping tables or definitions, transaction tables, program tables and communication tables can also be generated. These can be used to install menus, as well as programs that invoke and use those menus, in the target environment.

Report generation Report pseudocode can be automatically translated to report writer commands, or to programs required to implement the reports in the target environment. Relevant report writer tables or definitions can also be generated to install the reports, as well as the generated programs that produce those reports, in the target environment.

Screen generation Screen pseudocode can be translated to the target communication environment. This can generate screen-mapping commands required to implement the screens using the target communication facilities. Relevant screen-mapping tables, definitions, transaction tables, program tables and communication tables can be generated. These can be used to install screens, as well as the programs that invoke and use those screens, in the target environment.

Final system documentation This can print documentation of the systems generated for the target environment. It can include all data base creation or file definition statements needed to install data bases or files in the target DBMS or file access method environment. All generated screen-mapping definitions and commands can be printed, with relevant transaction tables, program tables and other definitions needed to install menus and programs in the target communication environment. It can include all generated report writer definitions and commands, with relevant tables and other definitions needed to install report programs in the target environment. All programs in the target language, generated to use the designed screens and data bases (or files) for the generated application systems, can also be printed.

Migrate to target   This can transmit the generated and tested application systems and data bases to the target computer(s) for final installation and operation.

22.3 | THE FUTURE

In this future environment, the time-consuming, error-prone manual design and coding tasks of today's systems development methods will disappear. Business changes will no longer result in the redevelopment of large parts of existing systems, as so often occurs today with the traditional development methods. Instead, changes will be applied by users directly to the data model. Changed subject data bases and implementation clusters will be automatically derived. Menus, screens and reports, and pseudocode affected by the changes, will be automatically identified by software and regenerated. Changed systems will be translated again to target hardware, operating system, data communication, language and DBMS environments.

The high cost of conversion, in moving from one hardware and software environment to another, will also be dramatically reduced. It will become a matter of data conversion – a much simpler task than system conversion (or even complete redevelopment), as required today. Instead, the developed systems will be technology independent. They will be able to take advantage of available hardware and software, with automatic conversion and migration of designed systems to new execution environments.

No longer will systems development productivity inhibit organizational change. No longer will new hardware or software technologies require that earlier systems be scrapped. Instead, only USER CASP/CASE generation software for these new target environments will need to be developed. Previously developed data models will then be used automatically to generate systems and data bases for the new target environments.

In this future environment, the need to use large mainframes for systems development will diminish. These large machines will instead be used for high-volume production processing. All systems development will be carried out using networks of micros having sufficient data base capacity for analysis, design and generation dictionaries. These micros may be interconnected using local area networks and wide area networks. Systems will be analyzed, designed, generated and tested on micros. Only then will those systems be transmitted to large machines for processing. In the future, large computers will become high-volume 'execution peripherals' of the micros used for systems development using information engineering as described in this book.

INDEX